The Meaning of the Built Environment

AMOS RAPOPORT

The Meaning of the Built Environment

A NONVERBAL COMMUNICATION APPROACH

With a New Epilogue by the Author

THE UNIVERSITY OF ARIZONA PRESS   TUCSON

The University of Arizona Press

Copyright © 1982, 1990 by Amos Rapoport
All rights reserved

Manufactured in the United States of America
∞ This book is printed on acid-free, archival-quality paper.
94 93 92 91 90   5 4 3 2 1

Library of Congress Cataloging-in-Publication Data

Rapoport, Amos.
    The meaning of the built environment : a nonverbal communication
approach / Amos Rapoport ; with a new epilogue by the author.
        p.   cm.
    Reprint. Originally published: Beverly Hills : Sage Publications.
c1982.
    ISBN 0-8165-1176-4 (alk. paper)
    1. Environmental psychology.   2. Meaning (Psychology)
3. Nonverbal communication.   I. Title.
    [BF353.R36   1990]
    155.9—dc20   90-10742
                                                            CIP

British Library Cataloguing in Publication data are available.

to the Kauffmans:
Your exemplary ways prove your hospitable
~~spirit~~ — a direct result of your faith.
May God continue to bless your ministry
as you widen the welcome for Christ!
Fred Bernhard

Widening *the*
Welcome *of*
Your Church

Biblical Hospitality &
The Vital Congregation

Fourth Edition—Revised and Expanded
Study Guide Included

Fred Bernhard and Steve Clapp

Cover by Custom Maid Design

A LifeQuest Publication

bernhfr@bethanyseminary.edu

Widening the Welcome of Your Church

Biblical Hospitality & The Vital Congregation

Fred Bernhard and Steve Clapp

Cover design by Randy Maid
Page 7 drawing by Kimberly J. Haugh

Copyright © 1996, 1997, 1999, 2004 by LifeQuest. The first two editions of this book were published by The Andrew Center. The third edition and this edition are co-published by **LifeQuest**, 6404 S. Calhoun Street, Fort Wayne, Indiana 46807 and by **Brethren Press**, 1451 Dundee Avenue, Elgin, Illinois 60120.

This opinions expressed in this book are those of the authors and not necessarily those of the publishers.

Biblical quotations, unless otherwise noted, are from the New Revised Standard Version of the Bible, copyrighted 1989 by the Division of Christian Education, National Council of Churches, and are used by permission.

ISBN 0–9637206–9–4

Manufactured in the United States of America

CONTENTS

For Dorothy

PREFACE

After long neglect, the subject of meaning in the built environment began to receive considerable attention when this book was completed in 1980. This interest has continued, and indeed grown, since then. It is a subject that has concerned me on and off for a number of years. In this book I use my own work and much other material to show how a particular set of ideas and a particular point of view can provide a framework that makes sense of a highly varied set of materials.

I approach the problem from the perspective of environment-behavior studies (EBS), which I see as a new discipline, at once humanistic and scientific, concerned with developing an explanatory theory of environment-behavior relations (EBR). As usual, I emphasize the role of cultural variables and use examples from diverse cultures and periods, as well as a variety of environments and sources, to allow for more valid generalizations than are possible if one considers only the high-style tradition, only the recent past, only the Western cultural tradition, and only the formal research literature. At the same time, I emphasize the contemporary United States because it also seems important to consider the usefulness of this approach to the present. Although I have added new material, much has also been left out because details and examples can be multiplied endlessly. The attempt is to provide a *framework for thinking* about the topic and also both to illustrate and to recreate some of the reasoning and working processes as an example of a particular way of approaching problems. This involves working with small pieces of information and evidence from varied fields and disciplines that use different approaches. How these intersect and become mutually relevant is important—both generally (Koestler, 1964) and in EBS more specifically. The test of any valid approach or model is, in the first instance, precisely its ability to relate and bring together previously unrelated findings and facts. Since many were added in October 1989 (in the Epilogue), the approach seems to be working as intended. Since both the number and the diversity of studies that a particular approach can subsume is important, a large number of references were added in the Epilogue, although this review

9

of the literature also is neither systematic nor complete. This has implications for how to read this book. It can be read as a narrative, describing the argument in concise form, and any section can be expanded by following the references—or all the references could be followed to elaborate and expand the argument, revealing its full complexity. Since the new references have not been integrated with the old, both sets of references need to be used.

Frequently it is the unforeseen and not always intuitively obvious *relationships* that are important, in the environment itself (see, for example, Rapoport, 1968a, 1977) and in the development of new fields. They are frequently at the intersection of two or more previously unrelated disciplines—from social psychology and biochemistry to molecular biology, sociobiology, and EBS. I approach the topic from the latter tradition, recent as it is, and emphasize that it is significant more for how one thinks and what one considers than for specific information. I suggest that the way of thinking described in this book is of interest in this connection. It is also of interest because it is relatively direct and simple, unlike other approaches to meaning. It is also applicable to a wide range of environments (preliterate, vernacular, popular, and high-style) and topics (landscapes, urban forms, buildings, furnishings, clothing—even social behavior and the body itself). It is also applicable cross-culturally and, when data are available, historically. We may well be dealing with a process that is pancultural but in which the *specifics* are related to particular cultures, periods, and contexts. It also seems, as the Epilogue suggests, that mechanisms are being discovered that may explain how the processes that are postulated work.

As the dates of some of my earlier articles suggest, the ideas discussed in this book have been developing for some time. The specific formulation and basic argument, however, were first stated very much in the form in which they appear here in an invited lecture at the Department of Architecture of the University of Washington in Seattle in November 1975. I further developed this at a number of presentations at various universities between 1976 and 1978, began the manuscript in mid-1978, and worked on it in my spare time until completion of the final draft in March 1980. The School of Architecture and Urban Planning at the University of Wisconsin-Milwaukee helped with the typing. Some minor revisions and bibliographic additions were made in mid-1982. In October 1989, in addition to preparing the Epilogue and the references for it, I corrected a number of typographical errors and updated a few entries in the original bibliography.

1

THE IMPORTANCE OF MEANING

In what ways and on what basis do people react to environments? This is clearly an aspect of one of the three basic questions of man-environment studies, that which addresses the nature of the mechanisms that link people and environments (see Rapoport, 1977: 1-4). This book as a whole will discuss the nature of one such mechanism and suggest a specific approach useful in that analysis. Within the framework of that approach a number of specific methods can be used. One can use observation of behavior; one can use interviews, questionnaires, and other instruments; one can analyze historical and cross-cultural examples and trace patterns, regularities, and constancies; and so forth. One can also analyze written and pictorial material that has not been produced consciously to evaluate environments but in an unstructured, unself-conscious manner for other purposes. These may include, among many others, travel descriptions, novels, stories, songs, newspaper reports, illustrations, sets for film or television, and advertisements. Such material tends to show how people see environments, how they feel about them, what they like or dislike about them, and which attitudes seem to be self-evident (see Rapoport, 1969b, 1977).

One of my earliest published articles is an example of this type of analysis, and makes a useful starting point for the argument. This is because it fits into the model even though it clearly was not intended to do so. Using it as a starting point reinforces one important principle—that models of environment-behavior interaction must not only allow findings to be cumulative and allow us to make predictions (at least eventually); they must also make sense of a large variety of findings and studies done over long periods of time, in different disciplines and for different purposes.

In 1966 I came across several sets of comments by student teachers of English and by teachers of English participating in a summer institute, both at the University of California at Berkeley. The purpose of the problem set was a writing exercise without any instructions other than that the immediate reactions were to be given to whatever was being discussed. Writing was the essence of the problem—not the subject matter. Some exercises were about apples and paintings, about the campus, and the Berkeley Hills. But several sets were written in classrooms that had no windows and thus used the built environment as their subject matter in the indirect way described above.

These descriptions (as well as photographs of the three classrooms) are given in full elsewhere (Rapoport, 1967a). Here a selection will be given.

By student teachers of English (first-year graduate students):

That the room was used for musical purposes was obvious from the piano in the corner, music on the walls and the various instruments haphazardly scattered about; but what was also noticeable and contradictory to this musical, sensual confusion was the operating-room green walls, the bare surgical-like atmosphere further encouraged by the plain, long tables, austere, utilitarian chairs and the harsh, glaring white light.

Our claustrophobic triple hour seminar room contained by four perfect walls whose monotony is relieved by crude murals, each letting in a little of the outside, surrounds a bleak space around which embryo ideas openly float.

The low-hanging phosphorescent lights diffuse an uncomfortably revealing glare upon the myriad of objects which, in conglomerate dissaray, gives the large room a close, cluttered, multipurpose appearance.

The room is too clean, too large, too modern, too American; everything in it could be made of plastic.

The various bright colors found on the maps and charts hung on the walls appear in sharp contrast to the stark cool lines of the furniture of this room, thereby giving it the feeling of a pleasant though businesslike place in which to conduct class.

The room is a cluttered green box of institutional furniture lit by fluorescent lights and decorated with too many blotchily executed juvenile maps.

Other passages not included are purely descriptive or stress sterility, flickering lights, color, peacefulness, and so forth. Some can be interpreted as negative, while others seem positive. The comments by a group of English teachers tended to be more uniformly and strongly negative. A selection follows:

> The rectangular room was clearly a stern example of functionalism; the cold grey steel cabinets, ascetic light fixtures and the simple spare tables and chairs—enlightened in a dull fashion by the blond finish of the cupboards and closet—were a stern pronouncement of the threatening creative sterility of contemporary society.

> The large and almost empty windowless room with its sturdy enclosing and barren walls inspired neither disgust nor liking; one might easily have forgotten how trapped one was.

> Upon entering the doorway one must comment upon the tasteless array of greys, greens and browns which form an apparently purposeless airless chamber.

> It was very long and grey, that room with its yellow-grey walls, grey metal cabinets, long silver and brown chairs and tables; and the bulletin board which ran the length of it; all lit by narrow overhead lights which revealed it as a fit place to spend so many long grey hours.

The descriptions in both sets deal mostly with color, light quality, air-conditioning hum, and furnishings; the reactions seem to stress monotony, sterility, starkness, emptiness, isolation from the world, a boxed-in quality. What is of primary interest, however, in the present context, is the heavy load of affective and meaning-laden terms used in these descriptions, as well as indications that people use various environmental elements to identify the purpose of these rooms as well as their character and mood.

The meanings of environments

It appears that people react to environments in terms of the meanings the environments have for them. One might say that "environmental evaluation, then, is more a matter of overall affective response than of a detailed analysis of specific aspects, it is more a matter of latent than of manifest function, and it is largely affected by images and ideals" (Rapoport, 1977: 60). In a recent study that does what I did for rooms above, but at the scales of cities and through active probing, the findings are very similar and some of the phrases even echo those above. In that case, the images held of Phoenix and Tucson, Arizona, while containing descriptive and evaluative elements (which, in themselves, clearly have meaning for people), stress affective aspects and associations (Jackovics and Saarinen, n.d.). Similarly, in a recent study of the descriptions of the meaning of urban place in Britain, most responses consisted of affective words (Burgess, 1978: 17).

This also seems to apply to things other than environments. To give just one recent example—affect is most important in the interpersonal relations involved in health care (Di Matteo, 1979). This, as we shall see, is an issue of great importance for my argument, since affect is read on the basis of the nonverbal messages projected by the actors.

It can therefore be shown that people react to environments globally and affectively before they analyze them and evaluate them in more specific terms. Thus the whole concept of environmental quality is clearly an aspect of this—people like certain urban areas, or housing forms, because of what they mean. In Britain, places considered to be industrial, and hence smoky, unhealthy, dark, and dirty are disliked; places with a rural character, and hence quiet, healthy, and gentle, are liked (Burgess, 1978). Thus trees are highly valued not least because they indicate high-quality areas and evoke rural associations.

Material objects first arouse a feeling that provides a background for more specific images, which are then fitted to the material, "and in the case of environments affective images play the major role in decisions" (Rapoport, 1977: 50). This applies equally to classrooms, student dormitories, wilderness areas, housing, cities, recreation areas, and so on. In the example of the rooms with which I began, not only do we find this happening, but we could also ask the question, "What is the meaning of these rooms in terms of what they communicate about the attitudes of various actors in the design process, the university as client, and so on?" In all these cases the initial affective and global response governs the direction that subsequent interactions with the environment will take. It is a basic argument of this book that these global, affective responses are based on the *meaning* that environments, and particular aspects of them, have for people. (Although, clearly, these meanings are partly a result of people's interaction with these environments.) Thus it becomes extremely important to study such meanings.

Meaning also gains in importance when it is realized that the concept of "function," so important in the modern movement, goes far beyond purely instrumental or manifest functions. When latent aspects of functions are considered, it is quickly realized that meaning is central to an understanding of how environments work. This gains in importance when it is realized that latent aspects of function may be the most important, and that this applies to economics, to consumption, to all artifacts and social possessions, even to food (see Douglas and Isherwood, 1979).

Any activity can be analyzed into four components:

(1) the activity proper;
(2) the specific way of doing it;
(3) additional, adjacent, or associated activities that become part of the activity system; and
(4) the meaning of the activity.

It is the variability of 2, 3, and 4 that leads to differences in form, the differential success of various designs, acceptability, and judgments of environmental quality. Note that this typology relates in an interesting way to the hierarchy of levels of meaning, ranging from the concrete object through use object, value object to symbolic object (Gibson, 1950, 1968; see also Rapoport, 1977).

This suggests that meaning is not something apart from function, but is itself a most important aspect of function. In fact, the meaning aspects of the environment are critical and central, so that the physical environment—clothes, furnishings, buildings, gardens, streets, neighborhoods, and so on—is used in the presentation of self, in establishing group identity (Rapoport, 1981), and in the enculturation of children (Rapoport, 1978a). This importance of meaning can also be argued on the basis of the view that the human mind basically works by trying to impose meaning on the world through the use of cognitive taxonomies, categories, and schemata, and that built forms, like other aspects of material culture, are physical expressions of these schemata and domains (Rapoport, 1976a, 1976b, 1979a, 1979b). Physical elements not only make visible and stable cultural categories, they also have meaning; that is, they can be decoded if and when they match people's schemata.

Users' meanings and designers' meanings

One of the hallmarks of man-environment research is the realization that designers and users are very different in their reactions to environments, their preferences, and so on, partly because their schemata vary. It is thus *users'* meaning that is important, not architects' or critics'; it is the meaning of everyday environments, not famous buildings—historical or modern (see Bonta, 1979; Jencks, 1980; and many others). It is users' meanings that explain why nineteenth-century houses being restored in Wilmington, Delaware, have their porches removed (although they *are* part of the style) and shutters added (although they are *not*). The meaning of "desirable old house" matches the schema "colonial." This also helps explain the use of imitation American colonial furniture in the NASA lunar reception building in Houston (Time, 1967b: 34)—it means "home." A similar phenomenon is the use of the then-new material aluminum in an advertisement by Reynolds Aluminum (Time, 1967a) to reproduce "colonial" elements (see Figure 1).

This advertisement shows 49 uses of aluminum and the many ways in which this new metal can provide "handsome classic columns in front," siding, shutters, shingles on the roof, and so on. The basic arrangement itself, the total image, is traditional to an extreme degree. Note also the front doors, the decorative handles, the landscaping, the gas lamp on the lawn, the two welcome mats, and other elements.

Similar elements seem to be involved in the case of low-cost housing in Britain, where people were said to prefer and to be buying private houses that were of lower standard than public housing. One reason was ownership itself; another, I would argue, is the presence of elements that remove the "stigma of being a council tenant" (Hillman, 1976). If we look at such housing (which, incidentally, costs less to build than public housing) in Southport, the most striking elements that seem to remove the stigma are the small-paned windows, classical doorways, and small front yards with low fences (see Figure 2). It is these stylistic elements that help communicate the appropriate meanings. Also, clearly, latent rather than instrumental or manifest functions seem dominant.

Comparable kinds of elements are found in much more expensive housing in the United States. In this case we find the use of traditional, local elements in new housing, the recently completed Victoria Mews in San Francisco (by Barovetto, Ruscitto and Barovetto): bay windows, panels, brackets, railings, the overall shape—even construction techniques of nineteenth-century houses (Architectural Record, 1979). In fact, the whole current "neovernacular," "historicist," and "postmodernist" movements can be seen in these terms, although

HOUSE WITH TRADITIONAL ELEMENTS USED TO ADVERTISE USE OF ALUMINUM IN 49 PLACES, WHICH "TAKES CARE OF ITSELF". (BASED ON ADVERTISEMENT IN _TIME_, MAY 5, 1967).

RAPOPORT

Figure 1

these also represent designers' rather than users' meanings so that the elements used may not necessarily communicate (see Groat, 1979; Groat and Canter, 1979). This may be because of their metaphorical use, the excessively subtle and idiosyncratic nature of the elements used, the nature of the relationships among them, or their context,

HOUSING IN SOUTHPORT, ENGLAND
(BASED ON PHOTOGRAPH IN THE GUARDIAN, FEB 16, 1976 p 7)

Figure 2

which may be inappropriate—or neglected. This lack of communication of meaning supports the view that meanings are in people, not in objects or things (see also Bonta, 1979). However *things do elicit meanings;* the question is *how* they elicit or activate these meanings and guide them and, thus, *which* things or objects "work" best. Put differently, the question is how (and, of course, whether) meanings can be encoded in things in such a way that they can be decoded by the intended users. I assume, for the moment, that physical elements of the environment *do* encode information that people decode. In effect, while people filter this information and interpret it, the actual physical elements guide and channel these responses.

An analogous situation occurs in other domains. Thus while one speaks of crowding or stress as being subjective reactions, these are related to, and evoked by, physical (and other) environmental characteristics. In the perceptual realm, the experience of complexity is subjective, but clearly environments possess certain characteristics that produce the experience of complexity much more reliably and unequivocally than others. These characteristics can, in fact, be specified and designed (see Rapoport, 1977: ch. 4). Yet, in spite of the apparent importance of meaning—and particularly users' meaning—it is fair to say that the meaning aspect of the environment has been neglected in the recent past—particularly users' meaning has been neglected—and continues to be neglected (see Jencks, 1977).

Ironically, the development of man-environment studies, at least in their early days, led to an even greater neglect. The attempt to be "scientific," to apply positivistic approaches, led to a neglect of the fuzzy, "soft" aspects of the environment such as meaning.

Perceptual and associational aspects of the environment

To use a distinction between *perceptual* and *associational* aspects of the environment (see Rapoport, 1977: ch. 6), one could argue that in man-environment research, perceptual aspects have been stressed. One could argue further that the differential reactions of designers and the lay public to environments can be interpreted in these terms: Designers tend to react to environments in perceptual terms (which are *their* meanings), whereas the lay public, the users, react to environments in associational terms. A recent example of this is Hertzberger's old people's home in Amsterdam (Architectural Review, 1976; see Figure 3). This was designed in perceptual terms by the architect, but

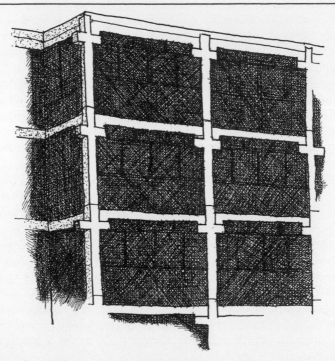

PORTION OF OLD PEOPLE'S HOME, AMSTERDAM, DESIGNED BY HERTZBERGER
(BASED ON PHOTOGRAPHS IN ARCH.REVIEW, VOL. CLIX, No 948, FEB 1976)

RAPOPORT

Figure 3

was evaluated in associational terms by the users, who saw the white frame and black infill elements in terms of crosses and coffins, that is, as having highly negative associations. Thus, even if one accepts the importance of meaning, one still needs to ask which group we are discussing, particularly since both designers and users are far from homogeneous groups. One thus needs to ask *whose* meaning is being considered.

In 1967, I wrote an article on meaning that was to have appeared as part of a special issue of the *Architectural Association Journal* that was later published, in revised form, as an early book on meaning from a semiotic perspective (Jencks and Baird, 1969). Both the special issue and the book stressed *architects'* meaning; my article (Rapoport, 1967b) questioned that focus and proposed that *users'* meaning was the more important. The argument of this book hinges on this distinction. The basic question—*meaning for WHOM?*—continues to distinguish the present work from most work on meaning; what has generally been considered is the meaning environments have for architects, or at least for the cognoscenti, the critics, those in the know. The question that must be addressed is: What meaning does the built environment have for the inhabitants and the users, or the public or, more correctly, the various publics, since meanings, like the environments that communicate them, are culture specific and hence culturally variable?

The point made is that the meaning of many environments is generated through personalization—through taking possession, completing it, changing it. From that point of view the meaning designed into an environment (even if it can be read, which is far from certain) may be inappropriate, particularly if it is a single meaning. What is wrong, I argued, is that we tend to overdesign buildings and other environments. That argument was based on a case study of a single major building (Saarinen's CBS building) as an exemplar (although reference was made to several other cases). It relies on accounts in the nonprofessional press (newspapers and magazines), since the universes of discourse of designers and the public tend to be quite different. The published material stresses the dissatisfaction of users with "total design" as opposed to the lavish praise this idea had received in the professional press. The nonprofessional accounts recount the dissent, opposition, resistance, and conflicts generated by the designers' prohibition of the use of any personal objects or manipulation of furniture, furnishings, or plants in order to preserve an overall aesthetic ideal.

The newspaper and magazine accounts stressed this element of conflict between users and the designers representing the company (and, one might suggest, their own values; see Rapoport, 1967b). The company and its designers wished to preserve uniformity, to safeguard the building as a "harmonious environment." They wanted to prevent a "kewpie doll atmosphere," to avoid having "things thrown all over" and "haphazard things all over the walls" thus turning the building into a "wall to wall slum" (Rapoport 1967b: 44). An aesthetician was put in charge to choose art, plants, colors, and the like to be compatible with the building, that is, to communicate a particular meaning. The users saw things rather differently and resisted. They tried to bring in their own objects, to put up pictures and calendars, to have family photographs on desks, to introduce their own plants. Some even brought suit against the company. I knew some people in the Columbia Records Division who fought these attempts at control—and won. In that case they saw the environment they wished as communicating that they were creative people, artists. This implied a setting that communicated that message, and that meant a cluttered, highly personalized environment.

This conflict described in the journalistic accounts can be interpreted in terms of a single designers' meaning conflicting with the various meanings of users. The argument in the article then shifts to a different, although related, issue having to do with the nature of design—of unstable equilibrium that cannot tolerate change (typical of high-style design) as opposed to the stable equilibrium typical of vernacular design, which is additive, changeable, and open-ended (Rapoport, 1969c, 1977, 1981). This then leads to a conclusion related to the need for underdesign rather than overdesign, of loose fit as opposed to tight fit, which is partly and importantly in terms of the ability of users to communicate particular meanings through personalization, by using objects and other environmental elements in order to transform environments so that they might communicate different meanings particular to various individuals and groups. The question then becomes how one can design "frameworks" that make this possible—but that is a different topic.

Two things seem clear from the above. First, that much of the meaning has to do with personalization and hence perceived control, with decoration, with movable elements rather than with architectural elements. Second, that architects generally have tended to be opposed strongly to this concept; in fact, the whole modern movement in architecture can be seen as an attack on users' meaning—the attack on ornaments, on decoration, on "what-nots" in dwellings and "thingamabobs" in the garden, as well as the process of incorporating these elements into the environment.

This argument can be applied with even greater strength to housing, where users' meaning is clearly much more central and where the affective component generally can be expected to be much more significant. "In the case of housing, giving meaning becomes particularly important because of the emotional, personal and symbolic connotation of the house and the primacy of these aspects in shaping its form as well as the important psycho-social consequences of the house" (Rapoport, 1968a: 300). In the study just cited, many examples were given showing the importance of personalization and changes as ways of establishing and expressing meaning, ethnic and other group identity, status, and the like. Such changes seemed important in establishing and expressing priorities, in defining front and back, in indicating degrees of privacy. A number of theoretical, experimental, and case studies were cited, and housing in Britain over a period of 10 years was evaluated in these terms. A series of photographs of housing in London, taken specifically for this article, showed the importance of the possibility of making changes, and it was argued that not only were designers opposed to open-endedness and seeking total control over the housing environment; they seemed systematically to block various forms of expression available to users until none were left. Finally, it was argued that when flexibility and open-endedness were considered by designers it tended to be at the level of instrumental functions (what I would now call "manifest" functions) rather than at the level of expression (latent functions). In other words, designers—even when they stressed physical flexibility—seemed strongly to resist giving up control over expression, that is, over meaning. Thus, for example, award juries praised the use of few materials, the high degree of integration, and the high degree of consistency, that is, high levels of control over the total environment (Rapoport, 1968a: 303).

It is in this sense that the discussion of open-endedness in housing is related to issues such as the importance of meaning, its variability among groups, the distinction between designers' meaning and users' meanings. This argument also reiterated and stressed the importance of decorative elements, furniture and its arrangement, furnishings, plants, objects, colors, materials, and the like, as opposed to space organization as such, although that could be important by allowing specific elements to change. An example is square rooms, which allow many arrangements of furniture that long narrow rooms make impossible. It was also suggested that different elements, arranged differently, might be significant and important to various groups and that this relative importance could be studied. This would then provide two important related pieces of information. First, it could reveal which elements, in any given case, need to be changeable by the users in order to establish and express important meanings, that is, which changes achieve personalization and what different individuals and groups understand by this term. Second, this would then define the less important, or unimportant, elements that could constitute the "frameworks" to be designed. The very definition of frameworks, it was further suggested, could be based on an analysis of various forms of expression in different situations.

How then could frameworks be defined? There may be constant needs common to humans as a species and a great range of different cultural expressions that change at a relatively slow rate. There are also rapidly changing fashions, fads, and styles. Frameworks could then possibly be defined in terms of the relative rate of change based on an analysis of past examples, particularly in the vernacular tradition. Other possible ways are in terms of the importance of the meaning attached to various elements; what is actually regarded as personalization, what degree of open-endedness is needed, and hence which areas and elements need changeability. It may be found that few areas are critical, and changeable parts may be relatively few in number. These are, at any rate, all researchable questions (Rapoport, 1968a: 305).

The result of this argument, in addition to a set of design implications and guidelines that do not concern us here, is that changes in expression by personalization may be more important than changes made for practical or instrumental functions; that they are not only natural but essential to the way in which people most commonly (although not universally) establish meaning.

Consider a recent example that both stresses this latter point and shows continued refusal by designers to accept this process. A set of changes and additions were made to Chermayeff's house at Bentley Wood; these changes were described as a "tragedy" (Knobel, 1979). All of the changes have to do with the *meanings* of elements that indicate home, as well as the meaning implicit in the *process* of change and personalization itself. Note that none of the changes are for practical or instrumental functions: arches in the hallway, elaborate wallpapers, a fireplace with historical associations, a doric entry portico, an elaborate front door with decorative door handles, a decorative rose trellis, and so on. These are all clearly associational elements. The criticism of these changes reflects different schemata and is couched in typically *perceptual* terms: "destroyed . . . sense of equilibrium," "disrupts inside-outside flow of the facade," "no longer as strong a sense of the openness of the house," loss of "simple, understated entrance" (Knobel, 1979: 311). The last criticism is particularly interesting in view of the historically and cross-culturally pervasive tradition of *emphasizing* entry.

The changes documented in the cases of other modern houses, not as large or lavish, can be interpreted in similar terms. For example, in the case of some of Martienssen's houses in South Africa (Herbert, 1975), they also consist of adding porches, pitched or hipped tile roofs, chimneys, "softening" garden landscaping, and so on. In the case of Le Corbusier's houses at Pessac (Boudon, 1969), one finds pitched roofs, chimneys, shutters, porches, hedges, flower boxes, small rectangular windows instead of horizontal bands, individualization of facades, traditional facades, and the like.

The meaning underlying such changes becomes clear in a recent detective novel in which the whole plot hinges on a modern house built by an architect. Other residents are upset; the house has a 78-foot long blank wall of rough reddish boards, hardly any windows generally, and a flat roof, and it is composed of two cubes. It contrasts with other houses such as a barn-red, white-trimmed ranchhouse on an immaculate lawn bordered by neat flower beds. Not only is it seen as an eyesore threatening the neighborhood and an insult, "It's not even a house! You can't call that thing a house! I'm damned if I know what you could call it" (Crowe, 1979: 4). The materials are "junk," without windows it looks like a tomb. Feelings run high: "Two orange crates would look better" (Crowe, 1979: 5). It's nothing but "damned cubes" and "boxes." The neighbors see it as crazy ideas, as opposed to "good normal homes" (Crowe, 1979: 7), and want it pulled down and a "regular" house built. What is a "good, normal home" or "regular house"? The modifications they would accept define it: "Put in windows, maybe a porch and a peaked shake roof. Paint it white, landscape heavily and it wouldn't look that different from an ordinary two storey house" (Crowe, 1979: 12).

This is clearly related to a schema, to the *concept* of a house. There are many ways of defining it (Rapoport, 1980a), and many of these involve meaning and associational elements as central, for example as Bachelard (1969) suggests. Hayward (1978) discovered, among young people in Manhattan, nine dimensions of home, including relationships with others, social networks, statement of self-identity, a place of privacy and refuge, a place of stability and continuity, a personalized place, a locus of everyday behavior and base of activity, a childhood home and place of upbringing, and, finally, shelter and physical structure. Given the population and locale, the fact that most of these have to do with meanings and associations is most significant, since one may expect these to be stronger among other populations and in other locales (see Cooper, 1971, 1978; Ladd, 1976). One may suggest that an important component of the associational realm is precisely the meaning the environment has for people, how these meanings are construed and what these meanings communicate.

However, partly as a result of considerations such as the above, the neglect of meaning in environmental design research is beginning to change. The growing concern about *perceived* crowding, density, crime, or environmental quality implies, even if it does not make explicit, the central role of subjective factors, many of which are based on the associations and meanings that particular aspects of environments have for people, which are partly due to repeated and consistent use and enculturation interacting with any pan-cultural and biological, species-specific constancies that may exist (see Rapoport, 1975b, 1979a).

The variability of standards, even the subjectivity of pain (Rapoport and Watson, 1972) and the subjective effects of stress (Rapoport, 1978b), leads to the inescapable conclusion that all stimuli are mediated via "symbolic" interpretation; that is, they depend on their meaning, so that meaning becomes a most important variable in our understanding of the environment, preferences for various environments and choices among them, the effects they have on people, and so on.

It should be noted that perceptual and associational aspects are linked: The former is a necessary condition for the latter. Before any meaning can be derived, cues must be noticed, that is, noticeable differences (Rapoport, 1977: ch. 4) are a necessary precondition for the derivation of meaning. These differences are needed and are useful for associations to develop. It is therefore interesting to note that among Australian Aborigines meanings of place are frequently stronger and clearer in locales where there are striking and noticeable environmental features (Rapoport, 1975a). Thus while the meaning of place is associational, having to do with significance, noticeable differences help identify places and act as mnemonics (Rapoport, 1980b).

In any case, however, the increasing interest in meaning is due to the overwhelming and inescapable evidence, from many cultures and periods, of its central importance. Consider just a few examples.

(1) When "primitive" art and, particularly, buildings of preliterate cultures are considered, they are generally considered perceptually. For example, the North West Coast Indian Dwellings and "Totem poles," Yoruba or Nubian dwellings, Sepik River Haus Tambaran in New Guinea, or Maori buildings are evaluated in terms of their "beauty," their aesthetic quality. If we wish to be more "scientific" we may evaluate their elaborate decorations *perceptually* and argue that they create a richer and more complex environment. Yet these decorations are *significant* and *meaningful*—their primary purpose is *associational*

in that they communicate complex meanings. This also applies to jewelry, body decorations, clothing, and other elements of material culture. Even the space organization of such buildings and their relations to the larger environment (the house-settlement system) have meaning and operate in the associational as well as, or more than, in the perceptual realm. This, of course, makes their real complexity greater still—their complexity is both perceptual *and* associational. Thus in order to understand "primitive" and vernacular environments, we must consider the meanings they had for their users (Rapoport, 1969, 1979a, 1979b, 1980b).

For example, in the case of India, it has been shown that all traditional built environments are basically related to meaning that (as in that of most traditional cultures) is sacred meaning. Architecture is best understood as a "symbolic technology"; it is described as *vastu-vidya*, the "science of the dwelling of the gods," so that cosmology is the divine model for structuring space—cities, villages, temples, and houses (Lannoy, 1971; Sopher, 1964; Ghosh and Mago, 1974; Rapoport, 1979b).

Of course, other traditional settlements are only comprehensible in terms of their sacred meanings, for example, ancient Rome (Rykwert, 1976), medieval Europe (Müller, 1961), China (Wheatley, 1971), Cambodia (Giteau, 1976), and many others (see Rapoport, 1979b).

(2) I have previously referred to the Mosque courtyard in Isphahan as an example of complexity and sensory opulence in the perceptual realm (Rapoport, 1964-1965; 1977: 188, 239). Yet the purpose of this remarkable manipulation of the full potential range of perceptual variables in all sensory modalities—color, materials, scale, light and shade, sound, kinesthetics, temperature, smell, and so on—was for the purpose of achieving a *meaning,* an associational goal. That goal was to give a vision or foretaste of paradise, both in terms of the characteristics imputed to that place and in terms of the contrast with the characteristics of the surrounding urban fabric. The full appreciation and evaluation of the quality and success of that design depends on an understanding of its *meaning* and the way in which perceptual variables are used to achieve and communicate it.

A similar problem arises with the medieval cathedral, which designers have tended to evaluate in perceptual terms—space, light, color, structure—yet the main significance of which *at the time* was in its meaning as a sacred symbol and *summa theologica*—a form of encyclopedia of theological meaning (see von Simson, 1953). Many more examples could be given, but the principal point is that historical high-style examples, as well as the preliterate examples described in point 1 above, must be evaluated in terms of the meanings they had for their designers and users *at the time of their creation*. This point was, of course, made with great force for a whole generation of architects and architectural students in connection with Renaissance churches, when they were shown not to be based on purely "aesthetic" consideration—that is, to be in the perceptual realm—but to be important sources of meanings and associations expressing important ideas of neoplatonic philosophy (Wittkower, 1962). Unfortunately, the lesson seems to have been soon forgotten, even though its significance seems clear for various types of environments. Consider two such types—urban space and vernacular design.

Urban Space. Regarding urban space, it can be pointed out that since sociocultural determinants are the primary (although not the *sole*) determinants of such organizations, it follows that meaning must play an important role in mediating between the stimulus properties of the environment and human responses to it (Rapoport, 1969e). This applies not only to built environments but to standards for temperature, light, sound, and so forth—even to pain. The reason, and the result, is that images and schemata play a major role in the interpretation of the stimulus properties of the environment. Wittkower's (1962) point about Rennaissance churches is applicable not only to various high-style buildings, but also to space organization on a larger scale—regions and cities (or, more generally, settlements). Sociocultural schemata are the primary determinants of form even on those scales and in turn affect the images and schemata that mediate between environments and people.

Urban form (and whole landscapes) can thus be interpreted. In many traditional cultures sacred schemata and meanings are the most important ones, and cities in those cultures can be understood only in such terms. In other cultures health, recreation, "humanism," egalitarianism, or material well-being may be the values expressed in schemata and hence are reflected in the organization of urban environments. Hence the widely differing nature of settlements and cultural landscapes in Spanish and Portuguese South America, in New England and the Virginias in the United States, in the United States and Mexico. Hence the differential impact of past or future orientation on English as opposed to U.S. landscapes and cities. Hence also the possibility, over long time periods, from Plato through Botero to the Utopian cities of our own day, of discussing the city as an ideal, a vehicle for expressing complex meanings. This also helps explain the transplanting of urban forms by colonial powers as well as by various immigrant groups. The centrality of schemata and images encoded in settlements and bearing meaning is constant; what varies is the specific meaning or schema emphasized or the elements used to communicate this meaning (Rapoport 1969e: 128-131). This also explains the different role of cities in various cultures, the presence or absence of civic pride, the varying urban hierarchies, and the very definition of a city, that is, which elements are needed before a settlement can be accepted as a city. Similar concerns influence the way in which urban plans are made—and whether they are then accepted or rejected—and also the differences among planners in different cultures and at different periods as well as the differences between planners and various groups of users (Rapoport, 1969e: 131-135). Without elaborating these points any further, I would just add that further work has only strengthened, reinforced, and elaborated these arguments about the primacy of meaning in the understanding of settlement form (see Rapoport, 1976a, 1977, 1979b, 1979c, and so on).

Vernacular Design. In the case of preliterate and vernacular design similar points need to be made, although clearly the specifics vary. In fact, the very distinction between vernacular and high-style design is partly a matter of the meaning attached to the two types of design (see Rapoport, forthcoming a). In the case of traditional vernacular the distinction, for example, between sacred and profane is far less marked than in contemporary situations, since it is the sacred that gives meaning to most things. Yet even in those situations there were areas of special sanctity—landscapes, trees, groves, hills, rocks, rivers, waterholes—or sacred built environments of some sort. Among the latter, sacred buildings or shrines have been important carriers of particular kinds of meanings—although not the only ones. Commonly such buildings have been assumed to be part of the high-style tradition and have been studied as high-style elements contrasting with the matrix made up of vernacular elements around them. Yet even among the vernacular buildings themselves it can be shown that, first, meaning plays a most important role; one can hardly understand such buildings or the larger systems of which they form a part without considering meaning. Second, among vernacular buildings one finds cues that indicate that there are buildings having differing degrees of importance or sanctity; in other words, among vernacular buildings there are sacred buildings, although they do differ from the corresponding high-style equivalents (Rapoport, 1968b). At the same time, the cues that communicate these varying degrees of importance or sanctity among vernacular designs tend to be rather subtle. This is because the models used in the design of such buildings and the elements used to communicate tend to be very widely shared and hence easily understood. Such cues can consist of any form of differentiation that marks the buildings in question as being in some way distinctive. Where buildings are colored it may be the absence of color—where they are not, the use of color; when other buildings are whitewashed, it may be the absence of whitewash—where they are not whitewashed, it may be the use of whitewash; it may be size, shape, decoration (or its absence), degree of modernity or degree of archaism, or many other cues (Rapoport, 1968b). In the case of vernacular design, as for urban space, it seems clear that later work has greatly strengthened, reinforced, and elaborated these arguments about the importance of meaning (see Rapoport, 1969c, 1975a, 1976b, 1977, 1978a, 1978c, 1979a, 1980b, 1981, and so on).

The importance of associational aspects continues in our own culture—even if the specific variables involved may have changed. An environment may no longer be a model of the universe—as a Navaho hogan or Dogon dwelling or village are—but it still reflects meanings and associations that are central, and even explains particular perceptual features (see Rapoport, 1969c, 1977).

(3) In U.S. suburbs, houses must not be too different—a modern house in an area of traditional houses is seen as an aesthetic intrusion, but the aesthetic conflict mainly has to do both with the meaning of style and with the deviation from the norm. This also applies to excessive uniformity, as in one legal suit that argued that a particular house was too similar to the one next door (Milwaukee Journal, 1973; see Figure 4). It is the meaning of the subtle differences within an accepted system that is important in communicating group identity, status, and other associational aspects of the environment while accepting the prevailing norms (see Rapoport, 1981).

(4) In evaluating student halls of residence, it was found that overall satisfaction was relatively independent of satisfaction with specific architectural features and had to do more with the character and feel of the building, the general image, and its positive or negative symbolic aspects or meanings (Davis and Roizen, 1970), that is, the associations

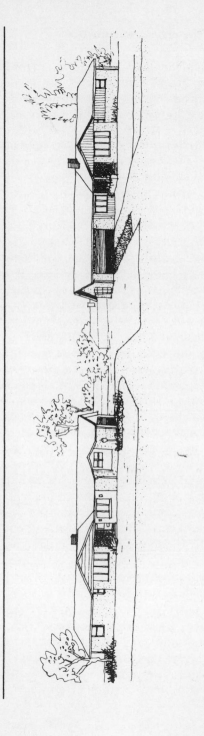

TWO ADJOINING HOUSES, W. DAISY LANE, GLENDALE, WIS.
(BASED ON PHOTOGRAPH, MILWAUKEE JOURNAL, SEPT. 26)

RAPOPORT

Figure 4

it had for students, which seemed to be related mainly to the notion of *"institutional character."* The important question, of course, that this book addresses (at least in principle) is which physical elements in the environment will tend to communicate that character or image defined as "institutional" by particular user groups.

(5) In a large study in France of reasons for the preference for small, detached single-family dwellings, respondents saw no contradiction in saying they preferred such dwellings because they provided "clean air" and, later in the same interview, complaining that washing hung out on the line got dirty because of the dirt in the air. Clearly it was the *meaning* of the space around the house that was important and that was expressed in terms of the image of "clean air" (Raymond et al., 1966; compare Cowburn, 1966). Two interesting, and most important questions concern the minimum space necessary for the meaning of "detached" to persist and the possibility of other elements communicating meanings that are adequate substitutes (see Figure 5).

(6) In a recent major study of the resistance of suburban areas in New Jersey to multifamily housing, particularly high-rise apartments, it was found that the reasons given were based on economic criteria, for example, they cost more in services needed than they brought in in taxes. Yet, in fact, particular mixes of housing could be advantageous fiscally. The commission studying this problem, consisting of economists, political scientists, government people, and so on, finished up by discussing perceptions and meanings. The perception of these dwelling forms as bad had to do with their *meaning.* They are seen as negative, as symbols of undesirable people; they are seen as a sign of growth, whereas suburban areas wish to maintain an image that is rural. The obtrusiveness of apartments, particularly high-rise apartments, destroys this rural self-image. Also, people moved to suburbs to flee the city and its problems—they see the apartments as tentacles of the city that they fled and that is pursuing them. The meanings of these buildings are also seen as reflecting *social evils,* as indicating a heterogeneous population, whereas the residents wish to live in homogeneous areas (New Jersey County and Municipal Government Study Commission, 1974). In other words, it is the meaning of particular building types that influences policy decisions.

Many other examples could be cited and can be found in the literature (for example, see Rapoport, 1977). But there is an important more general and theoretical argument that also stresses the importance of meaning—this has to do with the distinction already intro-

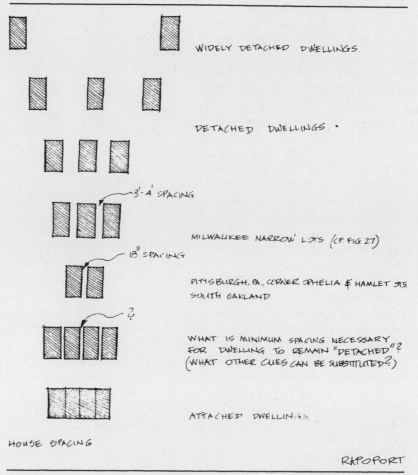

WIDELY DETACHED DWELLINGS.

DETACHED DWELLINGS.

3'-4' SPACING

MILWAUKEE NARROW LOTS (CF. FIG 27)

18" SPACING

PITTSBURGH, PA., CORNER OPHELIA & HAMLET STS. SOUTH OAKLAND

?

WHAT IS MINIMUM SPACING NECESSARY FOR DWELLING TO REMAIN "DETACHED"? (WHAT OTHER CUES CAN BE SUBSTITUTED?)

ATTACHED DWELLINGS.

HOUSE SPACING

RAPOPORT

Figure 5

duced between manifest and latent functions and, more specifically, the distinctions among an activity, how the activity is done, associated activities, and the meanings of the activity. It appears that the meaning of activities is their most important characteristic, corresponding to the finding that symbolic aspects are the most important in the sequence of concrete object, use object, value object, symbolic object (Gibson, 1950, 1968; Rapoport, 1977). Thus, even in "functionalist" terms, meaning becomes very critical.

To use an urban example of this (to be elaborated later), one finds that *parks* have important meaning in the urban environment. Their very presence is significant, so that even if they are empty—that is, not used in a manifest or instrumental sense—they communicate meanings of positive environmental quality of the areas in which they are located (Rapoport, 1977). This is clearly the reason for the importance of recreational facilities—which are desired by the majority but are used by very few (Eichler and Kaplan, 1967: 114; Rapoport, 1977: 52-53). Similarly, while most people express a need for common public open space in residential areas, it is because these "increase the attractiveness," "increase the space between units" (that is, lower perceived density), and so on, rather than for "walking around," "using for recreation," and so on—in fact, they are not so used (see Foddy, 1977). They all have the latent function of acting as social and cultural markers.

Such meanings, like most others, are evaluated in terms of the purposes of settings and how they match particular schemata related to particular lifestyles and hence, ultimately, culture. But the principal point has been made. Meaning generally, and specifically users' meaning, has tended to be neglected in the study of man-environment interaction, yet it is of central importance to the success of such a study.

2

THE STUDY OF MEANING

There is increasing interest in the study of meaning in a number of disciplines. Without reviewing the large and complex literature, a few examples can be given. In anthropology one finds the development of symbolic anthropology so that the "idea of meaning . . . provides an effective rallying point for much that is new and exciting in anthropology" (Basso and Selby, 1976: vii); there is also an interest in the study of metaphor (see Fernandez, 1974) and, more generally, the development of structuralism. Meaning is also becoming more important in geography, with the growth of interest in phenomenology and "place" (see Tuan, 1974, 1977; Relph, 1976). It is, for example, proposed that the human world can be studied in terms of signs (which guide behavior), affective signs (which elicit feelings), and symbols (which influence thought; Tuan, 1978). However, in terms of the discussion in Chapter 1, the first two of these can certainly be combined; the third will be discussed shortly in a broader context. In psychology, also, the study of meaning is reviving and has been approached, to give just one example, through the concept of "affordance" (Gibson, 1977), which deals with all the potential uses of objects and the activities they can afford. However, the potential uses of objects are rather extensive, particularly once one leaves the purely instrumental and manifest aspects and includes the latent ones. These are closely related to culture, yet that is neglected; in any case, the notion of meaning in terms of potential uses is rather ambiguous. Moreover, this concept has not been used in environmental research, and the question still remains: Which characteristics of environments suggest potential uses?

Meaning has also been approached through particular methodologies. Most used has been the semantic differential (Osgood et al.,

1957), which has spawned a great number of environmental research efforts. More recently, one finds the related but competing use of the repertory grid, based on personal construct theory (Kelly, 1955). These, being "experimental" in nature, limit the kind of work that can be done, who can do it, and where. For example, it is very difficult to study meaning in other cultures, to use evidence from the past, to use already published material—all important in the development of valid design theory. Such theory clearly must be based on the broadest possible sample in space and time: on all forms of environments, all possible cultures, all accessible periods. Moreover, these methodologies are partly independent of particular theoretical orientations of how environments and meaning are related.

From a more theoretical perspective, it would appear that environmental meaning can be studied in at least three major ways:

(1) Using semiotic models, mainly based on linguistics. These are currently the most common.
(2) Relying on the study of symbols. These are the most "traditional."
(3) Using models based on *nonverbal communication* that come from anthropology, psychology, and ethnology. These have been least used in studying environmental meaning.[1]

It is the third of these on which I will be concentrating. This is partly because these models are the *simplest*, the *most direct*, and the *most immediate* and they lend themselves to observation and inference as well as to relatively *easy* interpretation of many other studies. There are also some other, although related, reasons that will emerge gradually as the subject is explored.

Let me begin by discussing, very briefly indeed, some of the problems presented by the first two ways of studying environmental meaning before turning to a preliminary, and then more detailed, discussion of the third.

The semiotic approach

Even if one were not critical of this approach, one could justify exploring others due to their much less common use. The widespread use of the semiotic approach makes it less important to review it again (see Duffy and Freedman, 1970; Jencks and Baird, 1969; Barthes, 1970, 1970-1971; Choay, 1970-1971; Bonta, 1973, 1975, 1979;

Preziosi, 1979; Sebeok, 1977a; Eco, 1972, 1973, 1976; Greimas et al., 1970; Groat, 1979; Dunster, 1976; Jencks, 1977; Broadbent, 1977; Broadbent et al., 1980; Wallis, 1973 [although Wallis actually overlaps the semiotic and symbolic approaches, stressing the latter]; and many others [see also the International Bibliography on Semiotics, 1974]).

Yet the use of semiotics in the study of environmental meaning can be criticized. For one thing, there has been little apparent advance since its use began (see Broadbent et al., 1980). Another criticism is that even when interesting empirical work on meaning is done apparently within the semiotic tradition (for example, Krampen, 1979), it does not really need, nor does it relate to, semiotic theory. Moreover, in that case much of what that theory is meant to do (such as classification) is done better by other approaches, such as cognitive anthropology, ethnoscience, cognitive psychology, and so on. Similarly, other promising studies of meaning apparently within the semiotic tradition (for instance, Preziosi, 1979; Bonta, 1979) would do as well without those theoretical underpinnings.

Moreover, if everything can be a sign, then the study of signs becomes so broad as to become trivial. (This, as we shall see below, is also the problem with symbols. It also weakens the applicability of the structuralist model when one tries to apply it to the built environment.)

While in the long run such linguistic models may prove extremely powerful and possibly even useful, and some potentially hopeful examples can be found (Preziosi, 1979; Bonta, 1979), at the moment their usefulness is extremely limited and their use may even create problems. One such problem with semiotic analysis, which is a particular case of the use of linguistic models more generally, is the extremely high level of abstraction and the rather difficult and esoteric vocabulary full of neologisms, which makes much of it virtually unreadable. I must confess that I personally find these aspects of semiotic analysis extremely difficult to understand and even more difficult to use. While this may be a personal failing, I have found that many other researchers and practitioners, and most students, have also had great difficulty with them. Thus a recent graduate thesis on meaning by a mature student who was a faculty member referred to the "rigid theoretical framework" of semiotics, its "very complex technical jargon" and "its terminology usually so complicated that it is totally beyond the grasp of the uninitiated and apparently becoming more so" so that it is "hopelessly unintelligible" (da Rocha Filho, 1979)—and this was about one of the more readable efforts. As a result, it would appear that designers will encounter serious problems with such approaches and will resist tackling the important topic of meaning. This resistance will be compounded by the evident difficulty of *applying* semiotics—clear examples of actual environments and their analysis in reasonably straightforward terms tend to be singularly lacking.

If we accept the view that semiosis is the "process by which something functions as a sign," and hence that semiotics is the study of signs, then semiotics contains three main components:

- the sign vehicle (what acts as a sign)
- the designation (to what the sign refers)
- the interpretant (the effect on the interpreter by virtue of which a thing is a sign)

This formulation ignores many complex and subtle arguments about index, icon, and symbol as opposed to sign, signal, and symbol, and their definitions, relationships, and hierarchies (see one review in Firth, 1973). In fact, discussions of this apparently simple point can become almost impossible to follow, never really clarify the argument, and never help in the understanding of environmental meaning.

Semiotics, as the study of the significance of elements of a structured system, can also be understood as comprising three major important components; these, in my view, help us both in understanding some of the problems with semiotics and in taking us further. They are:

- *syntactics*—the relationship of sign to sign within a system of signs, that is, the study of *structure* of the system.
- *semantics*—the relation of signs to things signified, that is, how signs carry meanings, the property of the elements.
- *pragmatics*—the relation of signs to the behavioral responses of people, that is, their effects of those who interpret them as part of their total behavior; this, then, deals with the reference of the signs and the system to a reality external to the system—in a word, their *meaning*.

Generally, in semiotics, meaning has been regarded as a relatively unimportant, special, and utilitarian form of significance. Yet meaning, as those associational, sociocultural qualities encoded into environmental elements, characteristics, or attributes, would seem to be precisely the most interesting question. Another major problem, therefore, with semiotic analysis is that it has tended to concentrate on the *syntactic* level, that is, the most abstract. There has been some, although not enough, attention paid to the *semantic*—but hardly any at all to the *pragmatic*. Yet it is by examining which elements function in what ways in concrete situations, how they influence emotions, attitudes, preferences, and behavior, that they can best be understood and studied.

This book is precisely about this—*about pragmatics*. In a sense, one could argue that the stress has been on *la langue,* rather than on *la parole*—which is what any given environment represents and which should, in any case, be the starting point. It is not much use studying deep grammar when one wishes to understand what particular people are saying. Yet, in terms of our concern with the interpretation of how ordinary environments communicate meanings and how they affect behavior, the pragmatic aspects are the most important, at least in the initial stages. At that level, it is the embeddedness of the elements (and *their* meanings) in the context and the situation that are important—and that will be elaborated later. At this point, let me give an example I have used before (Rapoport, 1969d). We observe groups of people singing and sowing grain in two different cultures. In order to know the importance of these two activities to the people concerned, we need to know that in one culture the sowing is important and the singing is recreational; in the other, the singing is sacred and ensures fertility and good crops—the sowing is secondary. Thus in one case sowing is the critical thing; in the other, the singing. Alternatively, if we see a group of people standing around, yelling, and running, they may be doing one of many things. The situation and the context explain the events; knowing that it is a baseball game will put a different construction on the meaning of the actions. Thus it becomes important to define the situation and situational context and to realize that these are culturally defined and learned.

Consider an environmental example—the important meaning communicated through the contrast of humanized and non-humanized space (Rapoport, 1969c, 1976a, 1977). This frequently has to do with the establishing of place, and is often indicated by the contrast between the presence of trees and their absence. However, in a heavily forested area, a clearing becomes the cue, the element communicating that meaning; on a treeless plain a tree or group of trees is the cue (see Figure 6).

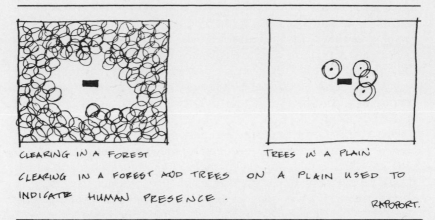

CLEARING IN A FOREST   TREES IN A PLAIN

CLEARING IN A FOREST AND TREES ON A PLAIN USED TO

INDICATE HUMAN PRESENCE.

RAPOPORT.

Figure 6

The reversals between the relative meaning of town (good) and forest (wild, bad) so common in early colonial America and the present meaning of forest (good) and town (bad; see Tuan, 1974), while they have to do with changing values, can, I believe, also be interpreted partly in terms of context. In these terms a steeple marking a small, white town in its clearing of fields among the apparently endless forest, dark and scary, full of wild animals and unfamiliar and potentially dangerous Indians, is the equivalent of a small remnant of unspoiled forest in an urban, or at least urbanized, landscape that covers most of the land and is believed full of crime and dangerous gangs. The context of each is quite different; the figure/ground relations have, as it were, changed.

In a town of mud brick in the Peruvian Altiplano the use of whitewash, reinforced by an arched door and a small bell tower, marks a special place—a church. In Taos Pueblo, the same cues are used to identify the church, in addition to a pitched roof contrasting with flat roofs, a freestanding building contrasting with clustered buildings, and the use of a surrounding wall and gateway (see Figure 7). In the case of a settlement that is largely whitewashed, it may be the use of color (as in some of the Cycladic islands of Greece), reinforced by size, the use of domes, and so on. Alternatively, it can be the use of natural materials, such as stone, in Ostuni or Locorotondo, in Apulia (Southern Italy). In that case the cue is also reinforced by other cues, such as size, location, domes, polychromy in the domes, special elements such as classical doorways or columns, and so on, to achieve the requisite redundancy (see Figure 8).

VILLAGE ON ALTIPLANO, PERU

TAOS PUEBLO, (S.W. UNITED STATES)

TWO CHURCHES SHOWING USE OF WHITEWASH & FORM TO CONTRAST WITH DWELLINGS BUILT OF IDENTICAL MATERIALS. (COMPARE FIG. 8). (BASED ON AUTHOR'S SLIDES).

RAPOPORT

Figure 7

In all these cases one's attention is first drawn to elements that differ from the context. They thus become noticeable, strongly suggesting that they have special significance. The reading of the meanings requires some cultural knowledge, which is, however, relatively simple; for example, the presence of the schema "church" (or, more generally, "important buildings," "sacred buildings," and so on).

It is also context that helps explain apparent anomalies, such as the highly positive meaning, and hence desirability, of old forms and materials such as adobe, weathered siding, half-timbering, thatch, and

LOCOROTONDO (APULIA, S. ITALY)
(BASED ON PHOTOGRAPH IN MERIAN, VOL 28, No4 (No YEAR GIVEN), p60-61)
HIGH STYLE INDICATED BY USE OF NATURAL STONE, POLYCHROME DOME, FALSE FRONT,
    DECORATION, SCALE, LOCATION ON CREST
VERNACULAR INDICATED BY WHITEWASH, SMALL SCALE, IRREGULARITY.

OSTUNI (APULIA, S. ITALY)
(BASED ON PHOTOGRAPH IN MERIAN, VOL 38, No4(No YEAR GIVEN), p62-63 & SLIDE BY C REISSER)
HIGH STYLE INDICATED BY USE OF NATURAL STONE, POLYCHROME DOMES, FALSE FRONTS, DECORATION, SCALE
AND LOCATION ON CREST & ALONG MAIN ROAD.
VERNACULAR INDICATED BY USE OF WHITEWASH, SMALL SCALE, IRREGULARITY.
        (COMPARE FIG. 7)

RAPOPORT

Figure 8

so on in Western culture and the equivalent meanings given *new*
forms and materials (galvanized iron, concrete, tile, and the like) in
developing countries (see Rapoport, 1969d, 1980b, 1980c, 1981).
This contextual meaning must be considered in design, and the failure
of certain proposals in the Third World, for example, can be interpreted in these terms—that is, as being due to a neglect of this important aspect (for instance, Fathy, 1973, can be so interpreted).

In linguistics itself, there has been increasing criticism of the neglect of pragmatics (see Bates, 1976)—the "cultural premises about the world in which speech takes place" (Keesing, 1979: 14). The development of sociolinguistics is part of this reevaluation; the point is made that the nature of any given speech event may vary depending on the nature of the participants, the social setting, the situation—in a word, the *context* (see Gumperz and Hymes, 1972; Giglioli, 1972).

In any event, it appears that the neglect of pragmatics and the concentration on syntactics almost to the exclusion of everything else are serious shortcomings of the semiotic approach.

The symbolic approach

Even if one includes some more recent versions, derived from structuralism, symbolic anthropology, and even cognitive anthropology, this is an approach that traditionally has been used in the study of historical high-style architecture and vernacular environments. It also has suffered from an excessive degree of abstraction and complexity. It also has stressed structure over context, but even in that case it seems more approachable and more immediately useful than semiotic analysis (see Basso and Selby, 1976; Leach, 1976; Lannoy, 1971; Geertz, 1971; Tuan, 1974; Rapoport, 1979b; among many others).

This approach has proved particularly useful in those situations, mainly in traditional cultures, in which fairly strong and clear schemata are expressed through the built environment—whether high style or vernacular. Many examples can be given, such as the case of the Renaissance churches already mentioned (Wittkower, 1962), other churches and sacred buildings generally (Wallis, 1973) or the Pantheon (MacDonald, 1976), the layout of lowland Maya settlements at the regional scale (Marcus, 1973), and the study of traditional urban forms (Müller, 1961; Wheatley, 1971; Rykwert, 1976). It has also proved illuminating in the frequently cited case of the Dogon (see Griaule and Dieterlen, 1954) or the Bororo (Lévi-Strauss 1957). It has also been useful in the study of the spatial organization of the Temne house (Littlejohn, 1967), the order in the Atoni house (Cunningham, 1973), the Ainu house, village, and larger layouts (Ohnuki-Tierney, 1972), the Berber house (Bourdieu, 1973), or the Thai house (Tambiah, 1973). Other examples, among the many available, are provided by the study of the relation between Greek temples and their surrounding landscapes (Scully, 1963) and more recent comparable examples from Bali and Positano (James, 1973, 1978). Note that in these latter cases the meaning first became apparent through observation—the locations of the buildings drew attention to something special, and hence important, going on within the context of the landscape in question. This was then checked more methodically; the interpretation of the meaning of these special elements required some cultural knowledge. In this way these examples come closer to the approach being advocated in the body of this book. Simple observation revealed quickly that something was happening. (This could have been checked in the cases of Bali and Positano by observing behavior.) By classification and matching against schemata the code was then read relatively quickly and easily.

I have used the symbolic approach in a relatively simple form. One example has already been discussed (Rapoport, 1969e); two more related examples will now be developed in somewhat more detail.

In the first (Rapoport, 1970b), it is pointed out that the study of symbolism (I would now say "meaning") has not played a major role in the environmental design field. When symbols have been considered at all, it was only in one of two ways. First, the discussion was restricted to high-style design and to special buildings within that tradition. Second, the discussion formed part of historical studies, the implication being that in the present context symbols were no longer relevant to the designer.

In the case of these special high-style, historical buildings, the importance of symbols has been recognized and well studied; examples are sufficiently well known and some have already been discussed briefly. But this kind of analysis has not been applied to environments more generally. In fact, the discussion is sometimes explicitly restricted to special buildings, specifically excluding "utilitarian" buildings, vernacular buildings, and, in fact, most of the built environment. Yet it is clear, and evidence has already been adduced, that this is not the case: Symbolism (that is, meaning) is central to all environments.

The definition of "symbol" presents difficulties. There have been many such definitions, all with a number of things in common (see Rapoport, 1970b: 2-5), although these need not be discussed here. The question that seems of more interest is why, if they are so important, they have received such minimal attention in design, design theory, and environmental design research. Many answers can be given; one is the difficulty in the conscious use of symbols in design and the manipulation of the less self-conscious symbols involved in the creation of vernacular forms. That difficulty stems from a number of sources—some very general (to be discussed later), others more specific.

Two among the latter are significant at this point—and are related. The first is the distinction proposed by Hayakawa (Royce, 1965) between discursive symbols, which are lexical and socially shared, and nondiscursive symbols, which are idiosyncratic. The argument follows that in the past there was a much wider area of social agreement about symbols and fewer idiosyncratic variations. Symbols in a given culture were fixed, known and shared by the public and the designers. A given environmental element would always, or at least in most cases, elicit the "right" responses (that is, those intended by the design) or at least responses within a narrow range. The choices were greatly limited by the culture and these limitations were accepted. This was so in preliterate, vernacular, and traditional high-style design. Under all these conditions the associations were much more closely matched to various forms and elements than is the case today. Today it is far more difficult, if not impossible, to design in the associational world, since symbols are neither fixed nor shared. As a result designers have tended to eliminate all concern with the associational world and have restricted themselves to the perceptual world; where they have not, the results have been less than successful.

Any attempt to design for associations at levels above the personal are thus difficult. This is one reason for the importance of personalization and open-endedness discussed earlier. Yet in any given cultural realm there are some shared associations that could be reinforced through consistent use. There may even be some pan-cultural symbols (Rapoport, 1970b: 7-8); yet variability today is the more striking phenomenon.

This brings me to the second, related study (Rapoport, 1973). This study begins by suggesting that the translation of symbols into form has certain common features in all forms of design—high style, vernacular, and popular. What seems to vary is the nature of the criteria used in making choices among alternatives that, used systematically, result in recognizable styles (Rapoport, 1973: 1-3; compare Rapoport, 1977: 15-18; 1980c). This involves a process of image matching that attempts to achieve congruence between some ideal concepts and the corresponding physical environments.

The question is then raised as to why popular design is disliked by designers even though it works well in many ways. In fact, one of the ways in which it works particularly well is in the consistency of use of models, particularly in chain operations. Given people's mobility and the need for environments that can be "read" easily so that comprehensible cues for appropriate behavior can be communicated, chain operations indicate very clearly, explicitly, and almost automatically what to expect. Seeing the relevant symbols, people know, without thinking, what behavior is expected of them, who is welcome, what level of "dressing up" is acceptable, and what food and services are available at what prices.[2] The cues are as clear, consistent, and comprehensible as in a tribal society and, in this way at least, such design is extremely successful and sophisticated. The question, then, of why such design is so strongly disliked by designers and other groups must be reiterated. The answer, in brief, is that the ideals incorporated in these images and schemata, that is, the values and meanings that are expressed, are found unacceptable. The result of this analysis is, therefore, that the problem is the variability in the symbols, images, and meanings held by different groups. These are not shared and, in fact, elicit very different reactions from various groups; mismatches and misunderstandings then follow.

As a result, there are problems with this approach. The above discussion deals with a specific problem: In nontraditional cultures such as our own it is difficult to use symbols when they are ever less shared and hence ever more idiosyncratic. This specific problem may, however, also affect other approaches to the study of meaning, although it seems to be exacerbated by relying on the notion of "symbol." But the use of the symbolic approach also presents more general problems to which I have already briefly referred and which I will now discuss.

These problems have to do with the common distinction between signs and symbols. Signs are supposed to be *univocal,* that is, to have a one-to-one correspondence to what they stand for because they are related to those things fairly directly, eikonically or in other ways; hence they have only one proper meaning. Symbols, on the other hand, are supposed to be *multivocal,* that is, they have a one-to-many correspondence and are hence susceptible to many meanings (for example, see Turner, 1968: 17). In this case correspondence is *arbitrary* and any part may stand for the whole. This then compounds the specific problem raised above since it compounds the difficulty of using symbols in analyzing or designing environments in the pluralistic situations that are now typical. There is also an even more general and basic question about the extent to which "symbolism" is a useful separate category, given that all human communication, and in some views much of human behavior generally, is symbolic. Some definitions of symbols tend, then, to be so general that, in effect, since symbol systems define culture (see Geertz, 1966a, 1966b; Basso and Selby, 1976; Schneider, 1976; Leach, 1976), *everything* becomes a symbol (as in semiotics everything becomes a sign!). Thus symbols have been defined as "any object, act, event, quality or relation which serves as a vehicle for a conception" (Geertz, 1966a: 5) and also as any "objects in experience upon which man has impressed meaning" (Geertz, 1966b). As we shall see below, one can look at environmental cues and analyze their meaning without getting into the whole issue of symbols, which can, and does, become fairly abstract (see, for example, Leach, 1976). In many cases, what used to be and is called symbolism can also be studied by the analysis of schemata and their meanings, for example by using cognitive anthropology approaches, so that settings can be seen as expressions of domains (see Rapoport, 1976a, 1977; Douglas, 1973b; Leach, 1976: 33-41). These in themselves, while simpler, are still complex. Moreover, one can frequently reinterpret major pronouncements on symbolism in terms of communication by substituting other terms in the text or leaving out the word "symbol" (as in Duncan, 1968). In a way, from a different perspective, the same point is made by the suggestion that symbols are neither signs nor something that represents or stands for something else; rather, they are a form of communication (McCully, 1971: 21). To say that A is a symbol of B does not help us much; the *meaning* of that symbol and what elements communicate that meaning still remain to be discovered.

Many analyses (for example, Leach, 1976), while discussing symbol systems (in this case from a structuralist position), in fact deal with culture as communication. What concerns them, basically, is that the "complex interconnectedness of cultural events [which includes environments and their contexts] itself conveys information to those who participate in these events" (Leach, 1976: 2).

The question is not that communication contains many verbal and nonverbal components—the question is how unfamiliar information is decoded, particularly expressive functions. Leach tackles this through signals, signs, and symbols that hopefully will reveal the patterning and information encoded in the nonverbal dimensions of culture, such as clothing styles, village layouts, architecture, furniture, food, cooking, music, physical gestures, posture, and so on (Leach, 1976: 10). He assumes that it will be like language without arguing this any further. Actually, we do not *know* that it *is* like language. Even if it is like language, we can begin with a simple, descriptive approach and get to structural analysis later. My approach will be to accept the task, about which we agree, to concentrate on built environments and their contents, and to try to approach the analysis more simply and more directly. This is, in fact, the major thrust of this book, that simpler approaches can be used to achieve more useful results in studying environmental meaning—at least in the beginning phases of this rather large-scale and long-range undertaking.

Interestingly, some studies of symbolism have made suggestions that I interpret as very close to my argument in this book. These suggestions are about the need to reduce the arbitrariness of symbolic allocation, which requires a stress on the social elements in symbolism and an interest in the processes of human thought and the role of symbols in communication (Firth, 1973). While this particular study does not even mention the built environment, the basic point that symbols *communicate*, that they are social, that they are related to status and represent the social order and the individual's place in it, are all notions that can be studied in other ways—notably through nonverbal communication. If culture is, indeed, a system of symbols and meanings that form important determinants of action and social action as a *meaningful* activity of human beings, this implies a commonality of understanding, that is, common codes of communication (Schneider, 1976). The question then is how we can best decode this process of communication.

The nonverbal communication approach

While this approach will be discussed in considerably more detail in the chapters that follow, a brief discussion at this point will help in comparing it with the other two approaches.

The study of nonverbal behavior has developed greatly in recent years in a number of fields, particularly psychology and anthropology (see Birdwhistell, 1970, 1972; Eibl-Eibesfeld, 1970, 1972, 1979; Mehrabian, 1972; Scheflen, 1972, 1973, 1974; Hall, 1966; Kaufman, 1971; Ekman, 1957, 1965, 1970, 1972, 1976, 1977, 1978; Ekman and Friesen, 1967, 1968, 1969a, 1969b, 1971, 1972, 1974a, 1974b, 1976; Ekman et al., 1969, 1971, 1976; Johnson et al., 1975; Davis, 1972; Argyle, 1967; Argyle and Ingham, 1972; Argyle et al., 1973; Hinde, 1972; Friedman, 1979; Weitz, 1979; Siegman and Feldstein, 1978; Harper et al., 1978).

The concern has been mainly with the subtle ways in which people indicate or signal feeling states and moods, or changes in those states or moods. The interest has been on their meta-communicative function and its role in changing the quality of interpersonal relations, forms of co-action, and the like. Studied have been the face and facial expressions, a wide variety of body positions and postures, touch, gaze, voice, sounds, gestures, proxemic spatial arrangements, temporal rhythms, and so on.

It has been pointed out quite clearly that people communicate verbally, vocally, and nonverbally. Verbal behavior is much more codified and used more "symbolically" than either vocal or nonverbal behavior. It thus seems incorrect, on the face of it, to argue that "language dominates *all* sign systems" (Jencks, 1980: 74; emphasis added), particularly in view of evidence that even language may be more iconic, and hence related to nonlinguistic reality, than had been thought (Landsberg, 1980). Be that as it may, however, all three—verbal, vocal, and nonverbal—act together; they may "say" the same thing or contradict each other, that is, reinforce or weaken the message. In any case, they qualify the interpretation of verbal discourse since they are less affected than verbal channels by attempts to censor information (see Ekman and Friesen, 1969a). Thus one finds that nonlinguistic somatic aspects of speech (paralanguage) greatly clarify spoken language. Tone of voice, facial expressions, and shared habits such as the meaning of relative physical positions, stances, and relationships of participants all help to clarify the meaning of spoken language well beyond the formal study of grammar, structure, and so on. In fact, it has been suggested that the sociocontextual aspects of communication, which are, of course, what one calls nonverbal, are the most important in the sense that they are the most immediately noted, that is, they are the "loudest" (Sarles, 1969).

Verbal and vocal behavior is received by the auditory sense, while nonverbal behavior tends to be perceived mainly visually, although auditory, tactile (Kaufman, 1971), olfactory (Largey and Watson, 1972), and other sensory cues may be involved—basically it is multichannel (see Weitz, 1979; Ekman et al., 1976). It is thus necessary to study a variety of other channels, although, so far, this has tended to be neglected (see Weitz, 1979: 352). Note that in the study of man-environment interaction itself, such as environmental perception, an analogous situation obtains: The visual channel has been stressed almost to the exclusion of all others, and there is even less stress on multisensory, multichannel perception (Rapoport, 1977: ch. 4).

I would argue that one such channel is the built environment. Yet, in many recent reviews of nonverbal communication (for example, Siegman and Feldstein, 1978; Harper et al., 1978; Weitz, 1979), there is nothing on the built environment, and even clothing and settings have tended to be ignored (see Friedman, 1979). Even if the role of the environment is not ignored, it is confined to space organization at the interpersonal, proxemic, extremely microscale level. At best, one finds scattered mentions of the built environment (see Kendon et al., 1975).

The concept of nonverbal communication in the environment can be used in at least two different ways. The first is in the sense of analogy or metaphor: Since environments apparently provide cues for behavior but do not do it verbally, it follows that they must represent a form of nonverbal behavior. The second is more directly related to what is commonly considered nonverbal behavior. Nonverbal cues not only themselves communicate, they have also been shown to be very important in helping other, mainly verbal, communication. They also greatly help in co-action, for example by indicating the ends of verbal statements. In that sense, the relationship is very direct and "real" environments both communicate meanings directly and also aid other forms of meaning, interaction, communication, and co-action. There are also methodological suggestions here for the study of environmental meaning. In nonverbal communication research, the links between different forms of communication have been studied by observing (or recording on film or videotape) cues and then making inferences. For example, how head and body cues communicate affect (Ekman, 1965; Ekman and Friesen, 1967) or how kinesic signals structure conversations among children (De Long, 1974). One can also study the amount of information provided by different cues—for example, by getting people to interpret photographs of situations, or the situations themselves.

Unfortunately, even in the study of nonverbal behavior, the stress has often been on its nature as a "relationship language" (Ekman and Friesen, 1968: 180-181), that is, on syntactics. Yet, because nonverbal behavior lacks the linearity of language, there has always been more awareness of pragmatics—both conceptually and methodologically there has always been a "simpler" approach rooted in pragmatics. There has always seemed to be an awareness that nonverbal communication could be studied either structurally, looking for the underlying system or set of rules somewhat analogous to language, or by stressing pragmatics, looking for relationships between particular nonverbal cues and the situation, the ongoing behavior, and so on

(Duncan, 1969). Thus in the study of nonverbal behavior both approaches have been used.

The stress, however, on the linguistic approach, with its high level of abstraction, has been unfortunate. Early in the development of the study of nonverbal communication the distinction was made between language as digital and dealing with denotation and nonverbal communication as analogic and dealing with coding; the analyses also needed to be different (Ruesch and Kees, 1956: 189). Thus environmental meaning, if it is to be studied as a form of nonverbal communication, is likely to lack the linearity of language (in semiotic terms, it is not "syntagmatic"). Environmental meaning, therefore, probably does not allow for a clearly articulated set of grammatical (syntactic) rules. Even in the case of body language, it has been suggested that there are a few aspects that may be coded in such a way that most members in a given community understand them. Most such cues, however, need a great deal of inference. This can be difficult, but guesses can be good *if the cues add up.* In other words, due to the ambiguity of cues their *redundancy must be great*—as I have argued elsewhere regarding the environment (Rapoport, 1977).

A role would also be played by people's readiness to make such guesses. This suggests that the insights of signal detection theory may usefully be applied to this type of analysis (see Daniel et al., n.d.; Murch, 1973). This argues that all perception involves judgments. In making judgments, two elements play a role—the nature of the stimuli and observer sensitivity on the one hand, and a person's willingness to make discriminations (his or her criterion state) on the other. Since all environmental cues are inherently ambiguous to an extent—that is, there is uncertainty (see Rapoport, 1977: 117, 150)—the criterion state, the observer's willingness to act on the basis of "weak" or ambiguous cues, becomes significant. At the same time, of course, signal strength and clarity, and hence thresholds, are still important; as we shall see, so are contexts—they help in drawing inferences from abiguous cues. Since designers cannot change the criterion state, they need to manipulate those aspects they can control: redundancy, clear, noticeable differences, and appropriate contexts (Rapoport, 1977). It also follows that since environments are inherently ambiguous, they more closely resemble nonverbal communication than they do language. Hence nonverbal analysis provides a more useful model than does language.

Environments and nonverbal communication also lack the clear-cut lexicons with indexical relationships to referents that language possesses. But it is frequently forgotten that in linguistics lexicons exist because of the efforts of descriptive linguists over long periods of time; linguistics began with dictionaries. It may be useful, therefore, to start with comparable approaches in studying environmental meaning by trying to relate certain cues to particular behaviors and interpretations—a point to which I will return. It is possible that "dictionaries" can be developed, as has been the case in the study of facial expressions (Ekman et al., 1972; Ekman and Friesen, 1975), kinesics (Birdwhistell, 1970, 1972), body movement (Davis, 1972), proxemics (Hall, 1966), gestures (Efron, 1941; Morris et al., 1979), and other types of nonverbal cues.

If we wish to study meaning in its full, natural context, we need to begin with the whole, naturally occurring phenomenon. This is what nonverbal studies have tended to do; so have ethological studies. In ethology, the view has been that a priori one cannot decide what to record and what to ignore: The important aspects are unknown. The first step is to describe the repertoire; the data themselves, then, inform subsequent research. Both conceptually and methodologically, the overlap between ethology and human nonverbal communication studies is very close.[3] For one thing, the behavior ethologists study is, by definition, nonverbal!! It is thus quite appropriate and significant that in ethology the first, and critical, step is to record repertoires and construct catalogues of behaviors—much as I am advocating here. In any case, such an effort, stressing semantics and pragmatics, seems potentially both more useful and more direct, particularly at the beginning, than a linguistic approach stressing structure and syntactics.

Note that all of these three approaches to the study of meaning, different as they seem to be, do have a number of general characteristics in common. These follow from the fact that in any communication process certain elements are essential (see Hymes, 1964: 216):

(1) a sender (encoder)
(2) a receiver (decoder)
(3) a channel
(4) a message form
(5) a cultural code (the form of encoding)
(6) a topic—the social situation of the sender, intended receiver, place, the intended meaning

(7) the context or scene, which is part of what is being communicated but is partly external to it—in any case, a given

This commonality links the three approaches described at a high level of generality. It suggests that in starting the study of environmental meaning through the use of nonverbal communication models, one does not preclude the others. Eventually, should this prove necessary or desirable, it may be possible to move to the use of linguistic models.

So far, however, environmental meaning has not been studied using nonverbal models, nor has the analysis of nonverbal communication really dealt with built environments and their furnishings, urban areas, and the like. The stress has been on human behavior at the microscale. It therefore seems useful to consider whether this approach can work when applied to built environments.

Notes

1. Note, however, the existence of a new journal (1976), *Environmental Psychology and Non-Verbal Behavior*, which may begin to redress this gap.
2. While making some editorial changes to this manuscript in mid-1982, I came across a postcard issued by Holiday Inn that illustrates my argument perfectly. In big letters, it says, "The best surprise is no surprise."
3. I will not, however, review the literature on ethology generally or on its relation to humans or its relevance to man-environment research.

3

ENVIRONMENTAL MEANING
Preliminary Considerations for
a Nonverbal Communication Approach

In line with the particular approach described in the preface, I will begin with an apparently very different and unrelated topic—one of the three basic questions of man-environment studies: the effect of environment on behavior (Rapoport, 1977). This is a very large and complex topic on which there are different views and of which there are many aspects that cannot be discussed here (see Rapoport, 1983). But one distinction that seems extremely useful, which will come up several times, is that between what could be called *direct* and *indirect* effects. The best way to clarify this distinction is through the use of two studies as examples.

In the first (Maslow and Mintz, 1956; Mintz, 1956), people were asked to perform various tasks—rate photographs of faces along various dimensions, grade examination papers, and so on—in a "beautiful" and an "ugly" room. Disregarding the meaning of these terms, and the validity and replicability of the findings (on which there is a sizable literature, of no interest to us here), it is found that human reactions and performance change in response to the effects of the characteristics of the two rooms: that is, these environments have some direct effect on the people in them.

In the second study (Rosenthal, 1966: 98-101, 245-249), the concern is with the effect of laboratory settings on how people perform in psychological tests. Only a few pages of a large book deal with this topic, but I found them seminal, since they got me started on this whole topic. In these studies there were still two rooms, but they were not "ugly" and "beautiful," but rather *impressive* and *unimpressive*. There were also experimenters present—dressed in certain ways, of certain age, mien, and demeanor—corresponding to the room that was their setting. In brief, one situation was of high status, the other of low status—and these influenced the test results on the highly standardized samples used.

The critical point is that the effects are *social* but the cues on the basis of which the social situations are judged are *environmental*—the size of the room, its location, its furnishings, the clothing and other characteristics of the experimenter (which are, of course, a part of the environment). They all communicate identity, status, and the like and through this they establish a context and define a situation. The subjects read the cues, identify the situation and the context, and act accordingly. The process is rather analogous to certain definitions of culture that stress its role in enabling people to co-act through sharing notions of appropriate behavior. The question then becomes one of how the environment helps people behave in a manner acceptable to the members of a group in the roles that the particular group accepts as appropriate for the context and the situation defined.

In all these cases, cues have the purpose of letting people know in which kind of domain or setting they are, for example, in conceptual, taxonomic terms whether front/back, private/public, men's/women's, high status/low status; in more specific terms whether a lecture hall or seminar room, living room or bedroom, library or discotheque, "good" or "ordinary" shop or restaurant, and so on.

That this is the case becomes clear from studies such as that of offices in the British Civil Service (Duffy, 1969), where it was found that the size, carpeting, number of windows, furnishings, and other elements of a room are carefully specified for each grade of civil servant. While this may appear nonsensical at first, on further reflection it makes extremely good sense. In effect, once the code is learned, one knows who one's interlocutor is, and is helped to act appropriately. The process is, in fact, universal, the main difference being that generally the rules are "unwritten" (Goffman, 1959, 1963)—whereas in the above case they appear in written form in manuals. Generally in offices location, size, controlled access, furnishings and finishes, degree of personalization, and other elements communicate status. An interesting question is what happens in open-space offices. In fact, other sets of cues tend to develop.

One can suggest that position, distance, and decoration in offices communicate social information about the occupant and about how he or she would like others to behave when in his or her room. How an occupant organizes the office communicates meanings about that occupant, about private and public zones, and hence about behavior. Business executives and academics, for example, arrange these zones very differently, so that status and dominance are much less important in academic offices than in business or government offices (Joiner, 1971a, 1971b). Location within an office building as indicating status seems so self-evident that it is used in a whiskey advertisement (see Figure 9), which shows a sequence of lighted windows in an office building as showing "the way to the top" so that one can now enjoy Brand X. Other advertisements also frequently use office settings with particular sets of elements to communicate meanings very easily and clearly and hence to provide an appropriate setting for the particular product being advertised.

It seems significant that, with relatively little effort, a whole set of cues can easily be described for this one type of setting. These cues provide information that constrains and guides behavior, influence communication, and generally have meaning; they provide settings for behavior seen as appropriate to the situation.

This point requires elaboration. The conclusion of the argument about indirect effects is that in many cases the environment acts on behavior by providing cues whereby people judge or interpret the social context or situation and act accordingly. In other words, *it is the social situation that influences people's behavior, but it is the physical environment that provides the cues.* A number of points that will be developed later will now be introduced; they are based on Rapoport (1979e).

People typically act in accordance with their reading of environmental cues. This follows from the observation that the same people act quite differently in different settings. This suggests that these settings somehow communicate expected behavior if the cues can be understood. It follows that the "language" used in these environmental cues must be understood; the code needs to be read (see Bernstein, 1971; Douglas, 1973a). If the design of the environment is seen partly as a process of encoding information, then the users can be seen as decoding it. If the code is not shared or understood, the environment does not communicate (Rapoport, 1970b, 1973, 1975b, 1976b); this

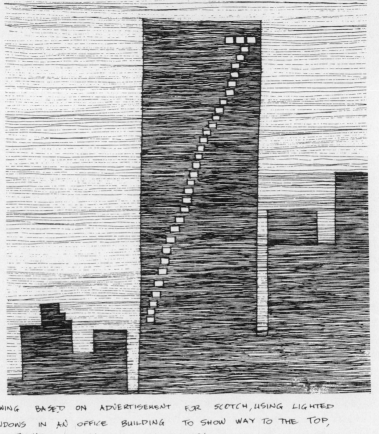

DRAWING BASED ON ADVERTISEMENT FOR SCOTCH, USING LIGHTED
WINDOWS IN AN OFFICE BUILDING   TO SHOW WAY TO THE TOP,
THE   REWARD BEING BRAND X SCOTCH

NOTE SELF- EVIDENT USE OF   HEIGHT TO INDICATE   HIGH STATUS
                               THREE - WINDOW OFFICE TO INDICATE HIGH STATUS.
(BASED ON ADVERTISEMENT IN COMMENTARY , VOL. 69, No 3, MARCH 1980, FOLLOWING p 12)
(SEE ALSO FIG. 21)
                                                      RAPOPORT.

Figure 9

situation corresponds to the experience of being in an unfamiliar
cultural context, culture shock. However, when the environmental
code is known, behavior can easily be made appropriate to the setting
and the social situation to which it corresponds. Of course, before cues

can be understood they must be noticed, and after one has both noticed and understood the cues, one must be prepared to obey them. This latter consideration did not exist in traditional situations and is a recent problem. Moreover, it is one over which designers have no control, although they can understand it. Designers can, however, have some control over the other two aspects—they can make cues noticeable and comprehensible. People need to be seen as behaving in places that have meaning for them (see Birenbaum and Sagarin, 1973), that define occasions (Goffman, 1963) or situations (Blumer, 1969a). In terms of behavior in environments, situations include social occasions and their settings—who does what, where, when, how, and including or excluding whom. Once the code is learned, the environment and its meaning play a significant role in helping us judge people and situations by means of the cues provided and interpreted in terms of one's culture or particular subculture.

It would appear that the sociological model known as *symbolic interactionism* (Blumer, 1969a), which deals with the interpretation of the situation, offers one useful starting point for an understanding of how people interpret social situations from the environment and then adjust their behavior accordingly. Note that I am not evaluating this model vis-à-vis others and that it is also clear that it needs to be modified for the purpose by considering some anthropological ideas and some notions about nonverbal communication with which this book deals. The specific question to be addressed is how environments help organize people's perceptions and meanings and how these environments, which act as surrogates for their occupants and as mnemonics of acceptable interpretations, elicit appropriate social behavior. In fact, it can be suggested that situations are best understood and classified in terms of the behavior they elicit (Frederiksen, 1974).

The symbolic interactionist approach to the definition of the situation can be summarized in three simple propositions (Blumer, 1969a: 2):

(1) Human beings act towards things (both objects and people) on the basis of the meanings which these have for them. [This central point is shared by other approaches, such as cognitive anthropology.]
(2) The meanings of things are derived from, or arise out of, the social interaction process. This is claimed to be specific to symbolic interactionsim. [Cognitive anthropology suggests that a basic human need is to give the world meaning and that this is done by classifying it into

various relevant domains and naming those. These domains often
correspond to the settings of everyday life; Rose, 1968; Tyler, 1969;
Spradley, 1972; Rapoport, 1976a, 1976b.]
(3) These meanings are handled in, and modified through, an inter-
pretative process used by people in dealing with the things which they
encounter. Meaning is thus not intrinsic and interpretation plays a
critical role [although, I would add, the interpretation is frequently
"given" by the culture].

It is the position of social interactionism that human groups exist
through action; both culture and social structure depend on what
people do: Interaction forms conduct. This view tends to neglect previous tradition (what we call culture) whereby we are shown and told
how to interact, what is expected of us, and what the relevant cues are.
We are told how to behave partly through the environment—the
objects of the world are given meaning partly by other people's
actions encoded in them.

Blumer (1969a: 10-11) speaks of physical, social, and abstract
objects, but in the built environment these are combined and interact;
most conceptualizations of the built environment stress this point—
that environments are more than physical (see review in Rapoport,
1977: 8). Thus one acts toward objects in terms of meaning, that is,
objects indicate to people how to act; social organization and culture
supply a fixed set of cues, which are used to interpret situations and
thus help people to act appropriately. In this connection the built
environment provides an important set of such cues; it is partly a
mnemonic device, the cues of which trigger appropriate behavior.

As already suggested, more stress needs to be given to the routiniz-
ing of behavior, the formation of habits, which is one thing culture is
about. It is this process that answers the question (Blumer 1969a: 136)
about how acts of interpretation can be given the constancy they need.
One answer, to be developed later, is that this is part of the enculturation process in which the environment itself plays a role (see Sherif and
Sherif, 1963; Rapoport, 1978a). It does this through the association
of certain environmental cues and elements with certain people and
behaviors; this is assimilated into a schema whereby these elements
come to stand partly for these people and behaviors; finally, these cues
can be used to identify unknown people prior to any behavior—or
even when the people are not there. At this point we begin, in fact, to
get a combination of symbolic interactionism, environment as communication, cognitive anthropology, the notion of behavior settings,

indirect effects of environment on behavior, and other important environmental themes—clearly the beginnings of a fairly large conceptual schema. Without considering that any further, let us continue with our theme: the insights that symbolic interactionism and its approach to the definition of the situation can provide.

The constancy of interpretation is partly the result of joint action that is repetitive, stable, and essential in any settled society (Blumer, 1969a: 17): Members of a culture *know* how to act appropriately in various settings; in fact, one definition of culture is in terms of people's ability to co-act effectively (Goodenough, 1957). Members of a culture also know the settings and the situations with which they are associated; different cultures have different settings, and the behavior appropriate to apparently similar settings may vary in different cultures.

The fixed cues and meanings encoded in the environment of any particular culture help make behavior more constant, that is, they help avoid the problem of totally idiosyncratic interpretation. This would not only make any social structure or cultural agreement impossible and hence make any social interaction extremely difficult, it is also likely that it would demand so much information processing as to exceed human channel capacity for such processing (see Miller, 1956; Milgram 1970; Rapoport, 1976b, 1977, 1980-1981).

In effect, in addition to the psychological and cultural filters people use to reduce alternatives and information, one important function of the built environment is to make certain interpretations impossible or, at least, very unlikely—that is, to elicit a predisposition to act in certain predictable ways. Settings, if people notice, properly interpret, and are prepared to "obey" the cues, elicit appropriate behavior. Environments in traditional cultures have done this extremely effectively and with very high probability of success. In the case of our own culture (with some exceptions, already discussed above), the degree of idiosyncrasy has greatly increased, making the process less certain and less successful. Environments and settings, however, still do fulfill that function—people do act differently in different settings and their behavior tends to be congruent; environments do reduce the choice of likely interpretations.

Consider theoretical suggestions from two different fields. Regarding art, it has been suggested (Wollheim, 1972: 124) that the observer does not do all of the interpretation. The better someone understands a work of art, the less of the content he or she imposes and the more is communicated: "The work of art should be to some extent a straight-jacket in regard to the eventual images that it is most likely to induce." If we substitute "environment" for "work of art" the parallel is very close, and the concept of culture shock followed by learning or accul-turation parallels that of aesthetic learning. It is also instructive to com-pare the traditional situation in art, with a fixed canon and lexical (shared) meanings and great persistence over time, with the con-temporary situation, with highly idiosyncratic and rapidly changing meanings, stressing novelty and in-group meanings. The parallel to environmental design is very striking.

In a more sociological context a useful suggestion has recently been made along the same lines that well complements Blumer's model. This is the suggestion that the definition of the situation is most usefully understood in terms of the *dramaturgical view* (Perinbanayagam, 1974; see also Britten, 1973; Goffman, 1963). This is useful because this perspective inevitably includes a stage, and hence a setting, props, and cues. This also makes it useful to combine the notion of the behavior setting (Barker, 1968) with that of the role setting (Goffman, 1963): The idea of "setting" becomes much more concrete.

The problem is always one of congruence between the individual's idiosyncratic definition of the situation and those definitions that society provides—and that are encoded in the cues of the various places and settings within which action is always situated. "Parties and railway stations did not just happen to be there: they were established as ways of eliciting a particular definition [of the situation] from who-ever may come along" (Perinbanayagam, 1974: 524). There is, of course, always some flexibility, some ability to redefine the situation, and the situation itself always presents some choice, but an appro-priate setting restricts the range of choices (Perinbanayagam, 1974: 528). *Such definitions are greatly constrained by environment,* and these constraints often are enforced through both formal and informal sanctions. This is the critical point, and the one on which this inter-pretation differs from Blumer's. Meanings are not constructed *de novo* through interaction in each case. Once learned, they become expectations and norms and operate semiautomatically.

Much of culture consists of habitual, routinized behavior that often is almost automatic; since the range of choices is greatly restricted in traditional cultures, the response tends to be *more* automatic, consis-tent, and uniform (Rapoport, 1969c, 1975b, 1976b, forthcoming). Once the rules operating in a setting are widely known and the cues identify that setting without ambiguity and with great consistency, these then elicit appropriate meanings (Douglas, 1973b), appropriate definitions of the situation, and, hence, appropriate behavior.

The definition of a situation can thus only arise when the parties to a transaction are at least minimally familiar with the customs of the group and have enough knowledge to interpret the situation in terms of the cues present (Perinbanayagam, 1974: 524). In other words, people must be able to interpret the code embodied in the built environment. In the current context they must be able to operate among different coding systems (see Bernstein, 1971), and this compounds the problem: Operating in pluralistic contexts can be very difficult indeed. Also, rapid culture change, modernization, development, and the like can lead to extreme difficulties in this domain and thus constitute a variable to be considered in policymaking, planning, and design (see Rapoport, 1979c, forthcoming).

In this connection behavior, clothing, hairstyles, and other similar elements can also elicit appropriate behavior in similar ways. In fact, all cultural material can act as mnemonic devices that communicate expected behavior (Geertz, 1971; Fernandez, 1971, 1974, 1977). Thus in the case of the Fang in Africa, the *Aba Eboka*, a religious structure for the syncretic religion known as the *Buiti* cult, forms a setting for a situation that is a miniature of the whole cultural system: It is a paradigm, or miniaturized setting, that reminds participants of a whole cultural system. By recreating a setting that is disappearing in its full-size form, it elicits appropriate behavior and proper responses. In this sense it reminds participants of a whole set of situations (Fernandez, 1977). Front lawns can play a similar role in our culture (Sherif and Sherif, 1963; Werthman, 1968); so can location, vegetation, materials, and other environmental elements (Royse, 1969; Duncan, 1973).

This last point will be discussed later in more detail. For now let us consider clothing, mentioned above. When clothing's role in providing identity and thus helping to define social situations breaks down due to lack of consistency, it becomes difficult to place people into categories, that is, to interpret their identities on the basis of costume; it also becomes more difficult to act appropriately (Blumer, 1969b). Traditionally, costume played an important role in this process (Roach and Eicher, 1965, 1973), as did facial scars, hairstyles, and many other similar physical, as well as behavioral, variables. This is important: When people can be identified as to type, potential situations are more easily defined; such people are no longer fully strangers (Lofland, 1973), and appropriate behavior becomes much easier.

Clothing is still used to classify people and is often selected to be congruent with given situations (Rees et al., 1974), but the consistency and predictability of such cues is now greatly reduced compared to traditional situations, in which costumes and other such markers had almost complete predictability; mode of dress was often laid down by law as well as by custom. Under these new conditions other cues, including the built environment, become more important (see Lofland, 1973; Johnston, 1971a). This also applies when knowledge of people (say within a small group), accent, "old school ties," and other similar devices cease to operate. Under all these conditions, as we shall see later, people's location in physical and social space becomes more important—and is often indicated by the settings in which they are found. These settings themselves are identified by various cues—if these can be "read."

Settings thus need to communicate their intended nature and must be congruent with the situation so as to elicit congruent acts. Settings, however, can also be understood as cognitive domains made visible. This conceptualization has two consequences: First, there are important, continuing relationships to culture and to psychological processes, such as the use of cognitive schemata and taxonomies, that tend to be neglected in the sociological literature. Second, conflicts can easily arise in pluralistic contexts when settings may elicit different meanings and behaviors—or where particular groups may reject meanings that they in fact fully understand.

Thus, at the same time that environments become more important from this point of view, they also tend to lose clarity and have less congruence with other aspects of culture; meanings become idiosyncratic and nondiscursive rather than shared and hence discursive or lexical (see Hayakawa, in Royce, 1965). To compound these problems, environments also become less legible—various cognitive domains lose their clarity and become blurred, their intended occupants and rules of inclusion or exclusion become less clear; codes multiply and are thus unknown to many. Environments cease to communicate clearly; they do not set the scene or elicit appropriate behavior (see Petonnet, 1972a). While there are also clear consequences of cultural and subcultural specificity and variability (Petonnet, 1972b; Rapoport, 1976b, 1977; Ellis, 1972, 1974), one finds, in broader terms, major differences between traditional (mainly vernacular) and contemporary environments. The congruence present in traditional cultures and environments, the rules of the organization of the environment—

of space, time, meaning, and communication—have tended to disappear. These rules were congruent with each other, with the unwritten rules of culture, with the ways in which situations were defined, with the ways in which settings were defined, and with the rules of inclusion or exclusion of people. As a result they elicited the expected behaviors. Today these processes do not work nearly as well—there are major incongruences all along the line among various cultures and subcultures and, not least, between planners and designers on the one hand and the various publics on the other.

The significant point for the purpose of this argument is that the role of the built environment in limiting responses has been most important in the definition of the situation and thus in helping people to behave appropriately. Like culture, environments have traditionally had the role of helping people to behave in a manner appropriate to the norms of a group. Without such help behavior becomes much more difficult and demanding. A better understanding of this process should enable us to make greater use of this role of environments; hence this book.

Many of the points just raised will be elaborated later. I will also discuss the ways in which environments transmit those meanings that define situations and, in turn, influence behavior and communication. At this point, however, one issue briefly mentioned above requires elaboration, particularly since it is intimately related to the whole issue of how meanings and learned behavior become habitual and routinized. This is the issue of enculturation (and acculturation) and the role of the environment in that process (Rapoport, 1978a).

Enculturation and environment

The question is basically how those codes are learned that allow the decoding of the cues present in the environment. It seems clear that commonly much of this learning occurs quite early in life, that is, during enculturation. For immigrants and during periods of rapid culture change or culture contact, this process may occur later in life and is then known as acculturation. The stress in social science has been on the role of verbal messages of parents, caretakers, and teachers; of reward and punishment. However, it seems clear that the environment plays a role. While little research exists on the role of the physical environment in the process of enculturation, some suggestive examples from varied cultures can be found (Rapoport, 1978a: 55-

56). While many settings play a role in enculturation, the role of the dwelling and how it is used is primary in influencing small children, often at the preverbal level.

It seems intuitively likely that those dwellings in which there are distinct male/female domains, clear rules about the inclusion or exclusion of certain groups, a clear relation between roles and various settings, and a clear and unambiguous use of various settings will convey different messages and hence teach different things to children than will those where all these are blurred—or absent. For example, we find the insistence on a front parlor in the rather small English working-class house and even in the barriadas in Lima, where space and resources are scarce (Turner, 1967); at the same time, we find that when the possible effects of reduced dwelling size in the United States are being discussed it is suggested that the first thing to be eliminated should be the formal living room (Milwaukee Journal, 1976). The effects of such decisions, and of the lifestyles and values they encode, should be considerable. It has also been suggested (Plant, 1930) and even demonstrated (Whiting, 1964) that children who sleep in the same room with their mother (or parents) develop differently from those who have their own room early. Similarly, one could posit that order versus disorder, or formality as opposed to informality—as indicated, for example, by the presence of living rooms versus family rooms, dining rooms as opposed to eating in the kitchen, or eating anywhere—would also have consequences and effects on children's enculturation.

To use an example I have used before: The differences between a family that takes formal meals together and one in which meals are grabbed informally at odd times are likely to be important (Rapoport, 1969c). In fact, it has been suggested that a meal contains a great amount of information that is culturally learned and can symbolize much (Douglas, 1974). Meals are, after all, social occasions that include appropriate settings, occur at appropriate times, occur in appropriate ways, include appropriate foods in the right order, and include or exclude certain categories of people and behaviors. In other words, they have certain rules associated with them. All these things children learn during the repeated process of participating in such occasions. The distinction between such formal meals and grabbing food at various times is precisely the difference between the restricted and elaborated codes (Bernstein, 1971). The relationship between these codes and the organization and use of the dwelling has been sketched out suggestively and persuasively by Mary Douglas (1973a). She suggests that spatial layouts that convey a hierarchy of rank and sex, in which every event is structured to express and support the social order, will produce a very different child than one in which no such hierarchy exists, in which each child's needs are met individually, and in which each child eats when his or her schedule dictates (Douglas, 1973a: 55-56). In one case the environment, in effect, imposes an order, a way of classification, the learning of certain systems, behaviors, and acceptance of social demands. In the other case none of this is demanded or learned—a very different order is learned (Douglas, 1973a: 81), and we would then expect different enculturation processes and results.

The English working-class dwelling clearly embodies, that is, encodes, many of the characteristics of the restricted code in the same way the elaborated code of middle-class families is embodied in their dwellings (Douglas, 1973a: 191) and also expressed through them. Certain middle-class families and dwellings have taken the elaborated code in terms of individualized routines, mealtimes, and so on to that very extreme posited as hypothetical by Mary Douglas. The relationship of this to changes in the social order and consensus offers many interesting questions. As just one example—Would one see in this the conflict between the open plan of the architect and the resistance to it by many users? A related point was made by Rosalie Cohen at an EDRA 4 workshop (not published in the proceedings). This referred to the possible effect on the conceptual styles of children of the very different social organizations encoded in the physical environments of schools, specifically, the likely impact on the cognitive styles of children of open classrooms, with simultaneous activities, lack of classification and nonlinearity, as opposed to traditional classrooms—separate settings, each for a specific purpose, with its label and consecutive, linear use. She suggested that this would greatly influence the process of categorization of activities, simultaneity or sequential thinking, linearity versus nonlinearity, work habits, behavior and rules about ignoring concurrent activities, and so on. In other words, different rules would be learned in these two settings, and the learning of such rules is an important part of the learning of culture, or enculturation.

In its most general terms the environment can then be seen as a teaching medium. Once learned, it becomes a mnemonic device reminding one of appropriate behavior. If one accepts the view that environments are somehow related to culture and that their codes

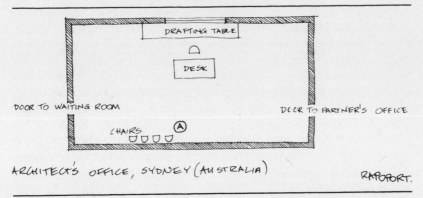

ARCHITECT'S OFFICE, SYDNEY (AUSTRALIA)

RAPOPORT.

Figure 10

have to be learned, since they are culture specific, then the role of the environment in enculturation (and acculturation) follows as a very likely consequence. In turn, this learning influences the degree to which environmental cues can be decoded easily and behavior adjusted easily to various settings. The topic of enculturation thus forms an important link in the development of the argument about how settings communicate meaning.

To summarize: Human behavior, including interaction and communication, is influenced by roles, contexts, and situations that, in turn, are frequently communicated by cues in the settings making up the environment; the relationships among all these are learned as part of enculturation or acculturation. The fact is that we all rely on such cues in order to act appropriately, although clearly some people are more sensitive than others. A personal anecdote, relating to offices, may help to make this clear.

This example concerns an architect in Sydney, Australia, who had had training in social science. His office was set up as shown in Figure 10. After they had been used by visitors, chairs were always replaced at point A. The architect then observed how entering visitors handled these chairs and where they sat. Three possibilities existed: A visitor could sit on a chair in place at location A; he or she could move it forward part way toward the architect's desk or all the way right up against his desk; or the visitor could even lean over the architect's desk, with his or her elbows on it. The architect felt that these three behaviors communicated ever higher degrees of status and self-confidence, and he acted accordingly. He felt that the results supported his assumptions and he found the system most helpful. In terms of our discussion, he clearly used these cues to identify the potential situation and modified his behavior accordingly.

The relationship between behavior and seating has long been known and can be intepreted both as communicating roles, status, and so on and as being dependent on context, as, for example, in the case of various tasks (Sommer, 1965), jury tables (Strodbeck and Hook, 1961), seminars (De Long,1970), and other group processes (Michelin et al., 1976), among many others.

All these indirect effects operate by establishing the context: Before elaborating this point it is useful to note that this has methodological implications regarding the possibility of establishing "lexicons" discussed above. In effect, the study of meaning, considered as pragmatics, can best occur by considering all its occurrences in *context*. The array of different meanings associated with any given cue can only be determined by surveying the possible kinds of contexts in which it occurs. This point has been made about symbols. The meaning of a given symbol or cluster of symbols cannot be determined simply by asking, "What is the meaning of A as a symbol?"; rather, it is necessary "to inspect the normative usage of A as a symbol in the widest array of possible contexts" (Schneider, 1976: 212-213). Clearly, one can substitute "cues" for "symbols" without loss of clarity and do so for elements in the built environment.

Since all behavior occurs in some context, and that context is based on meaning, it follows that people behave differently in different contexts by decoding the available cues for their meaning—and these cues may be in the physical environment. Thus context becomes an important consideration for the study of meaning and is, in fact, being stressed more and more in various fields; here again the different approaches to the study of meaning overlap to some extent. This overlap is due not only to the increasing interest in context in various disciplines but also to the fact that it has been discussed in general terms. Thus furniture arrangement, posture, conversational style, kinesics, and nonverbal behavior in general have been used to illustrate the importance of context and attempts have been made to apply contextual logic to analyzing these at a high level of abstraction (De Long, 1978). Regardless of the particular formulation and approach, a strong argument is made for the high general importance of context— although I will use it, once again, much less abstractly. This has long been known from perception—for example, the impact of context on changing the value of different colors, as in the work by Albers. Size, height, and other such variables are contextual—as in the Ames perspective room illusion and other optical illusions. This is also shown by the well-known experiment in which the same water may be experienced as both hot and cold depending on previous exposure. An urban analogue of what are essentially adaptation effects is the finding that the same city can be experienced as either drab or interesting, depending on which cities were experienced before (Campbell, 1961). Similarly, the same town can be seen as clean, safe, and quiet, or dirty, dangerous, and noisy, depending on whether one came to it from a metropolis or a rural area (Wohlwill and Kohn, 1973).

Social communication and context

Behavior vis-à-vis others, social communication, is often a result of judgments of others based on physical cues—such as dwellings, furnishings, consumer goods, food habits, or clothing. For example, clothing may have a stigma effect and thus reduce communication, but that effect of clothing will depend on the context—dirty or torn clothing worn while working on a car or in the garden will be evaluated quite differently than would the same clothing worn at a party or in a restaurant. This will have further differential effects depending on the subgroup at the party and the type of restaurant.

That clothing communicates and is used to project quite explicit messages about identity, status, group membership, and so on is clear from the recent spate of books and articles on how to dress for success, including the development of computer-programmed "wardrobe engineering" for success. One consultant advises people, at $50 per hour, how to dress for success—he points out that when a person enters a room many decisions are made about him or her based solely on appearance—mainly clothing. These judgments include economic and educational levels, social position, sophistication, heritage, character, and success. He stresses that many people feel that it is unfair to judge people by how they dress, but it is a fact (Thourlby, 1980). The implication is that particular suits or dresses, eyeglasses, colors, ties, shirts, and so on, their organization, and arrangement make a difference in the messages communicated and hence success in business (Molloy, 1976). The specificity of the recommendations also suggests that this is context specific—a suggestion that is quickly confirmed. Thus a New York appeals court barred a Roman Catholic priest from wearing clerical garb while serving as a lawyer in a criminal trial; it was held that this mode of dress would be a continuing visible communication to the jury that would prevent a fair trial (Hiz, 1977: 40). Clearly, in other contexts the use of such garb *would* be appropriate. Note also that to communicate particular ideological, religious, and social stances some priests and nuns dispense with clerical garb altogether.

Clothing generally has been used to communicate identity and has clear meaning. There is a large literature on dress, clothing, and fashion and their meanings which offers a useful paradigm also regarding the environment. Like built environments, dress has many purposes, one of which is to communicate status (meaning); other purposes include self-beautification and magico-religious requirements (both involving meaning), protection from the elements, and so on (Roach and Eicher, 1965, 1973). Dress indicates identity, roles, status, and the like and changes in fashion indicate changes in roles and self-concepts in society (Richardson and Kroeber, 1940). Dress is related to ideal body types, to activities, and to posture, all of which are culturally variable. Fashion communicates meaning by color, line, shape, texture, decoration, value, and so on and is used to communicate group identity. This it did particularly well in traditional societies in which it expressed ethnic and other forms of group identity and was used to place people in social space; it was frequently prescribed for different groups (Lofland, 1973). Clothing was thus dependent on culture, an important form of context.

There were also *proscriptions* about its use—sumptuary laws—applied to dwellings as well as to clothing, the purpose of which was to prevent the use of particular elements by various groups as a way of preventing them from expressing high status. This works much less well in modern societies, where meaning generally cannot really develop due to wide choice, mass production, haphazard use, rapid change, and so on (much as in built environments). But this very rapidity of change may, in fact, add importance to fashion as a way of defining particular elite groups—taste leaders (Blumer, 1969b). It is the ability of clothing to communicate meaning in traditional societies and its much lesser (although still present) ability to do so in modern societies that have led to the disappearance of the ability to place people in social space (Lofland, 1973), a process also helped by hairstyles, body markings, and many other variables (Rapoport, 1981). When all these cues disappear, as we shall see later, environmental cues gain in importance.

In all these cases, however, context plays a role; the meanings are influenced by the setting. For example, wearing a tie (or not wearing one) depends on the context. In the case of students in Britain, where dress style has important meaning, wearing a tie was seen as having different meanings depending on whether the student was en route to a class or an interview (Rees et al., 1974). More generally, the clothing worn and the context are manipulated together, to establish or eliminate social distance, to express conformity, protest, or whatever. Thus bright clothing worn by experimental subjects led to greater personal distance (Nesbitt and Steven, 1974). This can be interpreted as being due, at least partly, to judgments made about the wearers. For example, informal clothing will be read as appropriate in an informal situation but will be viewed quite differently in a formal context, where it may communicate protest, lack of care, or ignorance; other cues will, in turn, help define the context. In the study cited above, in a Southern California amusement park the bright clothing probably had less effect than it would have had in a variety of other situations; the cultural context will also play a major role.

Wristwatches also have latent meanings quite independent of their role in showing time. They seem to communicate sexual stereotypes, for example, the male as strong and function-related, the female as delicate and aesthetic (Wagner, 1975). If and when sex roles and stereotypes change, that is, new schemata develop, the decoding of these meanings will change and one can predict changes in watch styles and in their meanings—that is, these, too, are context specific. Most generally, one can argue that *all* goods and consumer items have meanings that organize social relations (Douglas and Isherwood, 1979); this is, in fact, their latent, and major, function.

In social psychology, also, one finds that the willingness to help others is strongly controlled by the setting and the context that the setting specifies (Sadalla, 1978: 279). This also plays an important role in evaluating and judging educational levels or medical states. In fact, even self-definition can depend on context!!! (See Shands and Meltzer, 1977: 87-88.) Subjective definitions of crowding also depend on context, so that the same number of people in the same size area is judged quite differently depending on the context—whether it is a library, an airport waiting room, a cocktail party, a conversational setting, or whatever (Desor, 1972). This is particularly significant for our discussion since, in effect, upon entering a setting containing a given number of people in a given space, a judgment is made whether it is "crowded"— that is, subjectively uncomfortable—or not, depending on the appropriateness in terms of an identfication of the situation through a set of cues that indicate "library," "waiting room," "cocktail party," or whatever.

In anthropology there has been increasing emphasis on context (see Spiro, 1965; Hall, 1976; De Long, 1978). In psychology this has also been the case, so that "one of the most replicable findings in psychology is the fact that our evaluation of virtually any event is partly determined by the context in which the event appears" (Manis, 1971: 153)—which is, of course, also the thrust of Barker's work, as we shall see below (for example, see Barker, 1968). In that case, the context is the behavior setting. In the case of perception, learning, and so on, the importance of context in noticing, recognizing, and understanding various ambiguous cues in different sensory modalities is quite clear (Neisser, 1967). It is also quite clear that inference also increases and improves when context exists (Bruner, 1973). Thus missing sounds are restored in sentences using context (Warren and Warren, 1970) and words and sounds generally are more comprehensible in meaningful contexts. Subliminally flashed letters are noticed, recognized, and remembered much better when embedded in words and meaningful syllables than when they form part of nonsense syllables (Krauss and Glucksberg, 1977). At the same time, while the *importance* of context is accepted in psychology and is growing, major interest in it is really only just beginning (see Rosch and Lloyd, 1978).

The importance of context in terms of signal detection theory is, of course, that it makes it easier to make reliable judgments about ambiguous stimuli. This is due to the presence of preexisting, learned "internal contexts," which provide the ability to match percepts with schemata; the context communicates the most likely schemata, it is predictive. The resemblance to the action of settings as a *type of context* seems clear.

In the case of nonverbal behavior, as in the cases discussed above, context seems important. Thus the role of the social setting (or context) is extremely important, since no human behavior ever occurs outside a social setting, so that spoken language, nonverbal behavior, and culture all play a role both in the production of behavior and its perception (see von Raffler-Engel, 1978). In linguistics, also, context is increasingly stressed (see Giglioli, 1972). The argument is, basically, that pragmatics must be stressed—that is, that meanings must be studied in contexts, considering the surrounding circumstances or "situation." Similarly, it has been argued that context is most important in the sensible construing of meaning in language. The context provides a pool of stored information on which both parties to a conversation can draw. This information, contextual and general, that speakers believe listeners share with them constitutes the cognitive background to the utterances (Miller and Johnson-Laird, 1976: 125). It is pointed out that children learn not just language but *social speech*, which takes into account knowledge and perspective of another person (Krauss and Glucksberg, 1977). This, then, leads adults also to be influenced by the context and the situation—so that directions asked by a "stranger" or a "native" elicit very different responses; note that "native" or "stranger" is communicated by a set of cues, many of which, such as accent, clothing, and so on, are physical and, certainly, nonverbal (Cook, 1971). Thus, in the case of language, context is established to a great extent by nonverbal elements (Sarles, 1969), many of which may be physical. Bilingualism provides a good example of context and of the potential relationship of linguistic analysis to our subject, if it is approached in terms of pragmatics, that is, language as *parole*, not as *langue*. Language, like behavior, varies with context. It not only varies with the social characteristics of the speaker, such as status, ethnic group, age, sex, and the like, but also according to the social context. Different contexts elicit different linguistic usages. These not only involve rules of appropriate or inappropriate (right or wrong) usage, but also assume certain cultural knowledge, the ability to elicit understanding with minimal cues, such as the "shorthand" of professionals or the special speech patterns of in-groups, based partly on the role, the audience, and so on. In some cultures, this is informal, in many others it is formalized (see Trudgill, 1974). Again, this distinction is found in environments; in some cases formalized and in others not.

The parallelism between sociolinguistic approaches to language and the approach to environments here being developed goes further. It has been argued convincingly (Douglas, 1973a) that the use of linguistic codes and the use of dwellings parallel each other closely in English working and middle classes. This is also implied in the finding that there are correlations, in Britain and the United States, between language and social status and group membership (Trudgill, 1974: 44-45) and the corresponding finding that different status groups have different environmental quality preferences, evaluating the same cues differently and, while capable of making social inferences by reading environmental meanings, interpreting cues differently (see Royse, 1969). While I know of no research trying to relate these two sets of findings, the relationship is rather likely as a hypothesis. Note, however, that we are using sociolinguistic, contextual, pragmatic approaches to language, rather than the formal, syntactic, abstract approaches criticized before.

Analogously, the cognitive background to appropriate behavior is provided by designed settings and the cues that communicate appropriate meanings. Once a group is known, its lifestyle (in the sense of the choices made) and behavior can be observed and the settings in which activities occur can be identified. This process can be quite straightforward. It is often done informally in descriptions, novels, and the way settings are used in films, television, and the like, and can be discovered by various formal or informal forms of content analysis; one brief example has already been given and more will be used later (Rapoport, 1969a, 1977). Frequently, a simple inventory of objects, furnishings, materials, and so on will reveal their meaning and the way in which they operate to let people know in which setting or domain they find themselves (see Zeisel, 1973; Jopling, 1974). It is striking how quickly, almost instantaneously, this process of reading occurs and how frequently novelists have taken it for granted.

Clearly, in these processes it is necessary to learn the cultural knowledge needed to interpret the cues—very much as, in the case of analyzing language, one needs to consider the cultural knowledge necessary to make language work. In *all* cases of communication, "pragmatic knowledge" is needed for such communication to work. The actors must have cultural knowledge upon which to draw in order to embed messages in social contexts; that is, even language utterances cannot be analyzed as an abstract system but must be considered within the context of the "culturally defined universe in which they are uttered" (Keesing, 1979: 33).

This cultural pragmatic context often provides the knowledge needed to relate perceptual and associational aspects. For example, in many traditional cultures there is a relationship between the noumenal world of invisible spiritual beings and the phenomenal, physical world of perception. These may coincide at specific places, which then become sacred. This relation may be "invisible" to outsiders (as in the case of Aborigines, Eskimos, and others) and must be known; it may, however, be indicated by various cues that can be learned (Rapoport,

1975a, 1977). This learning for members of a culture is the process of enculturation, for outsiders (including researchers) it is one of acculturation.

Consider a more "concrete" example—the mosque courtyards of Isphahan already mentioned (Rapoport 1964-1965, 1977). These can be experienced and described in terms of their perceptual characteristics in all sensory modalities, the transitions employed to reinforce these, and so on. In those terms they can be understood as the manipulation of noticeable differences in the perceptual realm to define a distinct place. This place is special, however, in associational terms (as already discussed) and this meaning, the knowledge how to behave, what to do—a whole set of appropriate rules—to enable one to act appropriately and co-act effectively requires much cultural knowledge. This last point is basic, particularly if culture itself is defined in terms of what a stranger to a society would need to know in order appropriately to perform any role in any scene staged by that society (Goodenough, 1957).

Thus in Quebec, at the moment, there is great interest in vernacular architecture and use of the "style neo-Quebecois" for suburban houses using elements of that vernacular such as particular roof forms, porches, windows, facades, and so on. To understand its meaning, however, so as not to misinterpret it, demands cultural knowledge—an awareness of the current cultural context, nationalism, separatism, strivings for ethnic and linguistic identity, and so on. Similarly, the impact on the development of Boston of neighborhoods like Beacon Hill and sacred sites, such as the Boston Common, churches, and burying grounds (Firey, 1961), demands a knowledge of the cultural context within which the environmental cues communicate.

Note that generally this process works much more easily for users of "vernacular" environments in traditional societies. These communicate much more clearly because the contexts and cultural knowledge are much more shared—in degree of sharing, extent of sharing, and so on (Rapoport, 1980b, 1980c, 1981, forthcoming). Recall that we have already seen that designers and users, and different user groups, perceive and evaluate environments differently so that meanings intended by designers may not be perceived; if perceived, not understood; and, if both perceived and understood, may be rejected (see, for example, Rapoport, 1977). In this process the understanding and acceptance of cultural knowledge and contexts are most important. Yet, as already pointed out, and to be elaborated later, given the approach here being developed, the discovery of cultural knowledge is possible and not too difficult.

The notion of role settings and the dramatic analogy of human behavior (Goffman, 1959, 1963) can easily be extended to the communicative and mnemonic function of settings and environments, which house appropriate behaviors and also remind people how to behave. Thus, considering settings as expressing domains (Rapoport, 1976a, 1976b, 1977) and considering the distinction between front and back, one finds markedly different behaviors in front and back regions. A particularly striking example is provided by the changed behavior of a waiter moving through the swinging door between restaurant dining room and kitchen (Goffman, 1963). I will have more to say later about these important cognitive domains, which lend themselves to very different behaviors (see also Rapoport, 1977). Here it may suffice to remark on an experience in Baltimore, where similar urban renewal projects, based on clearing out the interiors of blocks and replacing them with parks and playgrounds, worked as intended in some cases and failed in others (Brower and Williamson, 1974; Brower, 1977). It is most likely that a major part of this difference has to do with front/back behavior, since in the second case designs that helped people use the street worked well and transformed the environment. Note that the definition of front and back domains, identified with public and private and associated with appropriate behaviors, depends on particular cues.

Given the above discussion, it is clear that in terms of the effect of environment on behavior, environments are more than just inhibiting, facilitating, or even catalytic. They not only remind, they also predict and prescribe. They actually *guide responses,* that is, they make certain responses more likely by limiting and restricting the range of likely and possible responses without being determining (Wollheim, 1972; Perinbanayagam, 1974). Note that is order to guide responses—to tell people that they should act in such and such a way—the conditions we have been discussing must be met. Note also that Goffman (1963: 3) begins by reminding us that mental disorders are often defined in terms of behavior that is "inappropriate to the situation." Clearly the appropriateness of behavior and the definition of the situation are culturally variable. My interest here, however, is in the process whereby settings communicate the situation and thereby the rules that elicit the appropriate behavior. This is done through *inference* (as in much nonverbal communication), whereby settings are identified as stages where coherence prevails among setting, appearance, manners, behavior, and so on (Goffman, 1959: 3, 25). The rules linking these are unwritten, and may be "tight" in some cultures and contexts and "loose" in others (Goffman, 1963: 190-200). It is here where inference becomes important; for it to work the inference must be easy to make and should be made in the same way by all those involved, hence the need for cultural specificity, clarity, strong noticeable differences, adequate redundancy, and so on. Note, finally, that the same physical space may become several different settings, housing different occasions, and hence eliciting different behavior that is appropriate (Goffman, 1963: 21). Thus the same open space may successively house a market, a soccer game, a performance, a riot, and so on, each with appropriate behaviors. Similarly, as some students of mine found in Haifa, Israel, a single street corner may become a series of settings for different groups; in this case it is the people who elicit the appropriate behaviors. This has also been shown to happen in Hyderabad, India (Duncan, 1976; compare Rapoport, 1980b, 1980c). The consequence is that the uses of settings and appropriate behavior can become difficult since their invariance is destroyed. In general, successful settings are precisely those that successfully reduce the variance by clear cues and consistent use, which increase their predictability.

I have already commented on some of the reasons for the success of chain operations—they are among the most predictable settings in our environment. A similar observation was recently made starting from a very different perspective: that fast food restaurants, such as McDonald's, are settings for ritual behaviors with "an astonishing degree of behavioral uniformity" that may have been remarkably successful in producing behavioral invariance (Kottak, 1979). In terms of my paper on the definition of the situation, such settings restrict the range of behaviors appropriate in the setting, and do so effectively, because they are legible—their meanings are clear and unambiguous. In this legibility the consistency of use of various design elements is most important in achieving a degree of predictability unknown since tribal architecture. At a different level, other chain operations, such as hotel chains, achieve the same effects by providing the uncertain traveler with certainty as to price, food, service, layout, mattresses, language, and so on.

In this process the users play an active role: They interpret the cues. While they may be unable to notice the cues or, if they perceive them, to interpret them, and while they may be unwilling to act appropriately, in most cases when cues are noticed and understood people will act accordingly—the interpretation is restricted in range among members of a particular group sharing a culture, that is, it depends on shared cultural knowledge and behavior. The evidence is all around us that *settings work*—people know how to behave and are able to co-act effectively in shops, classrooms, discotheques, and so on. In effect, people enter settings many times a day, identify them and the relevant information, draw upon the applicable rules, and act appropriately.

A rather interesting and very general argument that bears on my discussion here has recently been made. This proposes that the notion of "aesthetics" be dispensed with and that, in effect, art be defined contextually—those objects and behaviors are artistic that occur in settings defined as having the purpose of housing works of art: museums, galleries, theaters, concert halls, and the like (Peckham, 1976). Thus, although Peckham starts from a totally different perspective, his conclusion is quite similar. While there is much in Peckham's book with which I disagree, this particular aspect—which I came across in 1978, after developing my argument independently—seems to fit the model based on a very different position, and hence starting point.

Note that in this view art objects are such because they elicit aesthetic behavior, that is, we play a role involving socially standardized behavior determined by convention: "A work of art is any artifact in the presence of which we play a particular social role, a culturally transmitted combination of patterns of behavior" (Peckham, 1976: 49). Both in the specific argument and generally, playing a role involves a setting—in this case one that defines the situation as "aesthetic." Once the situation has been defined, the appropriate behavior follows. This is no different from the process that takes place in a market, tribal dance ground, classroom, restaurant, or whatever (see Goffman, 1959, 1963; Rapoport, 1980b, 1980c). Using the dramatic analogy, in all these cases we have an actor, an audience, and a stage. That this concept can help in connection with very different problems indeed is illustrated by a case in which the nature and origin of megalithic tombs in Britain were greatly clarified by analyzing them in just these terms—as settings that housed ritual performances involving actors and audience and that thus had both communicative and mnemonic functions, eliciting appropriate behaviors (Fleming, 1972).

The form of these tombs was best understood by considering them as settings for rituals involving actors and spectators. The requirements of settings can then be specified and the actual forms tested against them—and understood. Clearly these are culture specific. In any given case, or for cross-cultural analysis, a knowledge of the rituals, their actors, and audiences and hence *their* requirements would be necessary to understand the meaning of the space organization and furnishings of such sacred spaces. Clearly, also, these settings are much easier to interpret when the actors and audiences, the *behaviors*, are present. It is thus the total situation—the setting, the furnishings, and the people in them—that explicates the meaning, partly through increasing redundancy, partly by providing referents and "lexicon" items (as discussed before). In other words, there are shared, negotiated meanings that follow certain rules. These involve certain social conventions and form a cultural code. This was one of my criticisms of the symbolic interactionist model discussed above—that the meanings are not negotiated afresh each time.

Clearly, cues are clearer and meanings more widely shared in some situations than in others: for example, in traditional (vernacular) situations more than in contemporary ones (Rapoport, 1980b, forthcoming).

Since the "objective" and "subjective" definitions of situations may differ, appropriate rules and behaviors *may be incongruent with each other.* The setting, while permitting a variety of responses, *constrains them.* Once the situation is defined culturally, behavior is limited if the cues are *noticed, read and understood,* and if one is *prepared to obey them* (that is, environments cannot *determine* behavior since one can refuse to act appropriately). The possibility of refusal to act appropriately is a new problem that was never encountered in traditional contexts; in those contexts, people tended to respond appropriately and almost automatically. Also, designers cannot influence this element, as they can the other two: They *can* make certain that cues are noticed and, once noticed, understood.

The mnemonic function of environment

The environment thus communicates, through a whole set of cues, the most appropriate choices to be made: The cues are meant to elicit appropriate emotions, interpretations, behaviors, and transactions by setting up the appropriate situations and contexts. The environment can thus be said to act as a *mnemonic* (Rapoport, 1979a, 1979b, 1980b, 1980c) reminding people of the behavior expected of them, the linkages and separations in space and time—who does what, where, when, and with whom. It takes the remembering from the person and places the *reminding* in the environment. If this process works, and this depends on the cues being culturally comprehensible, being learned through enculturation (or acculturation in some cases), it reduces the need for information processing, it makes behavior easier, since one does not have to think everything out from scratch. In effect, one can routinize many behaviors and make them habitual—which is one of the functions of culture generally. By suggesting similar, and limited, ranges of behavior, this process also helps prevent purely idiosyncratic interpretations, responses, and behaviors that would make social communication and interaction impossible—or at least very difficult.

This *mnemonic function* of the environment is equivalent to group memory and consensus. In effect, the setting "freezes" categories and domains, or cultural conventions. In effect, information is encoded in the environment and needs to be decoded. But environments can only do this if they communicate—if the encoded information can be decoded (see Figure 11). This is usually considered on small scales, but whole landscapes and cities can have that function, as in the case of the Cuzco area of pre-Columbian Peru (see Isbell, 1978). I have already suggested that in traditional, particularly preliterate and vernacular environments, this process worked particularly well, whereas in many contemporary environments it works less well (Rapoport, forthcoming b).

How well this process works can be very important indeed. It has been argued that anxiety ("the disease of our age") is generated in an individual when he or she has to choose courses of action without having sufficient grounds on the basis of which to make up his or her mind. At the same time, contemporary environments, physical and social, provide ever less information to help people make up their minds— less social information ("knowing your place," "family," and so on), less environmental information, less cultural information (Madge, 1968). These are linked, since environmental cues and mnemonics communicate social information and help make behavior more habitual (Rapoport, 1977).

The importance of decoding is also due to the fact that it is intimately related to culture and suggests the idea that environments, if they are to work, must be *culture specific*. This coding is also part of the general idea of ordering systems, cognitive schemata, and taxonomies that are very important—but these form a different topic (Rapoport, 1976a,

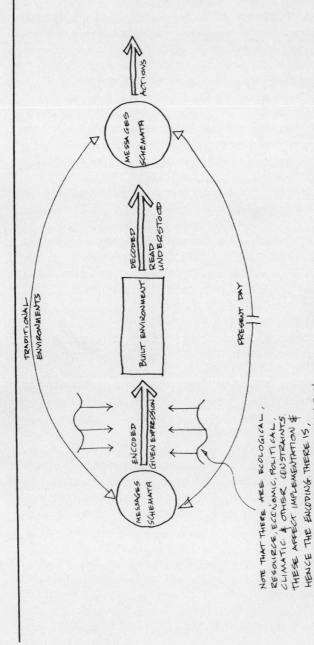

RAPOPORT

NOTE THAT THERE ARE ECOLOGICAL,
RESOURCE, ECONOMIC, POLITICAL,
CLIMATIC & OTHER CONSTRAINTS.
THESE AFFECT IMPLEMENTATION &
HENCE THE ENCODING. THERE IS,
THEREFORE, NO PERFECT TRANSLATION.
THE ATTEMPT IS, HOWEVER, TO
APPROACH AN IDEAL SCHEMA (CF. RAPOPORT 1977).
THESE CONSTRAINTS ARE IGNORED
HERE.

ENCODING/DECODING OF ENVIRONMENTAL INFORMATION

Figure 11

1977). However, it should be pointed out that these schemata, being part of the culture core (Rapoport, 1979c, forthcoming), help structure not only environments but also many behaviors. Hence the conceptual similarity between an environmental (for example, architectural) style and a lifestyle—both represent a set of consistent choices among the alternatives available and possible.

This I have called the choice model of design, where alternatives are chosen on the basis of schemata (Rapoport, 1976b, 1977) that correspond to the notion of lifestyle as a choice among alternatives in allocating resources (Michelson and Reed, 1970). It is interesting to note that this model developed from reading a paper on archaeology, in which it was pointed out that any artifact (in that case a pot) is the result of a set of choices among alternatives based on a "template" (Deetz, 1968). It thus encodes the template via a series of choices, so that any artifact encodes meanings, priorities, schemata, and the like, since it is the nature of the human mind to impose order on the world (Rapoport, 1976a, 1976b) by working through form (Douglas, 1975). Thus artifacts give expression to cultural systems that can be seen primarily as informational systems, so that all goods are part of an information system (Douglas and Isherwood, 1979); material and nonmaterial culture can be seen as *congealed information* (Clarke, 1968), that is, artifacts as outcomes of cultural processes encode information.

In archaeology, where the basic process is precisely one of "reading" material elements, the importance of "contextual analysis" has recently been stressed (see Flannery, 1976). Thus the meaning of archeological elements can be derived only if the context is known. This works on two ways: the objects, and the behaviors if known, help define the nature of the setting (on the difficulty of inferring behavior from archaeological data see Douglas, 1972; Miner, 1956); the setting, once and if known, can help define the nature of the objects found in it. I will return to the question of archaeology because the decoding of it is significant. From our perspective here, however, a more important consequence of the congruence of, and relation between, patterns of behavior and those artifacts called built environments is that the latter guide the former; they remind people how to act, how to co-act, what to do. They guide, constrain, and limit behavior without being determining.

When similar schemata control behavior and environments, we find maximum congruence between the meanings communicated by environments and the behaviors: culture as habitual behavior. In the same way we know how to dress, eat, use voice and body, and what manners to use, we also know how to use the environment—in fact, the environment helps us engage in these behaviors appropriately. The appropriate information and meanings reduce information loads by structuring the environment (a known environment is a simplified environment) and by structuring behavior correspondingly.

If, however, many contemporary environmental meanings are not clear, and if decoding (understanding the cues) becomes more difficult, what can be done? One important answer is that by increasing redundancy, the likelihood of messages and meanings getting through is greatly increased (Rapoport, 1977, 1980b, 1980c). The more different systems communicate similar messages, the more likely they are to be noticed and understood. This is important in language (which is highly redundant) but even more so in nonverbal or nonlinguistic messages, which tend to be less explicit, less clear than others.

We can see this operating in urban environments in two senses. The first is the finding (Steinitz, 1968) that when space organization, building form, sign systems, and visible activities coincide, meaning is much clearer and urban form much more legible and memorable. The other is that as the scale and complexity of social systems have gone up, the number of specialized settings, each with its special cues and appropriate behaviors, has gone up and the number of message systems has also gone up (Rapoport, 1980b). This helps us to interpret the point made by Venturi et al. (1972) about the separation of space organization and the eikonic and verbal message systems in modern cities and Carr's (1973) argument about their proliferation as meanings communicated by space organization have become less clear, as they communicate less effectively and surely than traditional urban and architectural spatial organizations. In those latter, location, height, domain definition, scale, shape, color, and the like all have unequivocal meanings. In modern environments, where they are much less clear, additional message systems of verbal signs, eikonic signs, and so on have had to be added and superimposed. This point has also been made by others (for example, Choay, 1970-1971) on the basis of semiotic analyses. These eikonic and verbal systems work best when they are clearly related to the space organization—that is, when redundancy is increased.

Also important is *consistency* of use, which, in fact, explains the effectiveness of traditional spatial organizations in communicating clear meanings. Traditional spatial organizations tended to be used in the same way in similar contexts and situations. Recall that this was also the point made above about the hypothesis that part of the success of chain operations of various types is precisely that they are used consistently and hence become highly predictable; they communicate very effectively. In other words, particular names and signs define not only environments but what they contain—types of beds, food, how one needs to dress, prices to be expected, what behavior is appropriate. They define behavior settings in the full sense of the word—milieu and the ongoing pattern of behavior (Barker, 1968), that is, the environment, the rules that apply, and the appropriate behavior. Note that much of this is done through physical cues.

Note an interesting point. Much of what I have been saying is, in fact, also the point made *implicitly* by Barker (1968). Recall that a principal point of his work is that the same people behave very differently in different behavior settings. But what does this different behavior imply? Although he does not make this point explicitly, it implies that settings communicate appropriate behavior. In fact, it is almost a corollary. In effect, what Barker is saying is that when people enter a setting, that setting provides cues that they understand, that they know what the context and the situation are, and hence what the appropriate rules, and behavior, are. This happens so naturally, and frequently, during our regular activity systems, that we take it very much for granted. We only notice the process when it *ceases to work, when we do not* understand the cues, the rules, the expected behavior—for example, in a strange culture (part of the process known as "culture shock"). In that case, we cannot draw on the available cultural knowledge necessary.

At the same time biculturalism, in environmental terms as in others, is possible—people can act differently, yet appropriately, in settings belonging to different cultures. This is, of course, the environmental equivalent of knowing a number of languages. This has been documented for Arabs in the United States and in their own homelands (Hall, 1966) and for Puerto Ricans in New York City in settings belonging to their own and to Anglo cultures (Hoffman and Fishman, 1971). In the latter case, it is clear that settings, defining situations, play a most important—if not crucial—role. It is the situation that determines behavior, but the setting defines the situation. Thus a *bodega*, a Puerto Rican grocery store, elicits Puerto Rican behavior, an Anglo supermarket more Anglo behavior, the Anglo work situation (and setting) totally Anglo behavior. Note that in these bicultural cases, settings often elicit both behavior and the corresponding language.

A most striking example of biculturalism is provided by a study of children involved in the cyclic migration of the Abalyia subclan of the Bantu in western Kenya. In this case, these children spend some time in a traditional, agrarian sociophysical setting in the "bush" and part of their time in an urban setting. The children behave quite differently in the different settings (Weisner, 1974) and each set of behaviors could be interpreted as appropriate to the particular setting. In that study, the particular role of *environmental* cues was not considered in any detail, yet these behavior shifts do make the basic point, particularly since the environmental cues were quite distinct. The specific role of environmental cues is shown by the case of the Lardil tribe of Australian Aborigines on Mornington Island. There, in the early days of acculturation, the mission station, described as "the compound," was clearly demarcated by fences. These fences became places at which "bush behavior" ceased and the new codes of mission behavior were observed (Memmott, 1979: 251). Two things may be noted: first, the different behavior in the different settings and, second, the role of fences as indicating places of transition and change. Aboriginal behavior also changes, to this day, when in a work setting or a residential setting, in a bush camp or a city, in a white pub or an Aboriginal one, and so on.

These are special cases. Yet, as already noted, many times every day we enter settings and places, pick up the cues encoded in them, decode the meanings, match them to the relevant and congruent schemata and cultural knowledge, and act appropriately. As we move from lecture hall to seminar room, from cafeteria to elegant restaurant, we adjust our behavior in response to cues in the environment that define the situation and context for us and help guide our behavior along predetermined paths. The cues even act in a predictive sense: We anticipate behavior and, for example, dress accordingly and appropriately before entering particular settings. The question, given the approach being discussed, is basically how we know that a setting is what it is, that is, which environmental and social cues specify the nature of the setting so that the appropriate behaviors are elicited. It is in dealing with this question that the nonverbal model seems useful, since the cues are clearly neither verbal nor vocal.

NONVERBAL COMMUNICATION AND
ENVIRONMENTAL MEANING

I take the nonverbal communication approach to environmental meaning to be something conceptually rather simple, which is the reason for using it. In order to keep it simple, the extensive literature on nonverbal communication, some of which is becoming very sophisticated and some of which is also at a high level of abstraction, will not be reviewed in any detail. For example, by 1972, an annotated bibliography on only some aspects of the subject contained 931 items (Davis, 1972) and the rate of publication has increased greatly since then.

I take three points of departure: There are nonverbal behaviors that are both extremely prevalent and extremely important; these both provide the context for other behaviors and also occur and are to be understood in contexts; nonverbal behaviors have been studied primarily by observation and recording and subsequent analysis and interpretation. Basically, the use of nonverbal models in studying environmental meaning involves looking directly at various environments and settings and observing the cues present in them, identifying how they are interpreted by users—that is, the particular meanings these cues have for human behavior, affect, and so on. This can be done easily and directly even without a major consideration of theoretical aspects of nonverbal communication.

This discussion, once again, is best begun by referring to a set of distinctions that apparently are unrelated to the topic and that were first proposed by Hall (1966). These comprise *fixed-feature, semifixed-feature,* and informal (better *nonfixed-feature) elements.*

Fixed-feature elements

Fixed-feature elements are those that are basically fixed, or those that change rarely and slowly. Most of the standard architectural elements—walls, ceilings, and floors—belong to that domain, as do streets and buildings in cities. Clearly, the ways in which these elements are organized (their spatial organization), their size, location, sequence, arrangement, and so on, do communicate meaning, particularly in traditional cultures, but in all cases they are supplemented by other elements. There are cases, however, when they still tell us much. For example, one can suggest that in any given case there are core elements (corresponding to elements of the culture core) that will persist while others, more peripheral, change (Rapoport, 1979c, forthcoming). Applying this notion to the Navaho, it is found that the settlement pattern seems more important than the dwelling (the hogan); at the same time, the hogan *is* invested with much meaning and is often used to identify the group so that its presence or absence is a good indicator of the degree of acculturation (Snyder et al., 1976, 1977). This is particularly interesting since that dispersed settlement pattern is derived from the Navaho's Athapascan (Canadian) forebears and is both characteristic of them and differs in important respects from both their Pueblo neighbors and the dominant Anglo-American culture (Jett, 1978).

Thus this settlement pattern both relates to the core values of the culture and *contrasts* with the other patterns around it. Interestingly, when in 1750 a nativistic revival of Athapascan culture occurred, it was marked by the introduction of the Blessingway as the central ceremonial ritual of Navaho religion; this specifically proscribed the building of communal, Pueblo-like structures and favored a return to a dispersed settlement pattern (Jett, 1978). At the same time, of course, other rituals, language, and a variety of nonenvironmental means are used. Moreover, hogans are typical of less acculturated Navaho and have, in any case, not been given up completely. Even individuals living in Anglo-type dwellings often build hogans in their backyards, particularly for those ceremonies (including Blessingway) most identified with Navaho culture. Clearly, the combination of settlement patterns and dwellings (which in the case of the Pueblo are inseparable) communicates clear meanings about group identity that are reinforced by many other, nonenvironmental, elements.

Among the Bedouin, also, the dispersed settlement pattern seems more important than the dwelling; although I have not seen any studies dealing with the *meaning* of that pattern, it probably has such meaning. What this suggests, however, is that the ordering principles of fixed-feature arrangements have meaning, although one group's order may be another's disorder. Thus one finds U.S. cities described by French observers as having no order while U.S. observers make the same comment about Moslem cities (Rapoport, 1977). The pattern of a "libertarian suburb" in California, which has important ideological messages for the builders and users (Barnett 1977), undoubtedly is seen by the surrounding residents as communicating disorder and messiness. Thus the ordering schemata are culturally variable and their "reading" in each case draws on cultural schemata. The people in the area see it as positive; the people outside see it as negative, as a stigma, and the area as a slum. With changing values it could be seen as a special place, and not negative, even by outsiders. Similarly, traditional African cities were often seen as disorganized by Europeans because their order reflected human relationships—social, religious, ethnic, occupational, kinship and lineage, hierarchical (Hull, 1976: 122)—rather than geometrical.

Semifixed-feature elements

Semifixed-feature elements range all the way from the arrangement and type of furniture, curtains and other furnishings, plants and "what-nots," screens and clothing to street furniture, advertising signs, window displays in shops, garden layouts and lawn decorations, and other urban elements (including the verbal and eikonic message systems discussed above). These can, and do, change fairly quickly and easily. Note that these become particularly important in environmental meaning in our own context, where they tend to communicate more than fixed-feature elements. Most people move into ready-made environments and fixed-feature elements are rarely altered. They tend to form a given, although the particular choice made does already communicate, in and of itself. Fixed-feature elements are also under the control of codes, regulations, and the like. While personalization and even gardens are controlled to an extent, the control is much less than for fixed-feature elements. Also, environmental preferences are frequently related to the degree of lack of outside control over personalization. This is one important (although obviously not the only) reason for the clear-cut preference for detached houses over other forms of housing, of ownership as opposed to renting, of townhouses as opposed to high-rise apartments, and so on.

Thus it appears that semifixed environmental elements are of particular importance in studying meaning in our current environment. At the same time, these elements have been used to establish meaning from earliest times. For example, in Çatal Hüyük, one of the earliest urban settlements, the distinction between residential rooms and shrines or ritual chambers is indicated primarily (although not exclusively) through semifixed elements of various sorts—that is, they are "furnished" differently and more lavishly than dwellings. If the "furnishings" were removed, they would convert back to "ordinary" rooms and dwellings (Mellaart, 1964, 1967; Todd, 1976; Rapoport, 1979a).

Also, when Pizarro first reached South America, he "knew" temples even though they were the same height and size, and of the same materials, as the dwellings. This was because they were covered in jewels and gold. Note that this was in a very different, never before seen, culture! Once these decorations were removed, the buildings would, in effect, revert back to dwellings.

An even more striking example is provided by the Ashanti Fetish houses in Africa, which are identical to dwellings in plan, construction, and even decorations. What is different are (1) the contents (sacred objects of various kinds), (2) the uses of space, (3) the activities that occur within, and (4) the occupants (Swithebank, 1969). This stresses the importance of semifixed and nonfixed elements, but also reemphasizes the importance of context. It is the relationships of these objects, behaviors, and people to the setting that have meaning and can be "read."

The use of fixed-feature and semifixed-feature elements to make inferences about behavior (that is, about nonfixed-feature elements) is the rule in archaeology, although we have seen that this presents problems; it is particularly difficult to read fixed-feature elements alone in terms of their meaning, although some inferences can be made. Yet archaeology does provide a most useful paradigm since meaning must be derived from artifacts alone in making inferences about behavior. Thus, in the case of ancient Tollan, in Hidalgo, Mexico, one could distinguish between front doors (decorated) and interior doors ("modest"). Decorative facings were used differentially and seem to indicate status; status indications are reinforced by the width of entrances, the use of porches consisting of roof and posts, with painted floors and wall plaster and decorative elements, and with spacious rear rooms almost identical to temple structures at Teotihuacan. Since, however, these rooms include utilitarian—nonritual—objects, one is dealing with a dwelling (Healan, 1977). Here it is the presence of semifixed-feature elements that clarifies the meaning of the space; the house groupings themselves, with houses with and without these status-indicating elements, suggest social relationships.

How meaning can be read from archaeological data is shown very clearly by the Maya Center of Lubaantun in British Honduras (Hammond, 1972). First, it proved possible to see that overall planning was involved, since a prodigious amount of labor and material resources were used to modify the topography in order to implement the plan. Since the planned layout was clearly important to the builders, one can conclude that the layout itself had important meaning. In this case, the superstructures had walls of poles and roofs of palm thatch, like Maya dwellings. All that was left were the stone bases, which were of varied sizes and heights. On the basis of these variables, the structures were classified into large religious, ceremonial, elite residential, and residential; that is, the meaning of structures was judged on the basis of size and the height to which stone extended. Location also seemed important, since not only were structures around any one plaza of one category, but centrality was related to importance—a religious core was surrounded by a ceremonial zone and a residential-center zone. These zones could be crosschecked by accessibility criteria, providing another instance of meaning in terms of public/private domains. Where ceremonial areas had low accessibility, it suggested that these particular activities were confined to special, elite groups.

The specifics are less important than the fact that, as is common in archaeology, the site could be read on the basis of its fixed-feature elements, although this was greatly helped by semifixed-feature elements. As already pointed out, in traditional societies fixed-feature elements communicate much more clearly, as cities such as Isphahan or Marrakesh will show; the hierarchy is easily read.

The difficulty of making behavioral inferences from archaeological data has already been mentioned (see Douglas, 1972; Miner, 1956). This difficulty has to do with the problems of interpretation where many elements are missing and cultural knowledge is absent. It also has to do with the existence of cultures with few fixed-feature or even semifixed-feature elements, such as Australian Aborigines and the like. In the case of the Aborigines, not only are important areas such as sacred places, story sites, and dance and initiation grounds often indistinguishable from the surrounding milieu, or the cues are so subtle that they are difficult for outsiders to see, they also disappear rapidly. Yet while these cues are present and these places are being used, their meaning *can* often be read quite clearly (Rapoport, 1975a). Therefore, conceptually, the argument stands: It *is* possible to read the meaning of the environments, including space organization, even among Aborigines (Rapoport, 1979a). Among Aborigines, as among other nomadic groups (see Rapoport, 1978c), it is also frequently necessary to keep spatial relationships fluid deliberately, to preserve avoidance and other interaction rules. This may *prevent* "freezing" the environment, so that even today this inhibits the use even of furniture among Aborigines—it is easier to shift position when sitting on the ground (Memmott, 1979). Yet while these behaviors occur they can be read so that the meaning of spatial organization can be decoded and understood, since it reflects sacred schemata, social structure, and hierarchy (such as among the Swazi people in Africa; Kuper, 1972).

Another, contemporary example in which the semifixed elements disappeared when the event ended not only shows the meaning of space but also the significance of boundaries. This is a photograph of two Latin American presidents, Carlos Lleras Rostrepo of Colombia and Raul Leoni of Venezuela, meeting in the center of a bridge spanning a river along their border. They embraced while toeing the border, then ate lunch at the precise center of the bridge, without leaving their respective countries (Time, 1967c; see Figure 12).

In our own culture, there is another possible reason why semifixed-feature elements may be more important, which has to do with the difference between designers and users. Thus it has been suggested that designers' stress on users' participation in the original design may be due to their own professional bias and training. Users, it is suggested, may be much more interested in decisions about furnishings, arrangements, and the like (Becker, 1977: 13)—precisely those elements that are here termed semifixed.

Thus in our own culture, both in domestic and nondomestic situations, semifixed-feature elements tend to be used much—and are much more under the control of *users;* hence they tend to be used to communicate meanings. Yet they have been ignored by both designers and analysts who have stressed fixed-feature elements. For example, among Nubians, traditionally, both house form and decorations were important (Fernea et al., 1973; Lee, 1969a). Upon the population's relocation after flooding due to the Aswan Dam, new, and most unsuitable, house and village forms were provided. These could *not*

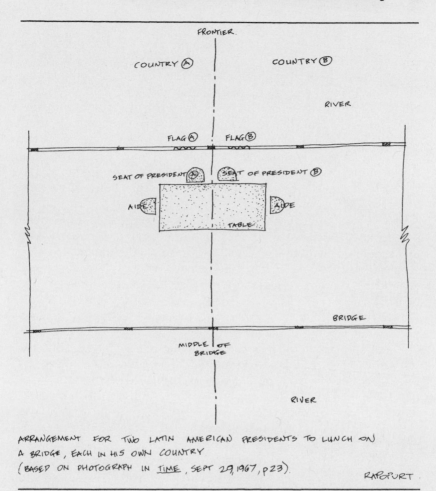

ARRANGEMENT FOR TWO LATIN AMERICAN PRESIDENTS TO LUNCH ON
A BRIDGE, EACH IN HIS OWN COUNTRY
(BASED ON PHOTOGRAPH IN TIME, SEPT 29, 1967, p23).

RAPOPORT.

Figure 12

be changed; however, colors and other external decorations were
changed immediately (particularly around doors; Lee, 1969a; Fernea
et al., 1973)—a suggestive point regarding meaning.

In our own culture, in the case of domestic situations, we find the
whole range of elements subsumed under "personalization"—internally, the use of colors, materials, pictures, curtains, furnishings, and
so on; externally, of colors, trim, shutters, mailboxes, street numbers,
decorations, planting, and the like. In nondomestic situations, we find
the changes occurring in urban shops and in roadside strip buildings
where the same fixed-feature elements can act as settings for dozens

of uses and activities through changes in the semifixed elements—decor, decorations, signs, and the like. Very few longitudinal studies have been done, but it is easy to think of examples if we have observed a shopping street or segment of roadside strip for any length of time. Increasingly, for example, one can observe gas stations converted for other uses. In one case, a gas station was turned into an Italian restaurant through some minor changes in a limited number of semifixed elements in plaster, chipboard, lighting (internally), and a sign and front door (externally). Another example might be a gas station converted to a bank through the addition of a mansard roof (as flimsy as a sign), a sign, a front door with decorative walls, and some decorative window panels.

The distinction proposed between "duck" and "decorated shed" architecture (Venturi et al., 1972) can be interpreted in terms of fixed and semifixed elements: A "duck" relies on fixed elements to communicate its meaning; a "decorated shed" relies on semifixed and changeable elements. This, of course, also has the economic advantage of being reused easily (see Rubin, 1979: 354ff). Note also that in nondomestic situations the meaning of particular elements becomes particularly easy to study: One can observe which elements are used for what and *which are changed how* when uses change. This corresponds to the observation, in nonverbal analysis, of facial expressions, gestures, and body postures and relating them to the context of particular situations, behaviors, interactions, and so forth; it is a very direct and easy method to use.

Given the fact that today most people move into ready-made environments, for example, housing, the study of meaning will necessarily be primarily in the semifixed-feature realm. For example, considering a group of Puerto Ricans inhabiting public housing in the South End of Boston, it was found that a particular "aesthetic complex" was developed internally, which communicated ethnic and other identity, that is, had meaning for the group. This consisted of the selection of certain decorative objects (often brought from Puerto Rico) arranged in certain ways, the use of specific colors, the use of particular furniture grouped in particular ways (space organization) and so on. Since external personalization was impossible, clothing, cars, and other devices were used as ways of communicating meanings having to do with group identity, and respectability—with "maintaining front" (Jopling, 1974). Note that it was observation—of rooms, their contents, people's clothing, cars, and so so—that first led to the notion of the *meaning* of the particular choices made.

Similarly, for the same ethnic group, but in New York City, it was through the observation of semifixed elements in living rooms (an inventory) that an understanding of the meaning of these settings was derived—that they represented "sacred spaces" (Zeisel, 1973). This meaning had clear design implications. In the same study, in the case of kitchens, it was the observation of women's behavior in kitchens (nonfixed-feature elements) and the appliances in kitchens that clearly indicated the meaning in this culture of kitchens and their latent functions—very different to those of Anglo kitchens. In the case of the Puerto Rican culture, status is gained during a party through a hostess being seen to produce food, being seen in the kitchen, and "performing" in front of an audience of her peers; in Anglo culture, a woman is seen as a good hostess when she apparently does no work, yet food appears as though by magic. The design implications were quite clear—an efficiency kitchen is unsuitable in this particular Puerto Rican housing because of the meaning of that setting.

Similar examples can be given from other cultures. In the case of the Apache, cooking involves the presence of others, with much social interaction (associated activities). The cooperative effort and the social aspects and companionship are the important (latent) aspects of the action of cooking. During holidays, feasts are held that involve the entire community. A great deal of room is needed to prepare the food. Similarly, the living space setting has meaning in terms of the behavior expected of guests. On arrival, one expects to sit peripherally around the room, far from others, with no conversation. When food is ready, and eating begins, talk and interaction also begin (Esber, 1972). Without large kitchens and living rooms, people could not behave appropriately. Again, *observation* was the key to discovering these meanings.

In Kenya, a complex set of culturally specific meanings attached to different rooms—the living room as "semipublic space," bedrooms as "private," and lavatories, bathrooms, and kitchens as "hidden"—were communicated by furniture and furnishings as well as by visibility. Curtains over doorways, types of furniture and their arrangement, and the like clearly communicated the above meanings, as well as domains of men/women, positive/negative, and provided cues as to where one should sit while entertaining and being entertained, where to eat, and so forth (Kamau, 1978/79). A clear distinction in meaning was found between eating as a social activity involving entertaining visitors and eating for nourishment. This was clearly indicated by the zoning within the living room, which stressed the maximum possible spatial separation between furniture groups: matched sofa and chairs (unmatched = less prestige), coffee table, end tables, and so on, on the one hand, and dining table and chairs on the other. Again, living rooms are furnished in specific and distinct ways in terms of furniture, objects, arrangements, colors, and the like, which provide information about the income of the men, the housekeeping abilities of the women, and the status of the family; it is a projection of the way in which they wish others to think of them and of the ways in which family members interact. Among bedrooms, rank is shown by the master bedroom being larger and having a better and larger bed, use of a bedspread, higher degree of cleanliness, and so on. Bathrooms and kitchens are regarded as unclean and shameful, and therefore are hidden; they are also the women's domain.

Note that the positive/negative nature of spaces reflecting the domains of men/women is found more generally, and is echoed in the correspondence between right/left and men/women (Needham, 1973). Note two more things: First, in all these cases, we are dealing with latent aspects of activities—how they are done, associated activities, and, particularly, their meaning—so that these are critical in the congruence of setting and activity; second, these complex findings, resembling semiotic and structuralist analysis in some cases, is done rather simply and in straightforward ways by observation of semifixed-feature elements and behavior—nonfixed-feature elements.

Nonfixed-feature elements

Nonfixed-feature elements are related to the human occupants or inhabitants of settings, their shifting spatial relations (proxemics), their body positions and postures (kinesics), hand and arm gestures, facial expressions, hand and neck relaxation, head nodding, eye contact, speech rate, volume and pauses, and many other nonverbal behaviors discussed previously. In fact, the study of nonverbal behavior has been developed in, and almost entirely restricted to, this domain; it is the nonfixed-feature elements that form the subject of nonverbal communication studies. The questions commonly asked concern what is being communicated, or hidden, by such behaviors as anger, revulsion, fear, or whatever, and also what role these behaviors play in interaction.

The task in applying the nonverbal model to environmental meaning is thus to move from the nonfixed-feature realm to the semifixed-

and fixed-feature elements, but asking comparable questions: What is being communicated? Why and by what means? What role do the cues play in behavior, social interaction, and so on? It is my argument, following what has already been said about semifixed elements, that the most productive first step is to try to bridge the gap between the work on nonfixed and semifixed elements, and to do it in the simplest and most direct way—by *assuming,* on the basis of the discussion thus far, that the environment acts as a form of nonverbal communication, and proceeding from there by direct observation, the analysis of existing studies, the content analysis of descriptions, and the like.

Some suggestions for the validity of this approach can be found in nonverbal communication studies in the nonfixed-feature realm. For example, one can use more than facial expressions of emotion and use the face itself—as an outcome of facial expressions over years. Thus it has been suggested (Ekman, 1978) that face information consists of facial sign vehicles that can be:

- *static*—These change, but very slowly. Included are bone structure, the size, shape, and location of eyes, brows, nose, mouth, or skin pigmentation—what one could call features.
- *slow*—These change more rapidly and include bags, sags, pouches, creases, wrinkles, blotches, and the like.
- *rapid*—These change very rapidly and include movements, skin tone, coloration, sweat, and cues such as eye gaze direction, pupil size, head positioning, and so on.
- *artificial*—These include glasses, cosmetics, face lifts, wigs, and the like.

The last category, of course, relates to *clothing, settings, and furnishings* that, with the face and body, lead to judgment of people—person perception, stereotypes, and the like (Warr and Knapper, 1968; Ekman, 1978). Like these others, facial characteristics are used to judge personal identity (race, gender, kinship), temperament, personality, beauty, sexual attractiveness, intelligence, state of health, age, mood, emotions, and so on. While the face is said to be the most commonly employed identity sign, clothing, furnishings, and settings are also thus used. Note also the interesting similarity of the division above into static, slow, and rapid with fixed-feature, semifixed-feature, and nonfixed-feature environmental elements.

For one thing, there has been at least some work on the meaning of semifixed elements, although not nearly as advanced as that on nonfixed. I have already referred to the use of inventories. These have long been used in anthropology. Also, as early as the 1930s, the condition and cleanliness of living rooms, furniture, and furnishings, their "orderliness" and impression of "good taste," which appear subjective, proved to be very effective indicators of social status (Chapin, 1938: 754, note 8) and, indirectly, lifestyle and the effect of rehousing. Although this finding was reported only in a footnote, it seems generally accepted and agreed that combinations of intentional and unintentional displays of material things, including humans, set the scene for social encounters. In judging public housing and other environments, the negative meaning of trash, bad maintenance, vermin, and other objects that communicate stigma has been used for some time (Rainwater, 1966). The contrary is also true—good maintenance and upkeep, cleanliness, underground wires, greenery, and the like all communicate positive messages and result in perceptions of high environmental quality, desirability, and satisfaction. This will be discussed in some detail later (see also Rapoport, 1977, ch. 2; Burby et al., 1976). The fact that physical elements in the environment are read easily and directly as indicators of social characteristics, and hence guides for behavior, has now been confirmed amply (Royse, 1969).

Note also that in discussing the use of photography in the social sciences (Wagner, 1979), it is taken for granted and self-evident that photographs (that is, visual images of nonfixed-semifixed-and fixed-feature elements of the world) can be interpreted. Thus in studies of skid row, shabby personal appearance, drinking in public, and the *setting of door stoops and alleys in a dirty part of the city* (Wagner, 1979: 31; emphasis added) match the public image of derelicts. In other words, they communicate "skid row" by being congruent with people's cognitive schemata. Photos of skid row settings communicate this through the types of people (their faces, clothing, postures, activities, and so on), the *ambience,* signs (such as signs saying "loans," "barber college," "Bread of Life Mission," type of hotel sign), and also the types of other shops visible.

One can clearly identify towns by the kind of clothing people wear, buildings, shop signs, and so on (Wagner, 1979: 147). A photographic record of a home setting would reflect religiosity, ethnicity, and elements of history, and might provide insights into psychological processes by revealing order or disorder (more correctly the *nature* of the order) through the artifacts and their arrangement, the inhabitants, their age, and "passage of life" (as shown by face, hands, and posture). Clothing would indicate economic well-being, taste, and possibly profession, while the manner in which it is worn and the posture might indicate psychological and emotional states (Wagner, 1979: 273). In other words, the nonfixed-semifixed- and fixed-feature elements would tell us much. In fact, such cultural inventories are so useful that, in the case of Native Americans in cities, the success of relocation can be measured reliably by the style and order of each home (Wagner, 1979: 281).

The analysis of U.S. urban landscapes and suburban dwellings also involves aspects of this kind of analysis although the approach is different (Venturi et al., 1972, 1976; Venturi and Rauch, 1976). Starting from a very different philosophical, ideological, and methodological position, Baudrillard (1968) has developed the notion that significantly, he calls *le systeme des objects*—"the system of objects." This corresponds to the notion of "the world of goods" (Douglas and Isherwood, 1979) and to the notion of an "object language" (Ruesch and Kees, 1965) that describes the messages encoded in material form, and that communicate their meaning both by their nature (material, shape, color, and so on) and through their arrangement, that is, their relationship to other elements (what I have called "context").

In fact, Ruesch and Kees's very early book on nonverbal communication is still possibly the most useful for our purposes. Since it is prior to most research in the field, and thus lacks some of the theoretical and methodological sophistication of more recent work, it comes closest to applying this approach to the environment, particularly to semifixed elements. It explicitly concentrates on pragmatics and stresses visual cues, observation, and context, employing both descriptions and photographs. Among issues considered are how roles are judged through clothing, activities, background and props; how groups, from dyads up, are identified by the settings and clothing that indicate the social situation; and how the rules of action are suggested by settings. Examples of shop windows, which indicate value and price through display techniques, houses, and neighborhoods are given. The stress is on the atmosphere or *ambience* of settings that indicates the activities in them, so that urban areas can be identified as commercial, industrial, or tourist. Similarly, the status of districts can be read and shops, bars, and restaurants provide cues for particular clienteles— bohemians, gourmets, neighborhood regulars, or connoisseurs. The book discusses how physical arrangements of settings guide, facilitate, and modify social interaction; how the physical environment expresses various identities—individual and of groups. It relates sign language (gestures), action language (walking, drinking, and so on), and object and spatial language (that is, nonfixed-, semifixed-, and fixed-feature elements). It concentrates on semifixed-feature elements (although it does not use that term), and stresses the nonverbal aspects of verbal messages, for example, the nature of lettering in terms of style, materials, color, and so on. It even addresses the issue of the interplay of biology and culture in nonverbal communication[1] and also has much to say about the importance of redundancy (which is called "mutual reinforcement"). All in all, Ruesch and Kees's book is not only still the most relevant published application of nonverbal communication to environmental meaning, it is also a veritable agenda for much research. It is a pity that it was not really followed up in the further development of nonverbal communication research. But even that provides a methodological approach based on *observation,* which is also summarized elsewhere, for a wide range of behaviors, including nonverbal, spatial, and others (see Weick, 1968).

Context greatly influences social interaction. While social context has rather dramatic and important effects upon interpersonal interaction, they are rarely taken into account; similarly, physical and other aspects of the total environmental contexts tend to be ignored (Lamb et al., 1979: 265, 269). Note that social interaction is studied by observation of nonfixed-feature elements and their subsequent analysis. The transfer of this approach to analyze semifixed- and fixed-feature elements makes things easier: the problem of the tempo of events, the fleeting yet critical cue, is missing. One has more time.

There are also many studies that, while nonexplicitly in this tradition, can easily be interpreted in this way; we have already discussed some, others will be discussed in more detail later.

The approach adopted here begins with an emphasis on semifixed-feature elements (although it is not confined to those). Some reasons for this have already been given. There is another: It can be shown that nonfixed and semifixed elements tend to covary, while the fixed-feature elements remain unchanged in the same situation. Consider an example of a conference that was photographed over a period of several days (Collier, 1967). At the beginning, people sat around maintaining formal body posture, formally dressed, wearing their identity labels. They maintained formal proxemic distance and their body language communicated comparable messages. They held coffee cups and saucers on their knees. At the end of several days all these nonfixed cues had changed—nothing was formal, personal distance was greatly reduced, body contact was often present, body posture was extremely informal, clothing expressed relaxed informality, coffee cups and other elements were scattered all over. The meaning of the nonverbal messages was quite clear. But it suddenly struck me that the furniture arrangements, the coffee cups, ashtrays, and the like, by themselves—that is, without the people present—would have communicated almost the whole story; a great deal of the meaning had been encoded in the semifixed realm. Nothing, however, could be deduced from the fixed-feature elements—the walls, floors, and ceilings. Note also that, at least initially, the arrangement of the semifixed elements (furniture) had an impact on human communication and interaction and guided it in specific ways.

Since our task is to apply to semifixed- and fixed-feature elements the nonverbal communication approach developed primarily in the nonfixed-feature realm, it is useful to begin with a brief review of that.

The nonverbal communication approach

In the nonfixed-feature realm many lexicons of the meanings of animal expressions and actions have been compiled, for example, of dogs, gulls and other birds, primates, and so on (for a recent review of some of these, see Sebeok, 1977b). In the case of humans the work of Ekman and his collaborators, Eibl-Eibesfeld, Birdwhistell, Hall, and others shows that a start has been made. Given the existence of some lexicons at least, the question is really twofold: Is the lexicon itself, that is, the set of possible devices, culture specific or universal? And, even if the lexicon is universal, do sets get picked that have universality (or commonality) or are they culture specific?

There are three major views about nonverbal communication in the nonfixed-feature realm: ⁺

(1) That it is an arbitrary, culture-specific system, hence similar to language in that respect. For example, there is an assumption of an analogy between kinesic behavior and language (see Birdwhistell, 1970, 1972). An extreme statement is that nonverbal behavior may be as culture bound as linguistic behavior (Lloyd, 1972: 25).

(2) That it is a pan-cultural, species-specific system and thus very different from language (see Eibl-Eibesfeld, 1970, 1972, 1979).

(3) A resolution of these conflicting views in an interesting model that, while rejecting the linguistic approach and concerned with how non-verbal behavior communicates feeling states, actually incorporates aspects of both (Ekman and Friesen, 1969b; Ekman, 1972).

In the case of the first two of these views, the argument is essentially about evolutionary versus linguistic models (Eibl-Eibesfeld, 1972; Leach, 1972). Some of the different findings may be due to the examination of different activities, for example, gestures versus facial expressions, which may have different degrees of cultural and biological components.

Cross-cultural studies by Eibl-Eibesfeld and Ekman and his collaborators indicate the existence of certain universal pan-cultural elements in facial expressions that seem universally, or at least very widely indeed, recognized. These, then, seem to be nonarbitrary and biologically based (see Darwin, 1872). What then is the role of culture? The model proposed (the "neuro-cultural" model; Ekman, 1977) resolves these two points of view in one way (the third approach above; Ekman and Friesen, 1969b; Ekman, 1972). The suggestion is that in the case of facial expressions, there is a universal, pan-cultural affect program involving facial muscles and their movements in association with states such as happiness, anger, surprise, fear, disgust, sadness, interest, and so on. The elicitors of these, based on setting, expectation, memory, situation, and so on, are culturally variable as are the display rules, that is, what is allowed where and when. These amplify or intensify, deamplify or deintensify, neutralize, blend, or mask the affect program. The outcome is a particular facial display, which, when interpreted, has affect and behavioral consequences in social interaction. The cultural differences, then, are due to differences in elicitors and display rules, and hence the blend, although the *elements* of expression are universal (see Figure 13).

This is clearly *not* a languagelike system. Note that not only are the elicitors of facial expression socially learned and culturally variable, but so are many consequences of an aroused emotion (such as whether it is expressed or hidden). At the same time, however, the facial muscular movement for a particular emotion, if it is displayed (that is, if displays rules do not interfere and inhibit it) are dictated by an affect program that is pan-human and universal.

The conflict between the two points of view can be approached in another way. Nonverbal behavior in the nonfixed-feature realm involves *origins*, or how these behaviors become part of a person's

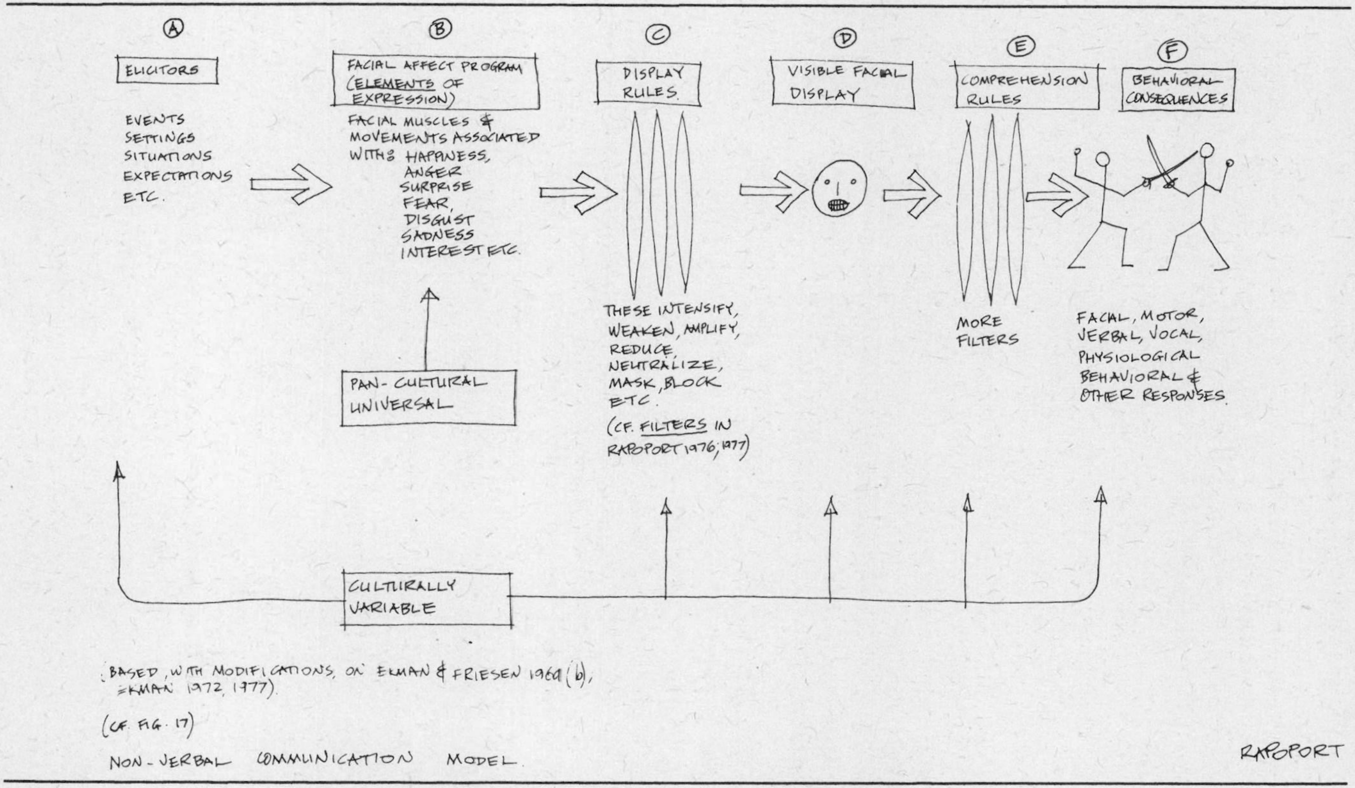

Figure 13

RAPOPORT

Non-Verbal Communication Model.

(cf FIG. 17)

Based, with modifications, on Ekman & Friesen 1969 (b), Ekman 1972, 1977.

A ELICITORS

EVENTS
SETTINGS
SITUATIONS
EXPECTATIONS
ETC.

B FACIAL AFFECT PROGRAM (ELEMENTS OF EXPRESSION)

FACIAL MUSCLES & MOVEMENTS ASSOCIATED WITH: HAPPINESS, ANGER, SURPRISE, FEAR, DISGUST, SADNESS, INTEREST ETC.

PAN-CULTURAL UNIVERSAL

C DISPLAY RULES

THESE INTENSIFY, WEAKEN, AMPLIFY, REDUCE, NEUTRALIZE, MASK, BLOCK ETC.

(CF. FILTERS IN RAPOPORT 1976, 1977)

CULTURALLY VARIABLE

D VISIBLE FACIAL DISPLAY

E COMPREHENSION RULES

MORE FILTERS

F BEHAVIORAL CONSEQUENCES

FACIAL, MOTOR, VERBAL, VOCAL, PHYSIOLOGICAL, BEHAVIORAL & OTHER RESPONSES repertoire (which is not of major interest here); *usage,* the circumstances of its use; and *coding,* the rules that explain how the behavior conveys information (Ekman and Friesen, 1969b). The argument about whether such behavior is innate, pan-human, or culture (or other group) specific applies mainly to origins. Usage seems clearly culture specific since it deals with the external conditions such as environmental settings, situations, roles, relationship to associated verbal and vocal behaviors, awareness of emitting the behavior and intention to communicate feedback from others, and whether the information is shared or idiosyncratic. Coding varies in terms of universality versus cultural specificity, and is of three types: *intrinsic,* which is eikonic and the act *is* the meaning; *eikonic* but *extrinsic,* although the appearance of the behavior is like what it means; and *arbitrary,* culture-specific extrinsic codes with no visual resemblance to what they signify.

On the basis of the three types of coding, one then finds three classes of nonverbal behaviors (for example, hand gestures): adaptors, illustrators, and emblems (Ekman and Friesen, 1972; Johnson et al., 1975).

- *adaptors*—These are the least intentional, most intuitive, exhibiting least awareness (note that one can have *object adaptors*—a potential link to our subject).
- *illustrators*—These augment or contradict what is being said, but have less precise meanings than emblems.
- *emblems*—These have exact verbal translations, with precise meanings known to all, or most, members of a group, and are deliberately used for messages, so that the sender takes responsibility for them. These can also be described as "symbolic gestures" (Ekman, 1976) and are the most "languagelike" (Ekman, 1977), or culture specific.

These tend to be studied using procedures derived from social psychology and linguistics. Different groups have different emblem repertoires, for example, varying in size (Ekman, 1976), which tends to correspond to language as in the case of "elaborated" or "restricted" codes (see Bernstein, 1971).

Thus emblems, being closer to language than illustrators or adaptors, show more influence of culture. Although even here one expects some commonalities across cultures, based on biology, these tend to be hidden by the cultural differences; the further from language, as in the case of adaptors and illustrators, the more the influence of biology and the less cultural variability is to be expected (Ekman, 1977; Hinde, 1972).

This, then, provides another way of resolving the argument— contradictory findings may be due to the analysis of different behaviors: adaptors, illustrators, or emblems. While these distinctions are proposed within the domain of gestures, one would expect them to be even more significant across types of nonverbal behaviors, for example, facial expressions versus gestures.

It seems intuitively likely that body positions (Birdwhistell, 1970, 1972), spatial relations (Hall, 1966), and gestures (Efron, 1941) are more arbitrary, emblemlike, and culture specific than facial expressions. One would also expect emblematic gestures to be most languagelike, particularly if studied verbally. This is, in fact, the case.

Recently an attempt has been made to study what are clearly emblematic gestures mainly through interviews—that is, verbally— although direct observation, still and cine photography, and the analysis of historical illustrations and descriptions were also used (Morris et al., 1979). A total of 20 of these gestures and their meanings were studied cross-culturally in 40 localities in 25 countries of Western and Southern Europe and the Mediterranean region, using 15 languages. In effect, the attempt was to build a lexicon of meanings by compiling diagrams of gestures both illustrated and described—the basic morphology, distinctive feature, selective symbolism, generic meaning, and specific message of each.

The gestures studied were assumed to vary from culture to culture. Since they can stand for abstract qualities, they therefore depend on convention, are culture specific, and may be meaningless in some cultures; their distribution may be wide or may be restricted to small groups (their geographic distribution was plotted so that the lexicon also shows spatial distribution).

Findings indicate that most of the gestures studied have several varied major meanings (some even in a single region); some of these meanings may be in conflict in different places. Some gestures have truly national meanings, others extend across national and linguistic boundaries, still others have boundaries *within* linguistic areas (often due to identifiable historical events), and still others are restricted to particular subgroups in a given population. Gestures change with time at different rates.

Apart from the fact that a lexicon *can* be prepared, and apart from methodological implication, some of the findings are significant for our purposes. While meanings clearly do vary, an examination of the histograms shows that many gestures have much more common meanings than others: constancy seems to be a matter of *degree* rather than being an either/or situation.

Second, hand gestures—particularly these emblematic ones—seem more variable than facial expressions, which have also been studied cross-culturally. Thus as one moves from facial expressions and adaptors through illustrators to emblems, the cultural variability and specificity tends to increase. The question, then, is what happens as one moves into the domain of semifixed- and fixed-feature elements—that is, are these elements primarily adaptorlike, illustratorlike, or emblemlike? In trying to apply this model to environmental cues in the semifixed- or fixed-feature realms, are there any universals—or are they all culturally variable? This is difficult to answer: So far there are no lexicons and hardly any research (which is urgently needed). But one may examine some of the evidence and some of what *is* known in a speculative mode. That evidence seems somewhat equivocal, but there does seem to be considerable variability; one cannot, however, say whether the elicitors and display rules alone are variable or whether the elements are also. Put differently, the question is twofold: Is the set of elements constituting noticeable differences in the environment, and upon which the designer in the broadest sense (Rapoport, 1972, 1977) can potentially draw, universal or culture specific? Within that set, even if the former applies, are there are commonalities in which specific cues get selected to communicate particular meanings (or are used to infer meanings), or is that particular repertoire culture specific?

A list of possible potential cues is easily listed (Rapoport, 1977: 229-230). Among these one can suggest the following as being particularly relevant (although this is not an exhaustive list):

physical elements
> *vision:* shape, size, scale, height, color, materials, textures, details, decorations, graffiti, furniture, furnishings, etc.
>
> spaces: quality, size, shape, enclosing elements, paving, barriers and links, etc.
>
> light and shade, light levels, light quality
>
> greenery, presence of planting, controlled versus natural, type of planting, arrangement
>
> age—new versus old
>
> type of order, order versus disorder

perceived density

level of maintenance

topography—natural or human-made

location—prominence, centrality versus periphery, hills or valleys, exposed or hidden, etc.

sound: sound quality—dead versus reverberant, noisy versus quiet, human-made sounds (industry, traffic, music, talk, laughter, etc.) versus natural sounds (wind, trees, birds, water, etc.); temporal changes in sound

smells: human-made versus natural, such as industry, traffic, etc. versus plants, flowers, the sea, etc.; "pleasant" versus "unpleasant," foods and the *type* of food, etc.

social elements
people: languages spoken, behavior, their dress, physical type, occupation, age, and sex, etc.

activities
and uses: intensity; type—such as industry, clubs, restaurants, residential, religious, fairs, markets, shops, recreation; separated and uniform versus mixed; cars, pedestrians, or other travel modes; cooking, eating, sleeping, playing, etc.

objects: signs, advertisements, foods, decor, fences, plants and gardens, possessions, etc.

temporal differences of various kinds

For example, if we consider planting, the very fact that different plant complexes in gardens are easily identifiable with particular ethnic groups, as we shall see later, suggests cultural variability. If we consider height, it is usually related to status, and is thus fairly common—the higher off the ground, either in person or in building form, the higher the status—but some interesting reversals can occur, as for example, between North and South Indian temples, where the height gradient in its relation to the degree of sanctity is reversed (see Figure 14). Yet the importance and sanctity of the temple *as a whole* is expressed in terms of height in both cases (see Figure 15).

Thus height, in the sense of above/below (in context), may well be an important universal category for indicating the meaning importance; certainly in the sense of relative *size* or *scale*, that is, the temple as a whole vis-à-vis the houses and other urban elements. This use of

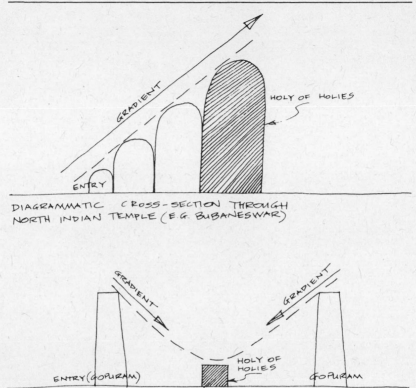

DIAGRAMMATIC CROSS-SECTION THROUGH
NORTH INDIAN TEMPLE (E.G. BUBANESWAR)

DIAGRAMMATIC CROSS-SECTION THROUGH
SOUTH INDIAN TEMPLE (E.G. MADURAI)

(BASED ON VISITS)

NORTH AND SOUTH INDIAN TEMPLES.

RAPOPORT.

Figure 14

height is so common cross-culturally (both in building elements and location) that examples soon become too numerous to handle; consider just the cathedral in a medieval city, churches in towns and neighborhoods, or the Haus Tambaran in a Sepik River village in New Guinea (see Figure 16).

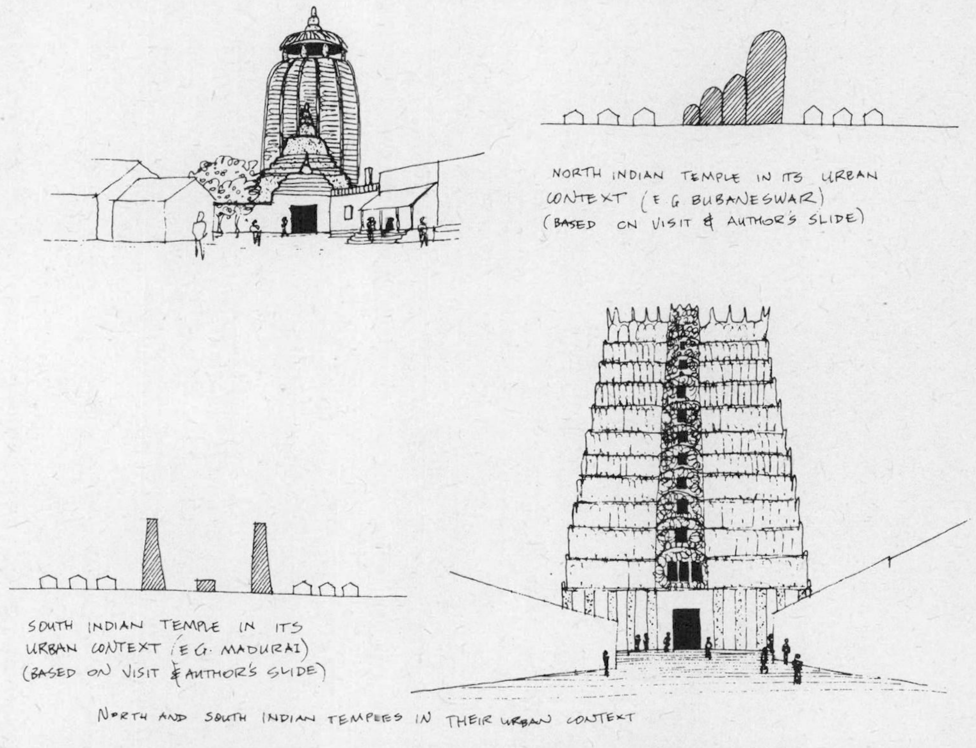

NORTH INDIAN TEMPLE IN ITS URBAN CONTEXT (E G BUBANESWAR) (BASED ON VISIT & AUTHOR'S SLIDE)

SOUTH INDIAN TEMPLE IN ITS URBAN CONTEXT (E.G. MADURAI) (BASED ON VISIT & AUTHOR'S SLIDE)

NORTH AND SOUTH INDIAN TEMPLES IN THEIR URBAN CONTEXT

RAPOPORT

Figure 15

109

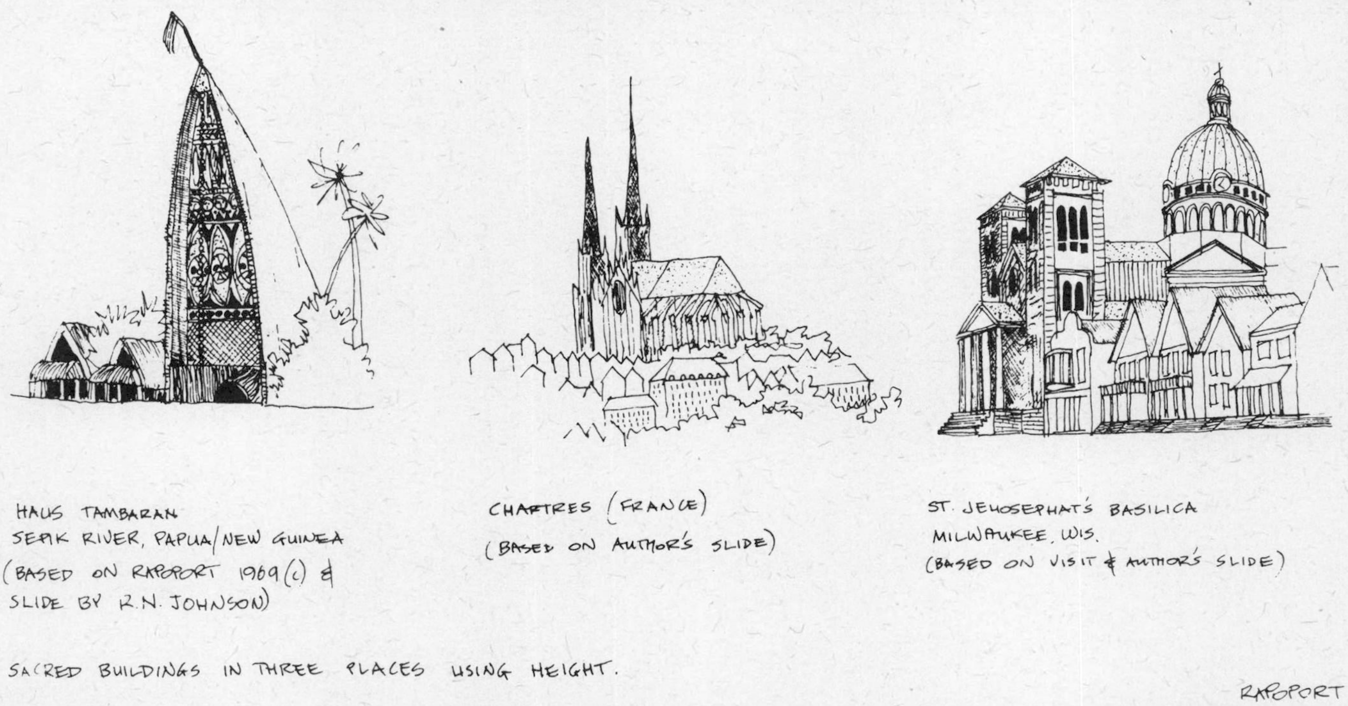

HAUS TAMBARAN
SEPIK RIVER, PAPUA/NEW GUINEA
(BASED ON RAPOPORT 1969 (c) &
SLIDE BY R.N. JOHNSON)

CHARTRES (FRANCE)
(BASED ON AUTHOR'S SLIDE)

ST. JENSEPHAT'S BASILICA
MILWAUKEE. WIS.
(BASED ON VISIT & AUTHOR'S SLIDE)

RAPOPORT

SACRED BUILDINGS IN THREE PLACES USING HEIGHT.

Figure 16

Note also that in traditional Thailand, commoners always had to be lower than nobles, and no one could be higher than the king, with implications for the design of buildings and settlements. Similarly, in Cambodia, nobles had raised houses and slaves were allowed only on the ground floor; redundancy was increased by restricting the use of tile roofs to nobles; commoners were restricted to leaves or thatch (Giteau, 1976). The use of podia, thrones, the "high table," and so on in the semifixed-feature domain and of bowing, kneeling, genuflecting, and even crawling on one's belly in the nonfixed domain also come to mind.

If we consider *centrality,* we find that while in most traditional societies central location *is* related to high status, there are cases in which this does not seem to be the case (that is, where there is no relation) and still others (such as the contemporary United States) in which reversals occur (Rapoport, 1977: 49). The differences, even today, between the United States and Italy (or even France) constitute almost a reversal (Rapoport, 1977; Schnapper, 1971). Yet the constrast between central versus peripheral location seems so widespread as to be almost universal. It is also found that the distinction or opposition between right and left, although universal—possibly related to our bodies' bilateral symmetry—is more variable in terms of meaning. While in most cases right is seen as positive and left as negative, there do exist rare cases of reversals (as in the case of China; Needham, 1973); once again, the context plays a role.

It may be useful to consider color in more detail, since there is evidence that it is one of the clearest noticeable differences (Rapoport, 1977). Some recent evidence suggests that color is much more clearly located in semantic space than are, for example, spatial relations, which tend to be more ambiguous (Miller and Johnson-Laird, 1976). This may partly help explain the greater utility of semifixed-feature elements for communicating meaning: Spatial relationships, per se, while critical in the organization of the perceptual world, are inherently ambiguous by themselves and also operate much less effectively in the associational realm. They are also much less noticeable as cues, whereas color is highly noticeable.

The question of specificity or universality in color applies to its perception and naming as well as the meaning. While this discussion is not directly relevant to the question of meaning, the centrality of color in semantic space makes this question worth addressing briefly, particularly since that which is not named, and hence not perceived *con-*

sciously, is unlikely to have major meaning and hence to be used as a cue.

In this area there also has been much argument, particularly whether the Sapir-Whorf hypothesis (that language influences perception) applies at all and, if so, whether in the strong, weak, or weakest form (for a good brief review, see Lloyd, 1972). The whole range of positions has been taken, but it appears that, while all human beings can discriminate color, the number of named categories, the salience of color, and the persistence of color as an attention-eliciting dimension vary with culture (Lloyd, 1972: 150). Color's position in the developmental sequence among children also varies (Suchman, 1966).

There does seem to be a universal, pan-human inventory of eleven basic perceptual color categories, from which various cultures draw all eleven or fewer. All languages, however, have two of the categories— black and white. If three are used, then red is next, if four, either green or yellow (but not both), and so on. There thus seems to be a clear, fixed sequence of evolutionary stages through which languages must pass as their color vocabulary increases; there are two temporal orders in this evolutionary sequence (Berlin and Kay, 1969).

If, however, one accepts the increasing variability as one goes from manifest to latent functions (that is, meaning) and from the concrete to the symbolic object, one would expect to find more variability and greater cultural specificity for meaning than for perception or naming. At first glance, this seems to be the case. Thus the color of mourning can be white, black, or purple; the Nazis used yellow as a stigma color, whereas it has the opposite meaning in Buddhism, and so on. In some cultures, such as the United States, color use seems to be arbitrary or random, whereas among the Navaho, colors are explicitly ranked in terms of good/bad (Hall, 1961: 104). In the latter case this may be related to the identification of colors with directions, which are clearly ranked. White is identified with east, blue with south, yellow with west, and black with north. Each is also related to specific phenomena, particular mountains, jewels, birds, and so on. Also, east and south (white and blue) are male, whereas west and north (yellow and black) are female (Lamphere, 1969). This relation between colors and cardinal directions is formed also in other cultures, even in the United States, where, however, these relations are not explicit and hence not widely shared and more idiosyncratic; for example, there are regional differences (Sommer and Estabrook, 1974).

But the evidence for the greater variability and cultural specificity between color and meaning is somewhat equivocal and ambiguous.

Thus the practice of using colors and color names to communicate affective meaning is found in many widely different cultures. Moreover, white is very commonly seen as positive and black as negative, not only in Western culture but among Siberian tribes, Mongols, some Africans, and American Indians. Although there may be exceptions, the evidence suggests considerable cross-cultural generality in the meaning of black and white and other colors and color names (Williams et al., 1970).

Black and white thus evoke positive and negative affective associations and meanings. These are more polarized in the West, where black has extremely negative meaning, than, for example, in Japan, where black and white tend to harmonize more and are seen more in terms of a complementary balance of opposites, although even in Japan white is still preferred. White is rated positively by Hong Kong Chinese, Asian Indians, Danes, English, Germans, and white Americans, whereas black is uniformly negative. These two colors seem to involve universal meanings (Goldberg and Stabler, 1973) modified by culture. Similarly, both white and black children in the United States attach negative meanings to black and positive meanings to white (Stabler and Johnson, 1972). Thus, while a few exceptions exist, black generally has negative connotations, white positive (Stabler and Goldberg, 1973).

It is quite clear, though, that colors generally do have meaning, both in themselves, by contrast with noncolors, and in terms of increasing the redundancy of other cues. For example, in ancient Peking, most of the city was low and gray; the sacred and hierarchically important section was centrally located, larger in scale, more elaborate, and higher, and the use of colors was restricted to that section.

Thus, generally, one finds many examples of explicit color meanings. One example is the complex color symbolism of medieval times[2] based on the notion that every object has mystical meaning. The colors used had four sources: (1) ancient religious archives and ceremonies of Iran, India, China, and Egypt, (2) the Old Testament, (3) Greek and Roman mythology, and (4) based on the other three, color meaning of nature. This included red for power (blood), yellow for warmth and fruitfulness (sun), green for youth and hopefulness (spring), and so on. There were clear and explicit rules for using color: (a) only pure colors were to be used, (b) combinations of colors to give tints corresponded to compound meanings, and (c) the rule of opposites, that is, reversing the "natural" meaning—thus green, which normally stood for youth and hope, could become despair (Blanch, 1972). Thus the use of color constituted an arbitrary system that needed knowledge of the cultural context to be read.

Although it seems rather equivocal, the cross-cultural generality of the meanings of colors other than black and white has also been strongly argued (for example, see Williams et al., 1970). While every culture has had its own expressive system of color meanings, and there were hence some variations, these have been widely shared among cultures (Kaplan, 1975). Yet many such arguments are not fully convincing. There is also the fact that colors seem to have some striking commonalities in their physiological effects, such as levels of arousal. Based on this, it has been suggested that since in all cultures colors are related to affect and mood, and since much of this relation is based on association with natural phenomena and the physiological impact of colors, the result is a widespread stereotyping of colors (Aaronson, 1970).

More importantly, and more generally, it is the presence or absence of color in a context—color as a noticeable difference—that is important. It usually indicates something special or important; thus the role of color in a monochrome or natural (for example, mud brick) environment, as in the cases of Peking or Isphahan already discussed. In such an environment a whitewashed building, such as a church, may stand out, as in the Altiplano of Peru or the Pueblos in New Mexico. Alternatively, a monochrome building (a church) reinforced by a change of materials, such as natural stone, may stand out in a polychrome, stuccoed setting (such as Mexico) or in a whitewashed setting (as in the case of Astuni in Apulia, already discussed) where it is further reinforced by location, size, height, form (domes and towers), and elaboration. In the case of materials or forms, age—old or new—also may indicate importance or status. Thus in the case of Rumanian village churches, emphasis, vis-à-vis dwellings, was obtained by the use of new materials; in the case of Pueblo Kivas, the contrast is achieved through the use of an archaic form.

There is clearly some uncertainty about the degree of constancy even in the nonfixed-feature realm, that is, nonverbal communication proper. It seems partly a matter of the kinds of cues, such as emblems or adaptors, gestures or facial expressions. In areas of overlap between nonfixed features and semifixed- or fixed-feature elements, the same condition exists. For example, male genital displays are extremely common among infrahuman primates. One also finds a correspondingly common reflection among humans in the widespread use of phallic figures as guardian figures and markers (Eibl-Eibesfeld, 1979: 43-46) found in many periods and among cultures as diverse as Europe, Japan, Africa, New Guinea, Polynesia, Indonesia, and ancient South America, to mention just a few.

In general, though, the survey above and other evidence suggests that in the case of environments, while constancies exist, the repertoire or palette grows and there is more variability and cultural specificity. Thus the reversals one finds in the meaning of environmental elements are striking: Mountains that were despised become sublime with the rise of the Romantic Movement (Nicolson, 1959); Roman ruins that were pagan, and hence evil, become remnants of a golden age with the Renaissance (as described in Rapoport, 1970b, above); the urban center has highly positive meaning in Italy and France, and negative meaning in the United States (Rapoport, 1977); the meaning of urban settlements vis-à-vis wilderness completely reverses in the United States in a comparatively brief time (Tuan, 1974: 104-105). If we compare Australian Aborigines and Northwest Coast Indians of North America, we find that among the latter the settlement pattern is determined by ecological and economic considerations; it is the dwellings, determined by ritual considerations, that are the bearers of meaning. Among the former, however, dwellings seem to respond mainly to instrumental forces (although this has recently been questioned; Reser, 1977) while the settlement patterns, in this case the movement pattern and relationship to the land (in themselves highly culture specific), are based on ritual and are most meaningful (Rapoport, 1975a, forthcoming c).

It thus appears that as one moves from the nonfixed realm, through clothing, to the semifixed- and finally fixed-feature elements, the repertoire, or palette, grows and there is ever more variability and specificity related to culture. In other words, the trend is to a more "languagelike" model, but one that is less arbitrary than language. Ekman's neuro-cultural model, however, comprising both constant and variable elements, seems useful, as does the notion of a global lexicon, which may be broadly limited to certain types of elements; from that, different groups may select repertoires more or less restricted in size and more or less constant in usage. We will know more when lexicons are developed and cues are studied historically and cross-culturally.

At the same time, one can see a constant tendency to stress differences—height, color, age, location, materials, layout, shape, or whatever are used to establish and stress differences. In most cases, a *distinction* or noticeable difference tends to be established between various elements; it is these that express meanings. For example, domains, such as sacred/profane, front/back, men/women, public/private, and so on, are distinguished; distinctive cues indicate that. The process seems universal, the *means* variable. There are probably limits to the means available and certain likely, or even almost inevitable, things might happen. Height will tend to be used and in most cases does indicate importance or sacredness; color will tend to be used even if specific colors vary; orientation tends to be significant, even if specific directions vary; centrality (for example, navel of the world, *axis mundi*) is common—although its meaning may be reversed; size or degree of elaborateness and other comparable elements will tend to recur and even tend to be used in certain ways rather than others. Thus height in the North and South Indian Temples is, in one sense, used in opposed ways in making sacredness within the temple, but in opposing temple/town height is still used to mark the sacred. This corresponds, for example, to the relation of up:down = sacred:profane or pure:polluted found among the Kwaio in the Solomon Islands (Keesing, 1979) and many other cultures.

It is interesting to examine status, hierarchy, prestige, and power. For one thing, they are related to social rank or dominance and these are almost universal, not only in humans but among many animals. In higher animals, status is related to *attention.* Human prestige striving is homologous with primate self-dominance, but the primate tendency for seeking high social rank is transformed into self-esteem, which is maintained by seeking prestige; the self or group is evaluated as higher (a significant word!) than others. To get attention, distortions of perception and cognition are used. In traditional cultures, culturally patterned strategies are used for this; culture contact often destroys these (Barkow, 1975). The built environment is one of these strategies, and in trying to establish prestige, height is, in fact, a very commonly used cue.

If we examine how space and physical objects communicate rank and power, we find height frequently used, although clearly this can only be understood in context. Many examples can be found. One very striking one has to do with the way rank was communicated in palaces. It appears that the Emperor of Byzantium had a throne that rose through mechanical means while those before him prostrated themselves (see Canetti, 1962)—a real-world analogue of the well-known scene in Charlie Chaplin's *The Great Dictator*. Other examples from Bangkok, Cambodia, and other places have already been given. This kind of cue is, I suspect, almost universally understood.

Horizontal space can also be used in this way, as in Versailles, Hitler's chancery (Blomeyer, 1979), or in the well-known example of Mussolini's office; many executive offices also use this. Redundancy is also used clearly to communicate rank and power clearly—height, horizontal space, decoration, materials, guards, and so on. Thus one can consider the palace of the pharaoh in ancient Egypt as a "ruling machine" (Uphill, 1972). Here a wide variety of architectural manipulation and ornament was used to produce a suitable feeling of awe in visitors. Note the implication that it was self-evident to all and that we can still so interpret it. The palace was a set of messages to communicate awe and subservience: absolute size, scale, settings, approach, spatial sequence, color, doorways, paneling, and other decoration, courtiers, costumes, furnishings, and many other elements were used to create a setting overwhelming in itself—and even more so in the context of the typical mud-brick villages and even larger houses. This contextual impact is, of course, critical in understanding any environment—a New England town in the seventeenth century in its clearing of fields contrasting with the dread forest; any humanized area in a real wilderness (such as a village in prehistoric times; Rapoport, 1979b); major monumental complexes or spaces, such as the Acropolis in the context of ancient Athens or the Maidan-i-Shah in the context of seventeenth-century Isphahan.

While in all these cases the meanings described would have been, and still are, immediately comprehensible since so noticeable due to redundancy, context, and the use of "natural" cues, the *specific* reading of the meanings requires some cultural knowledge. The codes must be known in order for the meaning of the order underlying buildings, cities, and whole countries to be understood. This was the case in Ancient Cambodia (see Giteau, 1976) and in the layout of the entire Maya lowlands, to give just two examples. These latter need to be interpreted in terms of a sacred model based on the quadripartite view of the universe and the consequent use of four capitals. This organization penetrates down to level of the villages, which also consist of four wards (Marcus, 1973). This is, of course, an ancient and common pattern; one of the earliest cities, Ebla, was structured in this way (Bermant and Weitzman, 1979: 155, 167), as were many other cities (Rapoport, 1979b). Similar models underlie Yoruba environments (Kamau, 1976) and Mexico, where a knowledge of ancient Aztec organization can help in reading the meaning of the organization of a contemporary small town such as Tlayacapan (Ingham, 1971). Thus knowing the underlying schemata, having internal contexts, helps in reading the meanings.

I have been discussing the fact that although context and cultural knowledge are important, many of these cues seem to be almost self-evident, although from the distant past and from very different cultures. This suggests the need briefly to consider again the suggestion made above that there may be regularities in the means available that may be likely, "natural," and almost inevitable. This may be interpeted in terms of the notion of evolutionary bases for behavior. One suggestion is that among more or less widely shared associations, there may be archetypal associations—that is, certain common responses to certain stimuli, or archetypes defined as the most likely schemata (see McCully, 1971). Another approach is that, due to evolution in particular conditions, the human species exhibits constancies in behavior, needs, and the ways things tend to be done, so that there are limits to the range of possible ways of doing things (Rapoport, 1975b; Hamburg, 1975; Tiger and Shepher, 1975; Tiger, 1969; Tiger and Fox, 1971; Fox, 1970; Boyden, 1974; Rossi, 1977).

It may also well be that not only is the repertoire or palette limited, but the rules of combination may be similarly limited. Here again, there may eventually be an area of overlap between the study of environmental meaning in terms of nonverbal cues and more formal structuralist, semiotic, symbolic, linguistic, and cognitive anthropology models. Note that many of these are based on the notion of oppositions—that is, contrasts—so that many theorists in the area argue that symbols occur in sets and that the meaning of particular symbols is to be found in the contrast with other symbols rather than in the symbol as such, so that individual symbols have layers of meaning that depend upon what is being contrasted with what (see Leach, 1976). This notion of contrast or opposition seems basic to discrimination or meaning, and forms part of the context that I have been stressing.

One of these common processes discussed above was the tendency of the human mind to classify the world into domains such as nature/culture, us/them, men/women, private/public, front/back, sacred/profane, good/bad, and so on; built environments often give physical expression to these domains (Rapoport, 1976c). Note that recently the strict binary nature of such oppositions has been modified by the realization that frequently an important middle term (or terms) exists that mediates or resolves the opposition. One example is provided by the concept of "field" as mediating between "village" and "bush" in various cultures; also, in the opposition "sacred/polluted," there is the middle term "ordinary" (Keesing, 1979: 23; Fernandez, 1977; Rapoport, 1979b). Among the Zapotec, one finds the graveyard used as the category mediating between the wild (field) and the domestic (house) domains; there one finds a whole gradation or continuum of terms defining domains that are expressed in terms having to do with fields, villages, houses, patios, and so on, and with concepts such as sacred, profane, good, bad, safe, dangerous, and so on. Knowing these clarified the environment and its meanings (El Guindi and Selby, 1976). Contrasts are thus often among expressions of domains; while the results may vary, the processes and rules are constant.

In defining domains, and in grouping environmental elements into domains, it is necessary to judge whether, and how, elements are the same or different. It has been suggested that there are five main modes of equivalence: perceptible (color, size, shape, position, and so on); functional (for what it is used); affective (emotional response such as liked or disliked); nominal (based on ready-made names in the language); and by fiat, that is, arbitrary (Olver and Hornsby, 1972). The use of equivalence criteria and their types are constant; the specific type used varies among different cultures (see Greenfield et al., 1972; Suchman, 1966).

Once domains are defined, and their equivalence or difference established, *cues* need to be used to make them visible. This is the role and purpose of the contrasts we have been discussing. For example, the modern movement in architecture, modern art, and all *avant-garde in itself* has meaning simply by contrast with what is *not avant-garde*, through being identified with an elite minority. This is, of course, the role of fashion today, as we have already seen (Blumer, 1969b). Equivalent to these is being modern in Third World environments through the use of modern materials, shapes, or gadgets, which we have already discussed; it is, in fact, a perfect analogue through contrast with the context, for example, "modern" houses, concrete floors, cement blocks, galvanized iron, and wood frame as opposed to "bush" houses with mud floors, mud and stick walls, and thatched roofs. Recall that in a setting of galvanized iron roofs it is the thatched roof that may have special meaning.

Without noticeable differences—contrasts—meaning is more difficult to read. For example, in Campo Rugia, a traditional neighborhood

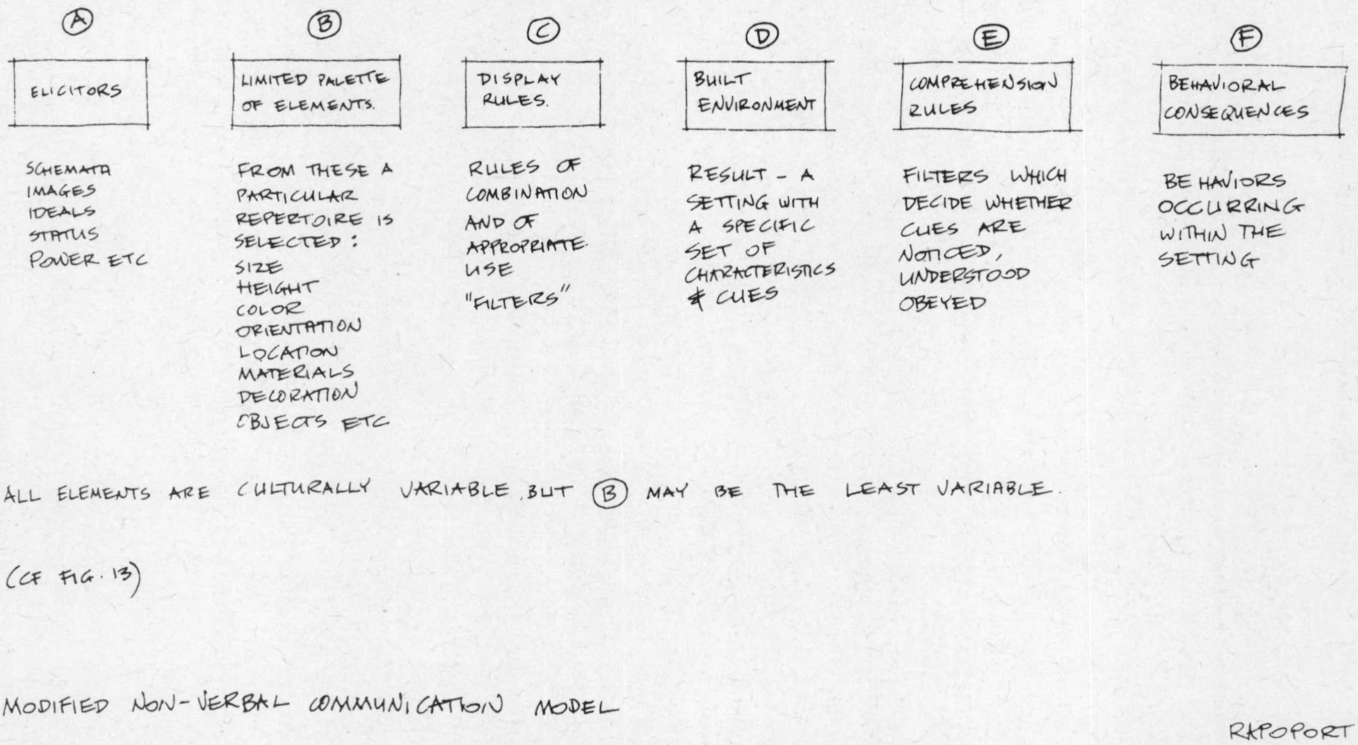

(A) **ELICITORS**

SCHEMATA
IMAGES
IDEALS
STATUS
POWER ETC

(B) **LIMITED PALETTE OF ELEMENTS.**

FROM THESE A PARTICULAR REPERTOIRE IS SELECTED :
SIZE
HEIGHT
COLOR
ORIENTATION
LOCATION
MATERIALS
DECORATION
OBJECTS ETC

(C) **DISPLAY RULES.**

RULES OF COMBINATION AND OF APPROPRIATE USE "FILTERS"

(D) **BUILT ENVIRONMENT**

RESULT - A SETTING WITH A SPECIFIC SET OF CHARACTERISTICS # CUES

(E) **COMPREHENSION RULES**

FILTERS WHICH DECIDE WHETHER CUES ARE NOTICED, UNDERSTOOD OBEYED

(F) **BEHAVIORAL CONSEQUENCES**

BEHAVIORS OCCURRING WITHIN THE SETTING

ALL ELEMENTS ARE CULTURALLY VARIABLE, BUT (B) MAY BE THE LEAST VARIABLE.

(CF FIG. 13)

MODIFIED NON-VERBAL COMMUNICATION MODEL

RAPOPORT

Figure 17

in Venice, windows vary greatly in size and form; this communicates the social meaning of dwellings. In the new neighborhood of Villaggio San Marco, the windows are all of the same size and form; they thus all seem to have the same importance and do not communicate (Chenu et al., 1979: 106, 110-111).

We have already seen that differences become more noticeable, and meanings clearer, when they are unique (one clearing in a forest, one colored building). Scarcity value is thus important in emphasizing absence or presence through contrast. For example, the shabby, non-manicured landscaping of upper-class areas (Duncan, 1973) communicates not only through matching the schema of "wilderness" and "simple, natural things," but by contrast with the prevailing suburban norm of manicured landscape. This landscaping becomes a *marker*. Similarly, since Venice has few arcades, they have a special meaning that indicates special areas of social importance, of interaction and meeting; they physically define the most important public places in the urban fabric. The two main ones are the Rialto—the business and financial center—and the Plaza San Marco—the political and religious center (Chenu et al., 1979: 76). Clearly, in Bologna, where arcades are the norm, their *absence* may have equivalent meaning.

Much work needs to be done in reviewing all these issues historically and cross-culturally. At the moment it still seems unresolved, but Ekman's model seems to be applicable whether semifixed- and non-fixed-feature elements tend to be more like emblems, illustrators, or adaptors; whether they are more like gestures or facial expressions (see Figure 17).

It thus appears that this approach, derived from nonverbal communication, can usefully be applied to environmental meaning, avoiding the problems presented by formal linguistic, semiotic, or symbolic approaches. Recall, however, the suggestion already made, reinforced by the above discussion, that by starting with this relatively simple, straightforward, and largely observational approach, one is in no way blocking its eventual integration with, and relation to, more formal linguistic, structuralist, semiotic, and symbolic analyses.

Notes

1. Interestingly, the authors were then at the San Francisco medical school of the University of California, where Ekman, whose work I will shortly discuss, has been working.

2. Note that this and many other studies on color are discussed in terms of "symbolism." As pointed out in Chapter 2, there is no loss in clarity when the concept "symbol" is omitted and the question, "What is the meaning of colors?" or "What do colors communicate?" is substituted.

5

SMALL-SCALE EXAMPLES OF
APPLICATIONS

Although many varied examples have been used in the discussion so far, it now seems useful to examine examples of the application of the approach advocated in more detail. While, in general, the examples will concentrate on our own time and Western culture, occasional more "exotic" examples will be used to stress specific points. In this chapter, smaller-scale examples will be examined; in the next, those at the urban scale.

As already pointed out, the advantage of this approach is that it is relatively simple and straightforward, involving observation and interpretation. Note that the early work of Ruesch and Kees, Hall, Birdwhistell, Ekman, and others involved observation and/or photography followed by analysis. This led to an index or catalogue of cues, which led to hypotheses tested by further observation or experiment. In this book, the suggestion is made that this early, relatively simple approach is extremely useful. Basically, one begins by looking and observing; one sensitizes oneself to see, observe, and understand: It is not a linear process, but one involving an intuitive "creative leap" once one has saturated oneself in the information (Rapoport, 1969d). This is, of course, also an analogue of design and of the use of man-environment studies in design.

The observation itself and the understanding become easier with practice, that is, as one develops this mode of thought. Clearly, one needs to intuit the meaning of what one sees; that intuition then needs to be checked systematically and in a more "linear" fashion. In both processes, of course, knowing the cultural context is extremely useful, but even that can be suggested by observation. In conventional non-verbal communication studies in the nonfixed-feature area, one can study both the encoding and decoding of the behaviors in an inter-action (Ekman and Friesen, 1972). In applying the approach to semi-fixed (and fixed-feature) elements one can also study the encoding (what setting would one provide for X) and decoding (what does this setting suggest or mean). One description of how this process might occur is given in the hypothetical example of how one might gradually comprehend the meanings of various elements in Spain, beginning with observation (Poyatos, 1976). Clearly, this process of gradual comprehension implies, as already pointed out, the need to acquire the cultural knowledge necessary to interpret the cues, that is, the con-text available to the users. At the same time, however, the early stages described involve a person, newly arrived in Spain, observing and recording various features in the environment: blending of offices and dwellings, the signs attached to balconies, film placards, sidewalk cafes, open-door bars, traffic, proxemic behavior, various smells, and so on; meanings can then be inferred and checked.

Spatial organization at small scales can communicate meanings at the level of semifixed elements. For example, if one considers court-rooms in several cultures (Hazard, 1972), the suggestion is that by observing the spatial relationships among five elements—judge's seat, defendant's seat, jury's seats, defending attorney's seat, and prosecut-ing attorney's seat—the major and essential features of the criminal justice system can be determined so that even an empty courtroom tells one a great deal (see Figure 18). Whether this is, in fact, the case is less important than the point that we can judge relative position, status, and the whole situation through such cues that, effectively, are in the semifixed realm, which is extremely significant for my argument. These cues may be very subtle, as a saw-cut in the bench behind which judge and prosecutor sit in Poland to make them distinct. For example, the jury is separate from the judge in the United States and Britain, and they retire separately to different places. In Geneva, the judge and jury retire together; in that case, the prosecutor is higher spatially than the defense attorney, accused, and witness stand. In other places, other variants are found. A significant point about the jury/judge relation above is that how and where they retire is significant. This clearly sug-gests that with people present, their dress, behavior, and interaction will communicate even more. For example, the nature of the judge's seat—its size, decoration, location, whether it is raised—will com-municate much. The judge's dress—robes, wigs, chains, or sashes of

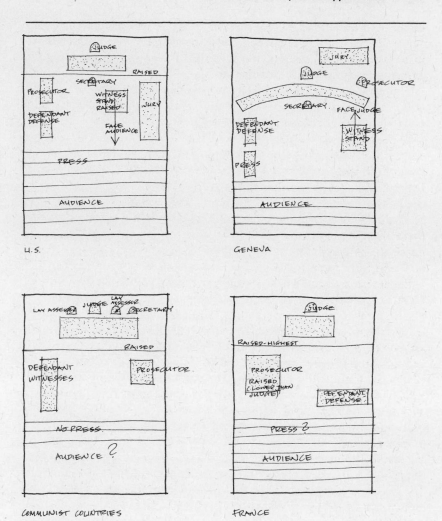

COURTROOMS IN FOUR CULTURES. NOTE THAT IN EACH CASE THE
FIXED-FEATURE ELEMENTS (WALLS) ARE IDENTICAL.

DRAWINGS BASED ON VERBAL DESCRIPTIONS IN HAZARD (1972)   RAPOPORT.

Figure 18

office—will add more; the nonfixed features, such as the usher's cry of "all stand" and the crowd's behavior, all add even more data.

Note that, moreover, one finds that clothing style, behavior, and "the subtle differences in the way lawyers and witnesses speak in the courtroom can have a profound effect on the outcome of a criminal trial" (New York Times, 1975). Thus these more typical nonverbal cues also play a role. The report also comments that the American criminal trial is a public ritual that is used to resolve conflicts. This is, of course, typical of all cultures; the discussion here bears on the setting for these rituals and it reflects them. Note that, once again, the fixed-feature elements communicate much less.

The advantage of such an approach is that it is simple enough conceptually to be used quickly and easily by practitioners and students. Basically one identifies sets of noticeable differences among environments and makes inferences about them. Once a single case is analyzed and relationships established, other comparable cases allow inferences to be made more easily, as we shall see below. One can also observe overt behavior and obtain demographic characteristics of populations to help interpret these meanings more fully.

It even becomes possible to disprove hypotheses in this way. Thus, for example, one student (Janz, 1978) compared semifixed elements in several hundred dwellings in an area on the South side of Milwaukee (a white ethnic, blue-collar area) with an area on the East side (a professional-academic, fairly high-status area, with a subsample of architects' dwellings there). He assumed that personalization would be higher on the East side. In addition to field analysis, he photographed the houses for further analysis. It soon became clear that personalization through semifixed elements was very much higher on the South side—in fact, what was typical of the East side was the *absence* of personalization. In other words, two different subculture codes were being used to which people conformed. The meanings communicated—"I am a good person who belongs here"—were communicated through both the presence and absence of personalization externally.

Various questions and subhypotheses could quickly be formulated. Was the lack of personalization on the East side due to lifestyle variables among the inhabitants so that the population established identity in other, nonenvironmental ways, for example, through professional achievement (see Rapoport, 1981)? Alternatively, other environmental means might be involved, for example, a group identity achieved through the architectural quality of the dwellings and overall character of the area that attracted people there in the first place and that would be damaged by major changes in the semifixed elements. Was the location of the area and residence in it sufficient to communicate a particular social identity that, on the South side, needed to be achieved through personalization? These questions, too, could be answered relatively easily.

It was also not too difficult for a student to begin to list the elements to be examined (that is, the *palette*):

external materials
colors
fences
planting and landscaping
visibility of house from street
visibility into house
shutters
awnings and decorations on them
mailboxes
street numbers
newspaper holders
external lights
handrails
signs on front of house
flagpoles and their location
air conditioners
storm doors
other objects

For each of these elements, many specific questions can easily be listed.

Similar questions and approaches can be used to study front/back distinctions. Thus lists of noticeable differences can be noted among fixed and semifixed (and even nonfixed) features that are used to indicate front or back. These can be, and have been, applied easily in the field by researchers, practitioners, and students. One can look at

the state of lawns
maintenance of houses
colors
presence and absence of porches

location of garages and cars
various uses and how treated
various objects
location of paths
landscaping
absence or presence of people, their dress, and behavior
presence, absence, or treatment of fences

and many others. (Inventories of this kind can also be used, both externally and internally, for many other studies.)

An example of one such study done by students examined the object language in two subculturally different residential areas in Urbana, Illinois (Anderson and Moore, 1972). The study investigated the demarcation of space through planting and fences, and began by observing and recording objects; a classification and typology easily followed. Then, qualitative evaluations and quantitative differences were studied. The process was direct, straightforward, and easy, and results were enlightening. The elements constituting the message content of the barriers used to demarcate space were also quite easily derived: location, materials, type, size, continuity. Other forms of boundary phenomena, such as markers (equivalent to point barriers), are quickly noted (even if not studied); they can then quickly be seen to relate to other studies of such markers. The presence or absence of semifixed-feature elements such as other planting, chairs, tables, sun umbrellas, or barbecues, and nonfixed-feature elements such as people and their activities could also be observed and used to clarify the issue. The study, like the Milwaukee example above, was done as project for a term paper and would hardly have been possible with more "sophisticated" means.

Another advantage of this approach is that many studies exist that can be interpreted in these terms: These begin to show patterns and exhibit relationships, enabling one to work in the manner described in the preface, that is, relating many disparate studies and integrating them into larger conceptual systems. An example is provided by a comparison of houses in some parts of Africa with those in the Sudan. In the former case, one finds granaries as major elements—in size, shape, color, decoration, location, and so on. These clearly are important in the meanings they have for people. In the Sudan, because of Islam, it is God who is honored rather than grain. Hence grain is stored in simple and unobtrusive granaries; it is mosques and tombs of saints that, in form, size, color, and so on, dominate the mud-brick villages

(Lee, 1974). The differences are clarified using cultural knowledge, but simple observation and listing of elements makes the point quickly and forcefully. In West Africa both elements are stressed—the meaning of granaries reflects the essential nature of grain and is expressed through most elaborate craftsmanship and use of the highest skills; the mosque has meaning as an expression of spirituality as the granary is a spiritual expression of material well-being. In other parts of West Africa, however, for example, among the Dogomba, it is not the granary but the doorframe of the compound portal that has the most meaning; among the Mossi, it is the doorway and lock (Prussin, 1972)—all judged on the basis of emphasis and elaboration. Thus, in the case of each of the West African groups, a different element communicates meaning; this is revealed through noticeable differences: elaboration, location, materials, decoration, and so on. Once noted, inferences can be made, the elements analyzed and interpreted, and the relevant cultural, contextual knowledge relatively easily obtained to check these interpretations.

Front lawns in our own culture provide a good example. Shortly after I arrived in Milwaukee in 1972, a rather interesting case occurred in the suburb of Wauwatosa, Wisconsin. Given the local climate, and the particular orientation of her house, a woman decided that she would have her vegetable garden in front—where a lawn is normally to be found in Anglo-American culture. The municipality was outraged, and many special council meetings were held. Court actions took place and the case eventually reached the Wisconsin Supreme Court. In the end, the woman was allowed to grow her vegetables, but what is far more interesting is the obviously strongly affective reaction to the attempt. Obviously a front lawn is independent of space organization—it is more than a certain number of square feet of grass. It must mean something very important—as we would also suspect from the anecdotal material on social pressures for well-maintained laws. But can one find more "scientific" evidence? It is, in fact, difficult to avoid it.

The central role of the lawn in communicating meaning is confirmed by studies done in new communities in California. In these new communities, after the purchase of the house, little money often remained available to residents. Yet, frequently, a lawn was put in and maintained while the house lacked adequate furniture (Eichler and Kaplan, 1967; Werthman, 1968). The importance of these lawns was in their meaning; they communicated adherence to a particular image that established a group identity and certified the worthiness of the individual to inhabit the particular area. Parenthetically (and to be discussed later), the whole area, and the meaning and purpose of planning, were seen as the creation of a particular image certifying and maintaining status, self-worth, and self-identity. In effect, the lawn becomes an expression of a particular message—the front region *par excellence.*

In almost all studies having to do with the environmental quality of residential areas, *maintenance* plays a most important role, that is, it is a most important component of that rather complex concept (for a review, see Rapoport, 1977: ch. 2). A most important (although, certainly, not the only) aspect of maintenance is the quality of the front lawn. The front yard and its lawn, its upkeep and layout, are indicators of the taste, status, and lifestyle of the family who owns it. The presence or absence of fences also has meaning, as we have already seen. In the United States, fences used to be common, but then disappeared. They were, and are, seen as communicating self-sufficiency, individualism, and nonconformity (Jackson, 1951). Note the role of context: Fences clearly meant something different before and after their general disappearance, and they mean something different in the United States than they do in Britain and other places where they are common. A fence where there are none or few has different meaning than a fence that is one among many: It is nonconforming in the former, highly conforming in the latter; in the former case it communicates attitudes about privacy, interaction, and boundary control, while in the latter it does not (see Figure 19).

There are, of course, areas of the United States where fences are still common and, at the moment, they seem to be proliferating generally in the United States. Their persistence, disappearance, and reappearance, and changes in their height, solidity, and so on, all have more to do with *meaning* than anything else; and so do the materials used or changes in their use (Anderson and Moore, 1972).

We already have seen that these meanings are part of the enculturation process and occur very early in life, providing the cues and standards for social comparison processes whereby people are judged. In Texas, for example, where both lawn and country gardens (bare earth and flowers) existed, quite young children judged people by these, with lawns seen as indicating higher-status and better-quality people (Sherif and Sherif, 1963). In other cultures, different devices are used to achieve similar ends. For example, in the Barriadas of

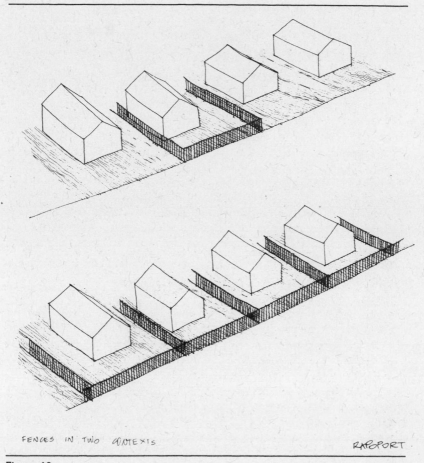

FENCES IN TWO CONTEXTS   RAPOPORT.

Figure 19

Lima, Peru, an elaborate front door is purchased often before a roof can be afforded—in a climate where roofs are, to put it mildly, a necessity (Turner, 1967). In other cases, front fences are used, such as in Puerto Rico, where elaborate wrought-iron grilles may cost more than the dwelling they enclose. The false fronts of frontier settlements in the United States and the false fronts among the Maya of Cozumel and generally in Putun-dominated Yucatan (Sabloff and Rathje, 1976) are other examples among many others that can be given (Rapoport,

1979a). What they all show is the important meaning of "front region" being communicated by the use of various devices.

An example of cues comparable to lawns and fences in a different culture is provided by the head-high, impenetrable beech hedges in front of houses in Denmark. These are grown from scratch and take between eight and seventeen years to mature; no interim boundary definers or privacy screens are used (Seligmann, 1976). The primacy of the *meaning* of this element, its latent rather than manifest function, is clear: The purpose is to establish front and communicate self-worth in the culturally appropriate way, even though Seligmann argues that in Denmark generally, front definition is of much lesser importance than in the United States. There are also other groups for which this is of less importance as part of a general lack of attention to dwellings and other environmental means generally to communicate status, identity, and so on (Duncan and Duncan, 1976; Rapoport, 1981). When front/back reversals occur, we find "inappropriate" behavior, as in the example of Baltimore cited above. Alternatively, an area may be defined as a "slum" on the basis of behaviors classified by one group as belonging in back regions occurring in front regions. Examples of how areas are read as urban slums in the Anglo-American realm might be the presence of garbage cans or people sitting in their undershirts drinking beer; in rural areas, the presence of stripped and cannibalized cars visible from the road (that is, a front region for most American travelers; see Rapoport, 1977: ch. 2, especially pp. 96-100). These larger scale examples will be discussed in more detail in the next chapter.

The analysis of lawns, country gardens, and hedges is based on the fact that one of the easiest ways of changing meaning is by the use of semifixed-feature elements such as planting. The very common use of such elements leads to their expressing meaning, and hence the use of gardens and plant complexes by cultural geographers as a culture indicator is significant (Kimber, 1966, 1971, 1973; Wilhelm, 1975; Anderson, 1972; Simoons, 1965). The implication of this is, of course, that gardens and planting patterns have meaning and, to those who can decode the meanings, can communicate ethnic and other group identities. The cultural specificity is striking, so that traditional Chinese gardens are of two types and, if the code is understood, can be shown to summarize and express Taoist and Confucian philosophies, respectively (Moss, 1965). In the former, man is seen as a natural being; in the latter, as a social being. Each of these positions has environmental implications. Thus the Taoist garden stresses irregularity, lack of symmetry, avoidance of axial vistas or avenues, a search for surprise, and intimacy rather than monumentality. In the Confucian view, gardens are less important than houses, palaces, temples, and other official or ceremonial settings—that is, the domain of culture. Confucian gardens also communicate that: hierarchically arranged and explicitly defined spaces, symmetry, rectangularity, and rectilinear direction change and axiality were sought; curvilinearity was avoided. In both cases, the specifics—layout, use of plant materials, rocks, water, and so on— follow from these ideals.

In the United States, also, the landscaping of dwellings can be "read" quite easily. It can be suggested that planting lawns, flowers, and the like is a mode of communication about the owners and the social situation. This, then, becomes the "chief, although not only, purpose of garden planning" (Anderson, 1972: 181). Again, the front/ back distinction often seems basic even when both yards are seen. Other binary oppositions are found: lawn/ground cover, cultivated flowers/wildflowers (= weeds), and so on. While in this case a semi-structuralist analysis is made, the "reading" is straightforward and simple, starting with the observed elements; there would be no less of clarity in using the nonverbal communication approach. It is significant that two subcultural groups, Mexican-Americans and Japanese-Americans in Los Angeles, transformed previously identical residential areas through planting and garden design: In the former case, with walled gardens, patios, little or no grass, bright flowers and flowering trees, cacti and so on; in the latter case, with grass, rocks, bonsai trees, stone lanterns, and so on (Rapoport, 1969c: 131, note 15).

Other elements of environments, such as suburban houses, can also be "read" in this way. Thus early twentieth-century U.S. popular houses were analyzed directly using the concept of audicule and trying to identify what was being communicated, the cultural meanings (Seligmann, 1975). These meanings are interpreted in terms of the interaction and conflict between communal roles and private identity, and other meanings. While the task of understanding the house as communicating certain life values by "decoding a set of signs" sounds semiotic (and does not use the approach of this book), it is done directly, straightforwardly, by beginning with observation and by identifying the elements. The analysis is concrete, clear, and, hence, useful.

Similar analyses have been done for the New Zealand suburban house (which I do not have) and the Vancouver house (Holdsworth,

1975). In this case also, although the nonverbal communication model is not used formally, the approach is effectively the one being advocated—observation and analysis. The use of wood, for example, is not due just to its local availability, but also to the fact that the brick urban world had negative connotations related to the nineteenth-century industrial city (Holdsworth, 1975: 4). The meaning of the detached house as *home*, of the fireplace and other elements, become clear from an analysis of advertisements. Individuality was important (again, partly in contrast to the English urban landscape, from where the inhabitants came) and the overall appearance of the house was influenced by the West Coast lifestyle—thus the impact of the Southern California bungalow in a very different setting and climate. Differences can be found between the working-class "home" and elite dwellings. The meanings of the latter can be so easily read, understood, and illustrated that they are used in advertisements (see Figure 20). The task is fairly straightforward and, given even a minimal knowledge of the context, can be relatively easily achieved.

The attempts to achieve the image of the freestanding house at high densities helps explain the use of narrow lots in nineteenth-century Milwaukee (Beckley, 1977), where the spacing between houses may be as little as four feet. In Pittsburgh, on the corner of Hamlet and Ophelia streets (in South Oakland), I recently saw houses about eighteen inches apart—they were still freestanding! (Recall the saw-cut in the Polish courtroom described above.) Another example of the meaning of freestanding houses in nineteenth-century working-class U.S. areas is provided by the "three-decker" house in Worcester, Massachusetts—it is a compromise between the economics of urban land and the ideal of the freestanding, single-family dwelling (Barnett, 1975). It is the *meaning* rather than the reality of the detached house that is important. Interestingly, with changing contexts and images, these same dwellings now often communicate negative meanings, and new elements are used in redevelopment in Milwaukee to communicate positive, and hence appropriate, meanings, as we shall see in the next chapter.

Similarly, by observing the spatial relationships of just two people (patient and therapist) in a psychiatric situation in a number of "schools" of psychiatry—Freudian, Jungian, Reichian, Gestalt, and so on—often expressed and expressible in furniture arrangements, or the absence of furniture, one can determine equally well the essential philosophy of the particular school (Goodman, 1959). One could add to this other examples, such as Morita therapy in Japan and various

DRAWING OF ADVERTISEMENT FOR SCOTCH SHOWING USE OF BACKGROUND SETTING TO COMMUNICATE HIGH STATUS. NOTE SELF-EVIDENT MEANING OF THE TWO MANSIONS (AND VERY LARGE LAWN). (COPY REFERS TO REQUEST TO BORROW CUP OF BRAND X SCOTCH)

(BASED ON ADVERTISEMENT, INSIDE BACK COVER, *COMMENTARY*, VOL 69, No. 2, FEB. 1980)

(SEE ALSO FIG. 9)

RAPOPORT.

Figure 20

135

ethnopsychiatric situations. This argument can also be extended to restaurants and to parliamentary institutions, where a comparison of the French Assemblée Nationale, the British House of Commons, and the U.S. Senate proves most instructive in the way meaning is communicated by the location of seating as expressing political philosophies.

Note that in many, if not most, of these cases, the cues are in the semifixed realm (and in the nonfixed realm when people are present)— the fixed-feature elements communicate much less.

6

URBAN EXAMPLES OF APPLICATIONS

Many dwellings together become residential areas and many gardens together become landscapes. More generally, *cultural land-scapes* are the results of many artifacts grouped together in particular relationships. They are also the result of the decisions of innumerable individuals. It is most striking that they can, and do, take on clear character. This suggests, of course, the presence of shared schemata among particular groups (Rapoport, 1972, 1977, 1980b, 1980c). It also suggests that once the schemata or codes are known, such land-scapes have meaning in terms of various forms of group identity and, moreover, that they can be read in the same way as smaller-scale examples—instantaneously. Also, since it is mainly, although not exclusively, semifixed- and nonfixed-feature elements that communicate meaning, the development of specific character at the areal level depends on some level of homogeneity. In a homogeneous area, personalizations and human behavior "add up" to produce strong, clear, and redundant cues; in highly heterogeneous areas they result in random variations with little or no meaning at the scale of the area. Also, particularly for residents, or users, the cultural knowledge needed to decode nonverbal behavior in the nonfixed- and semifixed-feature domains is much clearer in the one case than in the other (see Figure 21).

All these characteristics play a role in the relatively greater effectiveness of traditional environments in communicating to their users vis-à-vis contemporary situations. But even the latter frequently exhibit clear meanings given the persisting clustering of people in cities and regions by perceived homogeneity and the resulting cultural landscapes (Rapoport, 1977). Note that the main difference between

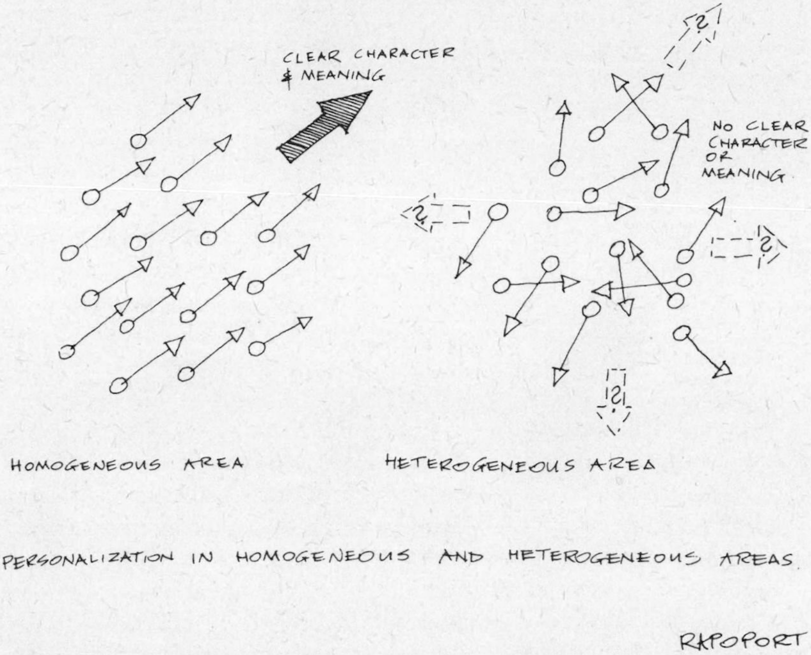

CLEAR CHARACTER & MEANING

NO CLEAR CHARACTER OR MEANING

HOMOGENEOUS AREA   HETEROGENEOUS AREA

PERSONALIZATION IN HOMOGENEOUS AND HETEROGENEOUS AREAS

RAPOPORT

Figure 21

these cases and the smaller-scale ones is that cues are collective rather than individual. Redundancy becomes even more important for clarity since even with extreme homogeneity a degree of variability is inevitable. Thus, at the area level, judgments are, theoretically, more difficult to make—more potentially discordant messages are present. Yet, as we shall see, judgments are made constantly, quickly, and easily. Possibly, given the importance of such cues in cities made up of very diverse individuals and groups, observers are prepared to act on the basis of very limited information; in terms of contemporary U.S. cities, for example, observers are ready to make judgments on the basis of minimal or uncertain cues.

Note, once again, that the process of understanding cultural landscapes is very analogous to that pertaining to interperson perception studied in psychology. There, individuals are required to make snap judgments about strangers on the basis of limited information—they make inferences on the basis of rules that seem quite regular and are based on the nonfixed-feature elements already discussed—facial expressions, skin, dress, speech, and so on. Often, stereotypical schemata are used to evaluate these perceived characteristics (Warr and Knapper, 1968; Mann, 1969: especially pp. 92-100; references in Rapoport, 1977; and many others). In the cases being discussed here, a wider range of cues, fixed, semifixed, and nonfixed feature, are being used to judge areas, and through them the character of groups.

An example of this process, and of the schemata used to stereotype and judge people, is provided by a group of architects who, in a particular case, classified large areas as slums even though, in fact, they were highly maintained and greatly improved. The judgments were made on the basis of the use of particular materials (such as fake stone and plastic sheeting imprinted with brick patterns) that the architects disliked and despised (Sauer, 1972); their comparison standard was based on different cues—materials replaced lawns—but the process was similar and so was the outcome. A *different* form of cultural landscape (in the context of architects' images) was judged negatively. Since people are judged by where they live, the group identity was negative or stigmatizing: Slums are inhabited by "bad" people.

The use of materials communicates meaning over and above space organization. Thus, in studying the early Mesoamerican village, one finds adobe first used in public buildings, replacing wattle and daub, and then gradually becoming used for houses—first elite and then nonelite. Thus, at that moment in time, adobe was equated with high status. In other cases, it may be brick or stone, human-made materials generally, and so on. The insistence on modern materials in the Third World already discussed is an example. But shape may also communicate in this way. For example, in large parts of the Middle East, flat roofs are now regarded as a mark of poverty. Pitched, tile roofs have become virtually a status symbol—people giving up necessary instrumental and manifest functions, such as work space and night sleeping space, for this purpose (Hodges, 1972; for other examples, see Rapoport, 1969c).

Thus people read environmental cues, make judgments about the occupants of settings, and then act accordingly—environments communicate social and ethnic identity, status, and so on. For example, environmental quality is often judged through maintenance (Rapoport, 1977). Maintenance itself is judged through a whole set of cues, which will become clearer shortly. In terms of identity and how it is communicated by group landscapes (see Rapoport, forthcoming a), it is of interest to examine immigrant groups in new environments. It is widely believed that, first, they tend to select landscapes like those "back home" because they have affective meaning, although this view has recently been challenged (see McQuillan, 1978: 138-139). Be that as it may, they do frequently transform the landscape through layout, space organization, buildings, plants, and so on. Thus one finds Ukrainian, German, Japanese, and other cultural landscapes in South America (Stewart, 1965; Eidt, 1971). Frequently, those groups that use familiar, traditional elements and that are able to create corresponding landscapes tend to be more successful in their settlement attempts (Eidt, 1971). This can be interpreted partly in terms of meaning: These environments are supportive because they are familiar, because they express elements of the culture core (Rapoport, 1979c, forthcoming a).

The cases of Australia and, particularly, New Zealand are even more striking: There, English landscapes have been recreated over large areas of the country (Shepard, 1969). Early topographic drawings of Australia and descriptions of other unfamiliar environments (such as the Great Plains of the United States) also clearly show the inability even to perceive the alien landscape and the negative connotations it has; the urge to transform it, to give it meaning through the use of familiar cues, becomes understandable.

It is also fascinating to study the landscapes created by various ethnic and cultural groups at smaller scales, for example, in the Middle East. Thus, in Haifa, Israel, areas settled by Germans in the nineteenth-century are quite different from others—they contrast house forms, shape and material of roofs (pitched and red tile versus flat), door details, and so on, establishing a "European" meaning. Similarly, vegetation is different (as on the German Carmel). In the context of that rather wild and remote place, at the time the area was settled the meaning was clearly important and very strong. In the plain of Sharon, descendants of Bosnian settlers in the village of Yamun, East of Nablus, can still be recognized through the fact that their houses have red tile roofs (Ilan, 1978). This differentiates them from their Arab neighbors, who live in traditional, flat-roofed houses. As a final set of examples, we find the treatment of various religious enclaves in the Sinai, Jerusalem, and the Judean desert. Their origins are clearly communicated—whether Greek, Italian, or Ethiopian.

All these are, of course, examples of the notion of cultural landscapes in geography as capable of communicating meaning and thus of being read. These not only embody values and ideals, but influence human behavior; they are systems of settings developed to elicit appropriate behaviors. To do that, they must be read. Similarly, archaeology, as we have seen, relies on the fact that the physical environment can be seen as encoding information, thus it can be decoded or read even if that reading may be difficult or inaccurate in some cases, as we have seen. Note that in archaeology also the reading can occur at the urban scale as well as at smaller scales. Thus in Monte Alban (Oaxaca, Mexico), a combination of fixed-feature and semifixed-feature elements were used in a *surface survey* to make inferences about the population, social structure, uses of areas, political organization, history, and so on (Blanton, 1978). Also, as already stressed, the extent to which environ-ments communicate these messages effectively depends on redun-dancy. In most cases, therefore, one finds multiple cue and message systems co-acting in order to provide sufficient redundancy for the message to ge through. This works particularly well in traditional and vernacular environments, where, for example, status and importance in a Southern Italian town such as Ostuni (see Figure 8 in Chapter 2) is indicated by location of buildings, their size, fenestration, features such as domes, towers, and pediments, materials, colors, and so on. But even in our culture this still works and is used for intergroup com-munication. Recall the example of Westchester County, where two distinct cultural landscapes were found that well communicated group identity (Duncan, 1973). Cues included street paving, street lighting, nature of planting (clipped or natural), house visibility, the presence or absence of colonial eagles, and the use of elaborate mail boxes or of rural mail boxes. While the respective landscapes were partly counter-intuitive—the more "scruffy" one indicated the higher-status group—the correlation between cultural landscape and group identity was extraordinarily high; once the code was known, membership could be read very easily and effectively. Note also the likelihood that the counterintuitive nature of the high-status landscape was a "cunning" way of marking that group and a subtle, and effective, way of exclud-ing the lower-status group.

Before returning to the United States to consider a range of examples, let us see how such codes work in different cultural milieus. For example, in Old Nubia, different groups along the Nile used tombs of saints to identify groups that also had different house and village forms. All houses, however, were decorated in very striking ways. When rehoused in uniform and highly unsuitable houses after the building of the Aswan Dam, the first thing the Nubians did was to begin to decorate the houses (Fernea et al., 1973). These decorations became the element communicating ethnic identity, that is, a specific meaning vis-à-vis the other inhabitants. A clear contrast was set up with the context. Thus noticeable cues are created—knowledge of the code then enables the meaning ("Nubians") to be read. In this case the cues are traditional; the contrast with the context of traditional environments may be set up through the use of modern materials and colors.

Thus a village may blend in with the local color (being built of mud brick) and look like a rock outcrop; houses may be beehive shaped—as in North Syria. More substantial dwellings of concrete or stone, with balconies or with grilles, and painted, indicate higher status, higher income, or contact with overseas relatives, even though they may be less comfortable, hotter in summer, and colder in winter. This is not unlike the distinction in India between houses of mud brick *(kutcha)* and of burnt brick *(pukka);* the meaning of the latter is clear from the English term *pukka sahib.* In Mexico and other countries of Latin America, and in many Indian or even Mestizo (or Ladino) villages, the double-story or painted (or both) dwellings will have similar communicative function (see Figure 22). This corresponds to the use of whitewash for a chapel in the Altiplano of Peru or the red or blue domes on churches in Mykonos (to which I refer in Rapoport, 1968b; see also Figure 7 in Chapter 2). In the case, however, in which the environment generally—that is, the context—is polychromatic (as in some Greek Islands, Italy, or Mexico), color will *not* have that role.

Changes in traditional environments also need to be understood in this way. For example, the change to Western, freestanding, "outward facing," European-style bungalows, new "suburban" location, the adoption of Western domestic furniture, furnishings, and equipment, and the consequent behavior in India was an indication of status: It was a marker. It began with elites, being a way of marking them, distinguishing between them and others (King, 1977). These changes were assertions about changing values and attitudes; they were markers of a particular group membership. Their major significance was in the realm of *meaning.* Note that these changes correspond to changes in the nature of the elite groups: Traditional elites do not need visible manifestations—their quality is *known* (see Duncan and Duncan, 1976). Clearly, all examples of the stress on new materials and forms

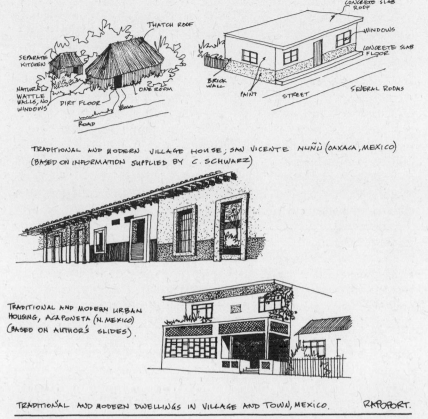

TRADITIONAL AND MODERN VILLAGE HOUSE; SAN VICENTE NUÑÙ (OAXACA, MEXICO) (BASED ON INFORMATION SUPPLIED BY C. SCHWARZ)

TRADITIONAL AND MODERN URBAN HOUSING, ACAPONETA (N. MEXICO) (BASED ON AUTHOR'S SLIDES).

TRADITIONAL AND MODERN DWELLINGS IN VILLAGE AND TOWN, MEXICO.   RAPOPORT.

Figure 22

are to be seen not in terms of comfort, improvement in livability, and the like, but as statements of meaning, about "modernity." They are in the associational realm.

In the Sudan, houses made of flimsy wood and grass are considered old fashioned and symbolic of the lowest economic and social classes; as soon as one can afford them, mud dwellings are used (Lee, 1969b). Similarly, the choice of house form, materials (such as red brick), and large windows (uncomfortable, but indicating modernity) all indicate prestige, which is equated with an identification with elements the meaning of which is *urban life;* the hierarchy, in ascending order, is wood and thatch, mud, and red brick. This sequence, which can be interpreted in terms of increasing distance from "nature" toward "culture" (Vogt, 1970), is particularly clearly developed into a code in Latin America.

In many parts of Latin America, the scattered, "haphazard" layout of Indian or rural areas, the proliferation of vegetation, and the use of "natural" materials contrasts with urban landscapes, which stress rectilinear, grid layouts, human-made materials forming what one could call an "urban wall," and an absence of vegetation, which is inside courts. The vegetation in plazas is controlled, for example, pleached, stressing its belonging to the domain of culture. Parenthetically, this vegetation then becomes a clear cue indicating "plaza" (that is, important place), which is reinforced through church steeples, arcades, light quality, activity types and levels, and so on. As a village becomes modernized and urbanized, these types of changes occur (Rapoport, 1977: 348). All relate to "distance to nature" as identifying status and membership in the two major groups: Indian and Ladino (or Mestizo), who also have clear status, low and high, respectively. In a study of San Pedro, Colombia (Richardson, 1974), a number of such cues indicated relative status: location—central as high status, peripheral as low; space organization—ordered and rectilinear as high status, scattered and straggly as low status; the presence of visible large masses of natural vegetation versus clipped vegetation localized in plazas (and in court interiors); materials—human-made (tile, brick, and so on) as high status, natural thatch, bamboo, and so on as low status.

Note three things. First, these are all environmental quality cues. Second, in other cultures, such as the United States or Australia, many of these cues are reversed: irregular layout, natural vegetation, and peripheral location would generally indicate higher status than an urban wall, absence of vegetation, and central location (we will return to this point later). Third, the cues described would, of course, be reinforced by other cues such as the types of people encountered, their dress, their behavior, the language spoken, the kinds of shops and what they contained, the presence or absence of markets, sounds, smells, and so on—that is, there would be a large range of noticeable differences (Rapoport, 1977) that would indicate status and, in this case, ethnicity. Also note that, first, while each cue by itself would hardly do it, all acting together and congruently could not fail to get the message across, because redundancy is high. Second, consistent and repeated use would lead to greater clarity of meaning since the response would tend to become almost automatic. In fact, the clarity of this code in Latin America may be due to the prevalence of this pattern.

In Las Rosas, Chiapas (Mexico), the center with whitewashed walls and red tile roofs unshaded by vegetation contrasts with the outskirts with thatched roofs, mud walls, and masses of greenery. People also act, behave, and dress differently, and Indians in the center "do not belong" and are unacknowledged by non-Indians (Hill, 1964). This is also clear from studies on the village of Ixtepeji (Kearney, 1972), for instance. In Latin America, these patterns (and others, such as unpaved streets versus paved ones, animals in the street, and so on) clearly communicate modernity, status, attitudes, and culture—a large set of basic attitudes (see Figure 23). Indians clearly use more natural features than Ladinos because they also conceive of their habitat differently in terms of ideas, beliefs, religion, social relations, and attitudes toward nature. The latter, for Indians, is so mystical, powerful, and compelling, that one tampers with it as little as possible—it is dominant. For Ladinos, nature is more objective, a "thing" that one can control, dominate, and exploit (Hill, 1964: 100, 103). Thus one can read more than just group membership and relative status; these cultural landscapes can be read to help decode major cultural attitudes.

Note that these patterns are formed elsewhere and may carry similar but not identical meanings, as in the case of Zanzibar, with the Moslem Stonetown and African Ngambo districts (Rapoport, 1977: 233). In terms of my principal argument, the significant point is that it is possible to look at these cultural landscapes, notice differences, and interpret them fairly easily without any complex symbolic or semiotic analysis. Note also the greater importance of redundancy and multiple cues in urban examples.

In simpler cultures, very subtle cues may suffice—or even no cues at all, that is, one may know what is necessary, but even then the mnemonic function of the environment may be useful. One example is provided by M'Buti pygmy camps, where, given the small size of the band, social relations are well known. Yet the direction of doorways communicates shifting social relations, which are changed overnight. In addition, spite fences are built to reflect changes in social relations (Turnbull, 1961). One knows these social shifts, but one is reminded by the environmental cues, which also tell returning members what has been going on. In addition, of course, changes and shifts in band composition reflect this in the nonfixed-feature domain. Similar events and devices are found among the Hadza (see Woodburn, 1972). To

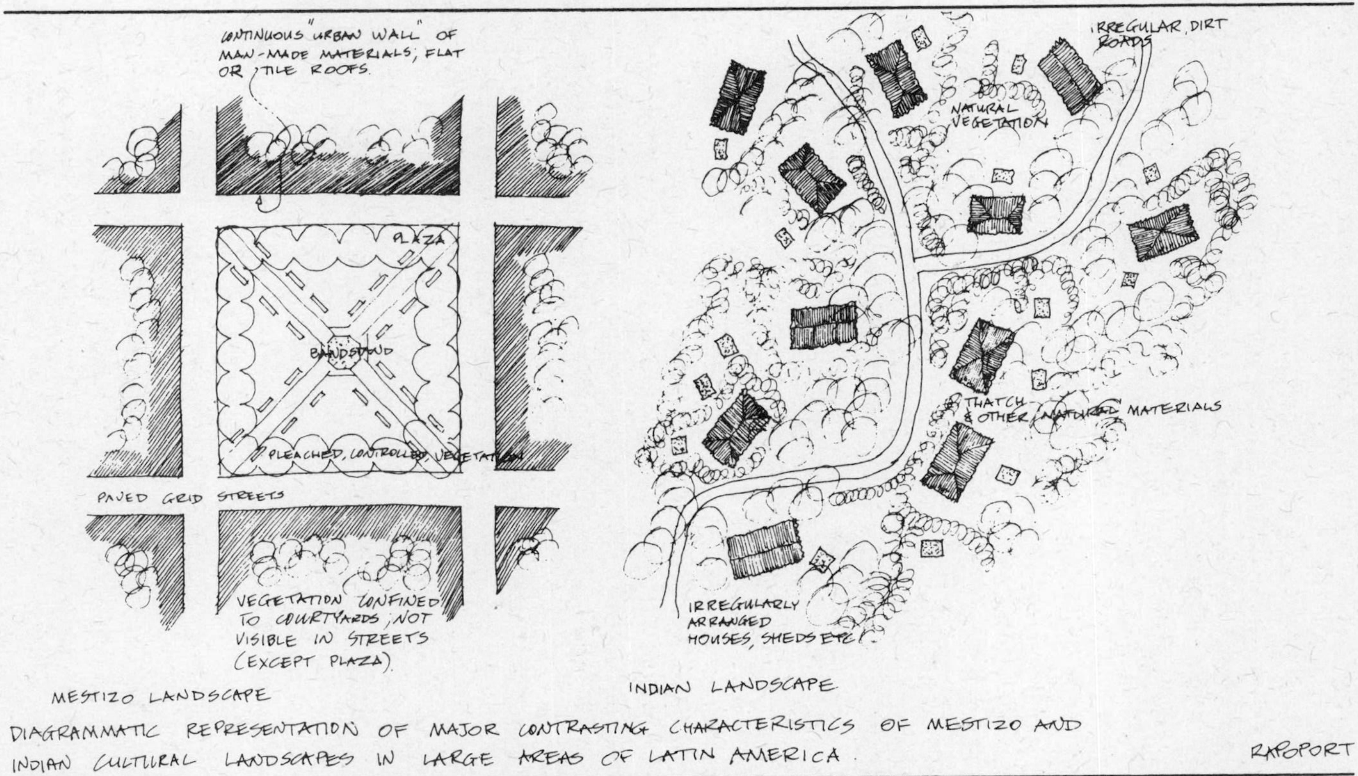
CONTINUOUS "URBAN WALL" OF MAN-MADE MATERIALS; FLAT OR TILE ROOFS.
PLAZA
BANDSTAND
PLEACHED, CONTROLLED VEGETATION
PAVED GRID STREETS
VEGETATION CONFINED TO COURTYARDS; NOT VISIBLE IN STREETS (EXCEPT PLAZA).
IRREGULAR, DIRT ROADS
NATURAL VEGETATION
THATCH & OTHER NATURAL MATERIALS
IRREGULARLY ARRANGED HOUSES, SHEDS ETC.
MESTIZO LANDSCAPE
INDIAN LANDSCAPE
DIAGRAMMATIC REPRESENTATION OF MAJOR CONTRASTING CHARACTERISTICS OF MESTIZO AND INDIAN CULTURAL LANDSCAPES IN LARGE AREAS OF LATIN AMERICA
RAPOPORT

Figure 23

reiterate: In all these cases, the social relations are *known*, but the environmental cues act as mnemonics for those who are there and as indicators for those returning after an absence.

Similarly, in the case of a !Kung Bushman camp, one knows where the fronts of dwellings are—they face the fire and the common space. At the same time, houses are built at least partly to indicate this. This becomes clear from the fact that sometimes houses are not built, but a hoop in put in the ground to indicate the location of the door and hence the front. Sometimes even with these hoops are not used. After all, the small group in question *knows* where the front is and how to behave. Yet, the house, or the hoop, helps remind people where men and women sit, what behavior is appropriate, and so on. Equivalents of the hoop—a freestanding gateway in an Arab village or Japanese farm—may indicate front or entry, the transition among domains, and hence behavior shifts (see Figure 24).

In other cultures, directions or orientation may indicate front—east among the Navaho or Bedouin, or west among the Wodaabe of Africa (Stenning, 1959). Clearly, such meanings need to be *known*, but the knowledge can be gained easily through observation. Privacy gradients, the meaning attached to various domains, can be indicated in very subtle ways: a change in ground surface, a small change in level, a bead curtain. In other cases much clearer barriers—that is, much more noticeable cues and greater redundancy—are needed (Rapoport, 1979a, 1980c). Clearly, the absence of cues or the use of very subtle cues, such as the use of swept earth among Australian Aborigines to indicate the private zone around the dwelling or a particular beam to indicate the private area within a Norwegian farmhouse (Rapoport, 1979a), depends on consistency of use combined with consistency of location. The clear understanding of these subtle cues also involves a knowledge of the rules regarding behavior defined by the situation and a willingness to follow these rules. Without all these conditions, the system would not work.

In other words, indication through physical cues may be less important in traditional cultures because things are *known*, partly through consistent use and partly through consistent, rigid, and shared rules. In our cities, known social aspects are still important but clear physical cues are needed. In traditional settlements, for example, cues are often not visible to the outsider at first glance, either being known and/ or indicated by subtler cues. They can, however, be discovered by observing behavior (who does what, where, when, and including or

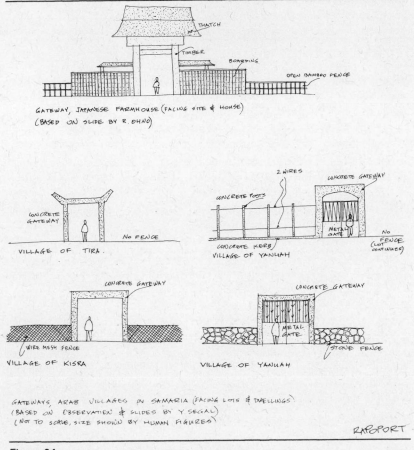

Figure 24

excluding whom) and also through more systematic studies. This applies to settlements of many groups—Pomo Indians (Rapoport, 1969c), Quebec Indians (Rapoport, 1977), Apaches (Esber, 1972), Australian Aboriginal camps (Memmott, 1979), and precontact African cities, where what appeared as random disorder, in fact, was organization based on social relationships (Hull, 1976: 122). All these cases can be illustrated through a generalized diagram (see Figure 25).

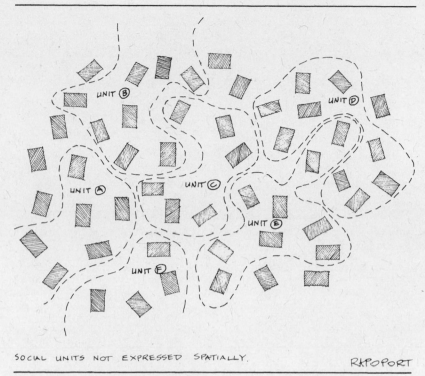

SOCIAL UNITS NOT EXPRESSED SPATIALLY.   RAPOPORT

Figure 25

Redundancy and clarity of cues

Note, however, how much clearer a Yoruba city made up of compounds or a Moslem or Chinese city made up of well-defined quarters
is—particularly when the physical definition is reinforced by a host of
semifixed- and nonfixed-feature elements. Physical cues, such as
walls, gates, colors and materials, and house styles, reinforced by
kinds of people, their dress, language, activities, sounds and smells,
and many other variables, combine to communicate social meaning.
In cities of more complex and pluralistic societies, with weaker rule
systems, such cues are even more important, thus higher levels of
redundancy are necessary. For example, being able to orient oneself in
a city, in terms of center-periphery and knowing where one is located,
is easy in a small, traditional city. In a large U.S. city, this is much less
clear. However, as one moves toward the (or a) center, one would

generally expect greater traffic density, greater difficulty in parking, more traffic lights, narrower streets, more shops, more signs (neon and so on), higher levels of activity, older buildings, run-down areas, tall buildings, and so on.

If all these cues add up, and reinforce one another, the indications could be quite clear; if not, less clear or unclear (Rapoport, 1977; Steinitz, 1968). This type of approach has even been used in suggestions regarding how clear cues and sufficient redundancy could be used to communicate such locational meanings in ideal urban transportation systems (Appleyard and Okamoto, 1968).

Thus, as one goes from preliterate, tribal (primitive) environments through traditional vernacular ones to modern ones, one could hypothesize that a curvilinear relationship would be found regarding the levels of redundancy and clarity of cues as opposed to a linear relationship among levels of redundancy and clarity required, thus defining a problem area (see Figure 26).

Clearly, the more complex and culturally pluralist the setting, the greater the required redundancy to produce sufficiently clear cues, particularly since many people are then "outsiders." In fact, most examples in such situations involve large numbers of cues so that noticeable differences are present; once one's attention is drawn to them, interpretation can follow. This interpretation requires cultural knowledge, but , as I have been arguing, this is not too difficult to obtain either by sensitive observation or other means. Consider the judgments about "overriding poverty" in the Kowloon City area of Hong Kong made by an English observer. These judgments were made on the basis of the general appearance of the area, which is said to be fully compatible with that hypothesis (Leeming, 1977: 156). Note two things: First, there is a matching of perceived characteristics against a schema or image, and second, these cues are sufficiently strong and redundant to draw attention to the area vis-à-vis other areas, that is, the context.

Among the cues making up that "general appearance" are:

- The "extreme antiquity" of the area (that is, age, with the notion that old = bad).
- This, in turn, is indicated by narrow streets and narrower lanes, frequent corners, and changes in level, including short flights of steps in the street.

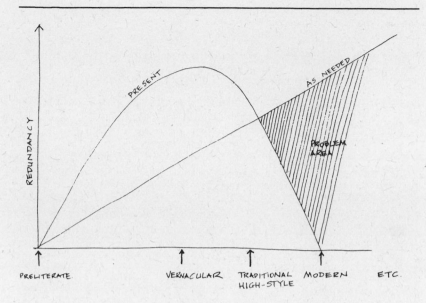

DIAGRAMMATIC RELATIONSHIP BETWEEN REDUNDANCY LEVELS
NEEDED AND PRESENT IN VARIOUS ENVIRONMENTS (HYPOTHETICAL)

RAPOPORT.

Figure 26

- Other cues include open drains, noise from factories, piles of rotting refuse in unfrequented spots, and lack of street lighting.
- In urban parts of Kowloon City: overhanging buildings, lack of light, gentle curves in most streets, high walls and gates in traditional building types, such as the Yaman and Temple.
- In village areas within Kowloon City: irregular placing of low buildings, occasional patches of vegetation.

In the case of North Carolina in the 1920s, a contrast developed (with social conflict consequences, that is, related to the organization of communication among people) between mill villages and new suburbs (Glass, 1978: 148):

mill villages	new suburbs
scruffy	tall houses
dingy	colors
parched	semiforest of cool green foliage
no cars (or old cars)	wide lawns
[unpaved streets]	trim hedges
	spacious, winding avenues
	many (and new) cars
	[paved streets]

Urban cues

Many such cues are still used in U.S. urban areas, and I will turn to those after commenting on graffiti. These are interesting because they have become major indicators of urban meaning yet are relatively new. They thus show that new types of semifixed-feature cues can develop and acquire meaning relatively quickly and easily. It has recently been noted (in connection with the use of a graffiti-covered wall in a Volvo advertisement) that graffiti are well known to have become associated with juvenile gangs, urban poverty, alienation, lawlessness, and racial minorities—all the "stereotypic components of the uncivilized world" (Rubin, 1979: 340-341). I am not concerned with the specific study, particularly since different interpretations are possible (as we shall see later). What seems important here is that many people would, in fact, quickly and easily make such inferences from these urban cues: It is clearly a majority view. They would use graffiti to judge environmental quality and hence desirability of areas, crime levels, and hence safety, the nature of resident groups, and so on. A very high correlation can be predicted between graffiti and negative judgments about a large set of urban characteristics. Since differing interpretations of graffiti are possible—for example, as signs of appropriation and as "territorial markers" (Ley and Cybriwsky, 1974), redundancy usually reinforces these judgments. This involves additional cues, such as location, cleanliness and litter, maintenance levels generally, lawns, houses, pollution levels, grilles on shops, boarded-up buildings, empty lots, mixed uses, absence of trees, and many other noticeable differences. These are all used to judge the nature of areas and their environmental quality, whether they are upgrading, stable, or declining.

How easily, quickly, and naturally these judgments are made can be seen initially from three examples: from scholarly research, a newspaper story, and a novel. For example, at a seminar at the Department of Geography, Hebrew University, Jerusalem, on December 26, 1979, Julian Wolpert was reporting on a major neighborhood study. Part of that study consisted of a windshield survey of environmental quality, improvements, and so on. This involved those cues that could be observed while driving down the street. Two things were of interest in terms of our discussion: first, the extremely high correlation of such judgments, made on the basis of a ten-minute trip per street, with household surveys involving a great deal more effort; and second, the selection of items or cues to be observed, the assumptions underlying their choice, and the fact that they seemed so self-evident as not to require comment. The cues observed included abandoned shops, quality of garbage pickup, upkeep of house facades, quality of landscaping (if any), gangs of young people hanging around corners, and the like.

In describing part of downtown Milwaukee that, according to a newspaper story, is "sagging," a set of cues is described that tell even a casual observer that "things are not as nice as they might be, while the visitor with a keen eye and understanding feet might come away with a much more negative impression" (Manning and Aschoff, 1980). Thus, while facades along West Wisconsin Avenue between N 4th and N 9th streets have been spruced up, alleys and back streets show the backs of these same buildings with rusting fire escapes, dirty and crumbling bricks, unlit electric signs, or failed or moved businesses. The character of the area is also indicated by

> transient commerce
> flattened beer cans
> broken wine bottles
> "the litter of losers who pass through the area"
> drunks on the street and other "characters" (which are judged by *cues*)
> vulgarity—adult bookstores and tawdry bars (which, themselves are
>   indicated by cues)
> surface parking lots
> vacant buildings with "squat, ugly faces"

incongruous, ill-advised uses of land that should be most valuable (that
   is, a mismatch with expectations; see Rapoport, 1977)
general atmosphere that scares people, who do not like the way
   downtown "looks"—that is, what the physical cues indicate

Note how self-evident all these seem to the journalists concerned.
Equally self-evident and taken for granted are the cues used to communicate meaning and to set a scene in the next example, from a
detective novel. Both of these examples, of course, are related to the
argument I have made before about the importance of analyzing
novels, newspapers, and the like (Rapoport, 1969b), which can be
used without engaging in formal content analysis (Rapoport, 1977).
   In this case (Childs, 1979: 90-92, 98), the attempt is to describe an
area of downtown Los Angeles. The contrast is made between a street
of beautiful nineteenth-century houses shaded by pale green trees
and a different area to which it suddenly gives way. That latter area
has:

no trees
weather-beaten old houses
cheap markets } (Note that these are inferences themselves
fleabag hotels } made on the basis of sets of cues.)
kids batting a softball around
graffiti on the sides of buildings
litter on the sidewalks
drifters and out-of-work laborers ambling in the streets,
   gathering in aimless groups
men with stubbled chins drinking cheap red wine and muscatel
   from bottles in paper bags
people in ragged, dirty overcoats huddling on benches
pawnshops
hotel with windows on the first two floors covered with heavy
   wire screens
grimy shops, some vacant, others with cheap secondhand goods
a jeweler specializing in 75¢ repairs on $5 watches
a dress shop with advertisements that no item is above $10
a bar with continuous topless entertainment

The description of a hotel lobby and hallway is similar, although on a
smaller scale:

a motley collection of couches in the lobby with stuffing poking out
   of holes in plastic covers

smell of decay
dim hallway with narrow strip of worn carpet running down the center
stale air
smell of aged urine
peeling brown doors

These add up to a "high class flophouse" (Childs, 1979: 98). This term is clearly an image or schema against which the perceived cues are matched.

The basic agreement between these three descriptions of areas on the basis of sets of cues, all from the United States, is extremely striking and impressive. So is the implicit fact that not only are the cues taken to be self-evident, but all that is involved is observation and fairly direct—and very rapid—interpretation. It is a simple process. It can be shown to work, and specific cues identified, through more systematic work. Consider two examples: the use of remote sensing, or of drawings or retouched photographs.

The very fact is significant that remote sensing techniques can be used to identify physical surrogates, which, in turn, seem to be good indicators of social and economic conditions of a given population and their area. In one study, nine such surrogates were found:

(1) land crowding
(2) condition of private free space
(3) nonresidential land uses
(4) litter
(5) condition of landscaping
(6) noise, hazards, and nuisance from transport systems
(7) nonresidential activities
(8) hazards and nuisances
(9) architectural styling—which needed to be checked on the ground

The last variable in turn included nine characteristics, including eight design features, as surrogates for the age, condition, and size of housing:

(1) variety of housing, that is, higher quality than subdivision
(2) block size or shape
(3) presence or absence of alleys, and sidewalk location
(4) lot shape, size of lot, site coverage, and setback
(5) orientation, shape, and spacing of houses
(6) garbage and driveway location
(7) roof design and materials

(8) location and design of chimneys and flues
(9) presence or absence of minor architectural features such as
    porches, steps, patios, etc. (Howard et al., 1974)

Basically, the high-quality environment is well maintained, has well-maintained vegetation, little litter, few vacant lots, good street upkeep, adequate but not too luxurious vegetation (Duncan, 1973; Royse, 1969), and few commercial structures. The opposite set of cues indicates a low-quality environment; clearly all these cues are remarkably similar to those already described—and still to be discussed.

Through the use of drawings or retouched photographs, it is possible to identify specific cues more rigorously. The former were used in Baltimore, where drawings of street facades had additions—such as people performing various activities, children playing, and so on, in the street or on the steps, occupying various locations in the street, window flower boxes and the like were added—and people made clear and explicit social judgments on that basis (Brower, 1977). Generally, the presence of recreation in the street was seen as a negative, low-status indicator (even when the people themselves actually engaged in such behavior—a difference between cultural *knowledge* and *behavior;* see Keesing, 1979). This influence of street recreation on areas being identified as slums has already been illustrated and is found generally (Rapoport, 1977).

An example of the latter is a major study by Royse (1969). By retouching photographs one variable at a time and showing the results to three population groups—upper, middle, and lower socioeconomic levels—it became possible to discover their preferences, but also how easily they judged the social meaning of areas, their status, the context and situation, and how these interacted in complex ways. It was quite clear that a large number of noticeable differences in the environment act as cues and allow people to make social inferences easily and to predict their likely actions and behaviors on the basis of those. Note that the three groups differed in the consistency of their inferences, the upper group being the most consistent and the lower group being the least. It was also fairly easy to discover the nature of specific cues—the presence of people and animals, *types* of people and animals present, planting, topography, and litter, garbage, materials, architectural details, and so on. Context was important once again. For example, a horse in a suburban setting had very negative meaning; in an exurban setting, the meaning was very positive, indicating high status through

inferred recreational patterns, implied density, and spatial cues, and,
hence, types of people. Note that "suburban" or "exurban," that is,
these contexts, were themselves inferred from cues present in a
single photograph.

Among the variables that changed the meaning of particular settings were: vegetation, which reduced the percentage identifying public
housing (which has negative meaning) as such; and black children,
which led to the identification of public housing as such (the presence
of white children had no impact). Appearance was important and
exterior maintenance influenced judgments greatly. Fences influenced quality and "friendliness," but context ("appropriateness") was
important. Materials such as asphalt shingles and aluminum screen
doors reduced the attractiveness for the upper and middle groups, but
not for the lower; all groups, however, identified them as indicating
lower-class people. Lower density was important to the upper group,
but not to the lower.

The form of planting also had meaning, but different meanings for
different groups. Thus the middle group evaluated highly manicured
planting positively and wild, natural landscape negatively. The high
group, on the contrary, saw the natural landscape as having much
more positive meaning. This fits in well with the different landscapes
found in Westchester (Duncan, 1973) and other high-status enclaves,
such as River Hills, Wisconsin (Rapoport, 1981). It suggests that the
distinction between neat and unkempt landscapes is interpreted in
two ways in the United States and that specific subcultural group
characteristics need to be considered; that is, meaning, like design
needs and environmental quality, is culture specific. It also reinforces
the major point that, generally, notions of environmental quality have
to do with the meanings they have.

For example, the rural image, which we have already discussed, is
what gives extremely different meanings, and hence environmental
quality ratings, to a village and a housing estate: the former being positive, the latter negative. In Britain, a village environment implies a
variety of architecture and a degree of "incoherence": different styles,
materials, roof pitches, buildings at different angles, "interesting" and
"intimate" groupings (in themselves inferential judgments), natural
vegetation such as gorse and heath grasses, mixed age and income of
people, and lack of uniformity generally (Architects Journal, 1979). In
other words, we find a series of cues that mean "village" since they are
congruent with the image of village—positive in this case, unlike, for

example, in a Third World context, where such cues may be seen as negative. In the case being discussed, a sales brochure makes clear that it is the "village image" that is being sold; it uses an affective evocative quote from Crabbe (without defining "village"): "Thy walks are ever pleasant; everything is rich in beauty, lively or serene" (Architects Journal, 1979).

Note how frequently planting and vegetation enter into the reading of meaning. In the United States generally, and the Anglo-American culture area more broadly, lush vegetation has a very different meaning to that traditionally found in Latin America, generally being identified with high status (Rapoport, 1977). Thus a student was able to show in a term paper that when trees are removed, for example due to Dutch elm disease, in the Midwest and in this case in Milwaukee, property values tend to go down compared to comparable areas with no tree loss; population decline is also greater in the former than in the latter (Schroeder, 1976). At the same time, as we have seen, subcultural differences are found relating to the amount of vegetation and its naturalness. However, even here the differences are smaller than in the case of other elements. Generally, in the United States it is found that there is more agreement about environmental quality of natural landscapes and nature than about human-made landscapes (Craik and Zube, 1976: 53)—although the evidence here being presented suggests that even in the human-made environment there is much agreement. This suggests that nature forms a domain separate from the human-made and is evaluated separately (Rapoport, 1977). Thus nature/culture as a distinction seems almost universal and is often expressed through the contrast natural/human-made or controlled; the positive or negative meaning of these, however, can change. Its changes can be studied historically—and have been. One example is the major change in the meaning given wild mountain scenery with the Romantic Movement (Nicolson, 1959). Similarly, in the United States over the past 200 years, a complete reversal has occurred between the meanings of city and wilderness. The former, once seen as positive, has become negative, and vice versa—their meanings as "sacred" and "profane" have reversed (Tuan, 1974). It is also possible to find adjoining cultural groups giving contrary meanings to environments. Thus, the M'Buti pygmies regard the forest as good, the plantations and fields as bad, whereas the adjacent Bantu farmers see the latter as good and the former as bad (Turnbull, 1961: 53-54). The pygmies also go through rites of passage as they move from one of these worlds to the other—for them the village is profane; for the Fang, it is the bush, or wilderness, that is profane and the village humanized and habitable (Fernandez, 1977)—a contrast similar to the two periods in the United States discussed above.

In terms of our earlier discussion, then, we find the use of a common set of variables setting up contrasts (in this case, natural/human-made) but with different meanings attached to them. But even here one finds some regularity. Thus if one considers high-income groups, who have maximum choice, one does find differing choices made; upper-class areas can have different environment quality variables, as was the case between Wahroonga and Vaucluse, in Sydney, Australia (Rapoport, 1977: 88-89). Yet, generally, in the Anglo-American culture, such choices tend to be closer to the Wahroonga, or rural image, model and it is such areas that we most easily and typically identify as "good" areas in neighborhoods in strange cities (Rapoport, 1977: 32). Thus in Detroit, historically, high-income areas can be identified through privacy, large lot size, accessibility to desired uses (recreation, parks, and the like) and distance from undesirable uses (the nature of these and the proximities can also be studied; Peterson and Worall, 1969), character of houses, exclusion of undesirable people, exclusive golf and country clubs, many recreational facilities generally, natural amenities, vegetation, and so on (Backler, 1974).

Underlying much of our discussion here, and many of the specific cues indicating environmental quality, is the general notion of *maintenance*, which influences appearance. One could argue that in many, although not all, of the cases under consideration, the meaning of the area is related to maintenance in its broadest sense. Thus, at the urban scale, changes indicating negative qualities include reduced maintenance and hence deterioration of houses, increased noise, increased traffic congestion, industrial and commercial development, street cleanliness, outmigration of "good" people and inmigration of "bad" people (for example, people manifesting delinquency or hippiness), signs indicating crime, violence, and delinquency (boarded-up shops, grilles on shops, graffiti, and so on), loss of services, and, above all, reduced green open space. These are all seen as urban threats and have negative meaning; they lead to a fear that crowding will develop (Carson, 1972). Note that many of these qualities are based on maintenance. Also, as we shall see, high perceived density is based on inferences made by matching perceived characteristics, many of which are related to maintenance, against certain contexts, images, schemata,

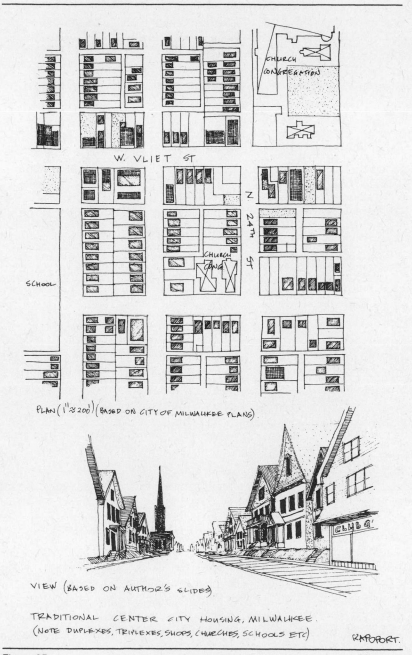

PLAN (1" ≈ 200') (BASED ON CITY OF MILWAUKEE PLANS).

VIEW (BASED ON AUTHOR'S SLIDES)

TRADITIONAL CENTER CITY HOUSING, MILWAUKEE.
(NOTE DUPLEXES, TRIPLEXES, SHOPS, CHURCHES, SCHOOLS ETC)

RAPOPORT.

Figure 27

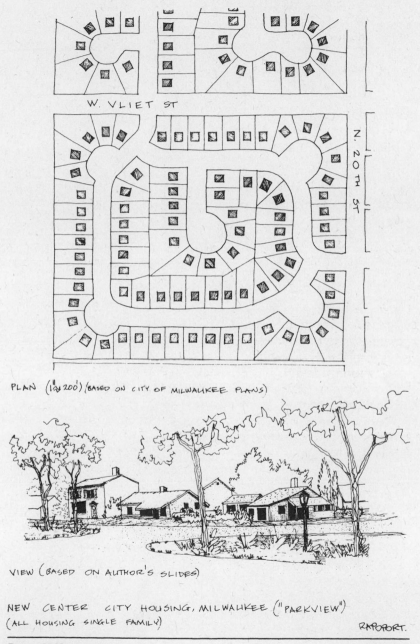

W. VLIET ST

N. 20TH ST

PLAN ($1\frac{1}{2}'' = 200'$) (BASED ON CITY OF MILWAUKEE PLANS)

VIEW (BASED ON AUTHOR'S SLIDES)

NEW CENTER CITY HOUSING, MILWAUKEE ("PARKVIEW")
(ALL HOUSING SINGLE FAMILY)

RAPOPORT.

Figure 27 Continued

and norms. Similarly, the sensory cues indicating positive environmental quality often include appearance of newness (that is, low perceived age and no obsolescence), appearance of expensiveness, high levels of maintenance with no deterioration or disorder, and harmony with nature, such as greenery, open space, naturalness, and privacy (Peterson, 1967a, 1967b). Greenery seems to be rather less important in the case of other countries, for example, the Netherlands (see Jaanus and Nieuwenhuijse, 1978). In this case, while green spaces had little influence on positive meaning, the absence of shops and restaurants, road and site layouts that communicate a feeling of spaciousness and privacy, an absence of monotony, and newness were important. The last was sufficiently important to lead to a higher ranking being given to high-rise development vis-à-vis old, traditional environments that designers would rank much more positively.

Suburban image

In the United States, the basic positive meaning of residential environments is still summed up by the suburban image. The variables that communicate that image are clearly revealed by new center-city housing in Milwaukee, Wisconsin; this image also *explains* the form of that development. The context is of two-story, nineteenth- and early-twentieth-century frame houses on narrow lots (see Beckley, 1977); the street pattern is a grid. The new housing is clearly meant to be "suburban," contrasting with the negative connotations of the above urban environment.

This suburban image, contrasting with the urban, includes the name "Parkview" (for downtown housing!; see Rapoport, 1977: ch. 2); curved streets as opposed to the grid; "superblocks" with culs-de-sac as opposed to "pass-through" streets; low perceived density as opposed to high perceived density; a mixture of one- and two-story houses as opposed to all two-story; mixed forms of housing as opposed to a single type, but of the "universal" suburban ranch-style variety rather than the midwest frame; low degree of enclosure versus high degree of enclosure; absence of corner shops, churches, and the like versus their presence; subdued colors as opposed to bright colors; low complexity versus high complexity; lawns, shrubs, and a variety of trees freely arranged versus large elms in lines along the streets (now gone due to Dutch elm disease). Note two things: the nature of the cues as well as the high level of redundancy; the use of many cues. This unmistakable message is reinforced in the actual experience of these environments, the transitions, and contrasts as one moves through them. This helps us further to understand the intended meaning and how it is communicated (see Figure 27).

Note that in the above case, fixed-feature elements play an important role in establishing meaning, although semifixed-feature elements—particularly vegetation—are important. Moreover, it is interesting to note that many of the cues agree well with a list of cues proposed as indicating low *perceived density*. The notion of that concept is that a variety of physical, associational, and sociocultural cues are used to make inferences about the density of areas. It is these inferences, not actual density in people per unit area, that are matched against norms and ideals to make judgments of acceptability and desirability (Rapoport, 1975c). A partial list of these hypothesized cues follows (from Rapoport, 1975c: 138-140; reference cites deleted); the suggestion is that not all need be present for environments to be judged as one or the other. Clearly the list of cues, the number needed to infer densities and hence the meaning of areas, and how these cues reinforce or cancel each other are subjects for research. At the same time, our discussion so far and the Milwaukee example support this notion (see also McLaughlin, 1976, which can be interpreted partly in these terms).

Dense	Not Dense
	Perceptual	
tight spaces	open spaces
intricate spaces	simple spaces

These terms are, of course, difficult to define at the moment. They can be discussed in terms of complexity. They also seem intuitively clear to most people—admitting that they are a matter of degree and affected by culture, adaptation levels, and so forth.

large building height to space (i.e., a large amount of subtended building in the field of vision)	low height to space ratio (i.e., little subtended building in the field of vision)
many signs	few signs
many lights and high artificial light levels	few lights and low artificial light levels

Dense	Not Dense
many people (or their traces) visible	few people (or their traces) visible
mostly human-made (little greenery)	mostly natural (much greenery)
high noise levels	low noise levels
many human-made smells	few human-made smells
many cars—high traffic density and much parking	few cars—low traffic density and little parking

Generally the number of physical, sensory stimuli that indicate the presence of people.

Associational/Symbolic

tall buildings, apartments, or offices may indicate high density even when spaces and other perceptual cues indicate low density	low buildings may indicate low densities even if other cues indicate the opposite
in residential areas the absence of private gardens and entrances	in residential areas the presence of gardens and entrances

The relative impact and importance of perceptual and associational/symbolic cues are important questions.

Temporal

fast tempos and rhythms of activity	slow tempos and rhythms of activity
activities extending over 24 hours per day	activities reducing or ceasing at certain times

Physical/Sociocultural

the absence of "defenses" allowing the control of interaction	the presence of "defenses" allowing the control of interaction

Generally, then, the same number of people in an environmental configuration that exposes them to others, or isolates them, would be read very differently (e.g., the presence of fences, courtyards, compounds, and the like).

Dense	Not Dense
high levels of "attractive stimuli"	low levels of "attractive stimuli"
the absence of other adjacent places for use—streets, meeting places, and so on	the presence of other adjacent places for use—streets, meeting places, and so on

Thus the availability of many nondwelling places—pubs, shops, streets, parks, and the like—that can be used by people and whether they are actually used (i.e., the house-settlement system) will affect the perception of density. Where they are present and used extensively, an area would be perceived as less dense because more effective area is available for use and activities and groups may be separated in space and time.

the presence of nonresidential land uses in a residential area and mixed land uses generally	the absence of nonresidential land uses in a residential area and absence of mixed land uses generally

This is in apparent conflict with the previous characteristics. In this case the presence of nonresidential uses leads to higher rates of information from the environment itself, more people visible, more traffic, and so forth. There are thus two contradictory effects with complex results.

Sociocultural

high levels of social interaction leading to social overload	low levels of social interaction and absence of social overload

This depends on culturally (and individually) defined desired levels as well as the form and effectiveness of defenses.

feeling of lack of control, choice, or freedom, leading to judgments of less effective space being available and hence of higher densities; control by environment	feeling of presence of control, choice, and freedom, leading to judgments of more effective space being available and hence of lower densities; control of environment

The alternative hypothesis, that lack of control means lack of pressure to make decisions and hence the perception of less density, is unlikely in view of evidence that lack of control is associated with increased stress and with the general argument that density is related to interaction and that privacy is the ability to control unwanted interaction.

These feelings may differ for various groups—by culture, age, sex, and so on.

Dense	Not Dense
social heterogeneity along some subjectively defined dimensions—hence increased unpredictability, reduced redundancy, and higher effective density in terms of information-processing needs, the inability to read symbols and cues, not sharing rules, and hence acting inappropriately	social homogeneity along some subjectively defined dimensions—hence increased predictability and redundancy and lower effective density in terms of information-processing needs, ability to read cues and symbols, sharing of rules, and hence acting appropriately

One example might be agreement about rules regarding private/public and front/back domains, nonverbal behavior, and so on. This suggests that density and crowding are related via privacy, defined as the control of unwanted interaction and also via social norms defining behavior appropriate to various density situations.

absence of culturally shared and accepted nonphysical "defenses" and control mechanisms for regulating social interaction	presence of culturally shared and accepted nonphysical "defenses" and control mechanisms of regulating social interaction
previous experience, socialization, and so forth at low densities (i.e., adaptation level at low densities)	previous experience, socialization, and so forth at high densities (i.e., adaptation level at high densities)

The impact of poor maintenance, litter, graffiti, reduction of greenery, high pollution levels and noise, untidiness, poor road surfaces, industrial invasion, and so on also fit into this framework. Their meaning is due to the fact that they are surrogates for people—or for particular types of people. Moreover, most of the studies dealing with environmental quality in Anglo-American culture are remarkably consistent, as we have seen, in attaching positive meaning to those cues that indicate low perceived density. This becomes even clearer when we consider suggestions for making townhouses and condominia more acceptable, that is, have them communicate more positive meanings. These are all related to indicating the lowest possible perceived density (and the associated higher status): the presence of recreational facilities (recall, however, that it is the latent aspect, the image and meaning of recreation, rather than use, or manifest aspects, that are important); good maintenance of landscape, dwellings, yards, and streets; houses not crowded and too close together, or spaciousness; good privacy; homogeneity with "good" people; low child density (an important variable in many studies, associated both with maintenance and perceived density); low noise levels; as much open space as possible, many trees, shrubs, lawns, and natural features; absence of nonresidential uses; absence of nuisances; pleasant views; short dwelling rows and individuality of dwellings, hence variety rather than monotony in design, and so on (see Norcross, 1973; Ermuth, 1974; Burby et al., 1976). That this interpretation is true is confirmed by the finding in Britain, among others, that the best predictor of satisfaction in residential areas is low perceived density—for example, expressed in terms of average number of stories of dwellings and the number of dwellings visible within 150 meters (Metcalf, 1977).

What the Milwaukee housing and the other examples try to do, then, is to communicate as many as possible of the positive meanings associated with residential areas and as few as possible of the negative ones: meaning and image are being manipulated in a particular way (although other ways are possible).

Consider a study in Atlanta in which well-being in residential areas was correlated with various environmental characteristics (James et al., 1974). These characteristics can be interpreted as cues, the meaning of which depends on a contrast between those seen as positive and those seen as negative.

Positive	Negative
much open space	congested
residential pocket away from the bustle of urban activity	proximity to libraries, public health centers, schools, sports fields, freeways
separated from traffic, railroads, and public facilities	high pedestrian densities and many visitors
distant from arterial streets and hence public transport	bare dirt; no lawns between buildings and streets
absence of outsiders	heavy littering
much grass, well-maintained lawns, uniform landscaping	presence of weeds
open space with natural vistas	front areas with vegetables, etc., rather than lawns and shrubs (i.e., diverse landscaping)
views of attractive human-made features	
few paved areas	little effort at landscaping
well-maintained landscaping	unkempt, vacant lots
many trees	few trees, bushes, or flowers
off-street parking	many parked cars (no off-street parking)
mainly private dwellings	
quiet	presence of commercial, industrial, fringe commercial, parking, and other nonresidential uses
narrow streets	
few traffic lights	
newness, indicated by "contemporary street patterns," i.e., curved streets, culs-de-sac, etc.	noisy
	one-way streets
	deterioration and poor state of repair of sidewalks
	many "for sale" and "for rent" signs

It seems clear that these elements correspond to notions of high environmental quality already discussed repeatedly in this book (see also Rapoport, 1977: ch. 2). It is also clear that the meaning of these elements has to do with the inferences made about the kinds of people living there and the potential interactions (since well-being is clearly correlated with social relations and interaction). We thus begin to see a potential relation between environmental meaning and social interaction or communication—a topic to be discussed in Chapter 7. At this point, it may be sufficient to suggest that the inferences made about people by reading physical environments influence and help organize social relations and interaction. I have argued in a number of places that interaction best occurs in what I call *neutral places* among homogeneous, owned areas (Rapoport, 1977). But two questions came up. First, what cues indicate neutrality—location, use, territory, and so on? This clearly requires cultural knowledge, since it may be a grocery, a teahouse, a men's house, or whatever. Second, what cues indicate "owned" areas, or defensible space (Newman, 1971; Suttles, 1968, 1972)? In this connection, much is made of "symbolic" boundaries, which, however, need to be noticed, understood, and "obeyed."

Actual physical boundaries are also important, particularly since movement and mobility, particularly their latent aspects, also have meaning. I have pointed out elsewhere that many traditional cities restrict mobility while the U.S. city stresses it and facilitates it *in principle* (Rapoport, 1977: 21). However, one finds that parks are seen as desirable not only because they can be used and, even more, because they are there as cues of positive environmental quality, neighborhood stability, low perceived density, and, generally, desirable areas. They are seen as desirable also because they can become a "no-man's land," keeping strangers out of neighborhoods. Recall that one set of cues of environmental quality had to do with the absence of strangers.

A striking example of the relation of this to mobility and its meaning is provided by a recent report that a federal appeals court refused a six-year long attempt by white residents of the Hein Park neighborhood in Memphis, Tennessee, to block a street called West Drive at its north end, where a large black area begins (Milwaukee Journal, 1979).

While this would, of course, reduce *actual* mobility and penetration, I would argue that the major purpose of this attempt was "symbolic"— it was at the level of meaning. What it tried to communicate was: This neighborhood is homogenous, "closed"; it was, if you will, the equivalent of walled developments (Rapoport, 1977). Significantly, the court's refusal was also on such grounds of meaning; the closure would, the court said, be a "badge of slavery." Thus mobility and equal access to all parts of the city, as well as their opposites, are seen at the level of *meaning*, as being about human *communication* or social relations, rather than in purely instrumental or manifest terms.

This relates to the discussion above of the environment as a mnemonic. One could argue that the blocked street is a boundary cue, marking perceived differences among two groups and setting up social boundaries, that is, attempting to exclude particular groups (see Barth, 1969; Wellman, 1978; Rapoport, 1977, forthcoming). Social boundaries, of course, are not necessarily spatial or physical but, once again, their perception, which must precede understanding and behavior, is helped by clear and unambiguous markers—noticeable differences of all kinds. This is, of course, related to our earlier discussion about boundary markers as objects (fixed feature or semifixed feature), boundary-marking rituals (nonfixed feature in time or space), doorways and thresholds, and so on. All communicate meanings the basic function of which is to reinforce basic cultural categories. Thus the whole notion of indicating boundaries by means of noticeable differences to delineate social groups, domains, and their spatial equivalents, and to define entry or exclusion, becomes very significant.

Context, once again, is important. Consider fences. Clearly, while all cultures distinguish among domains, and mark boundaries, the use of fences is much more variable. The question has been raised as to why fences are so common in Mormon areas. In that case, the analysis of fences tells much about Mormon culture (as can the analysis of other artifacts). As one subtle point: The number of gates indicated the number of wives a man had (Leone, 1973). Also, it is clear that in a place such as England or Australia, or some areas of the United States, where fences are common, they have different meanings than in places where they are rare. In the latter, again depending on context, they may indicate appropriation, concern, and good upkeep, or high crime-rates that make their use necessary. Their absence can similarly have two analogous, contrasting meanings.

It is important to mark boundaries, however this is done, and to contrast what these boundaries define or contain. By marking them, and the corresponding domains, noticeable and recognizable effective reminders and warnings are created. These tend to reduce or eliminate conflict, whether about appropriate behavior or appropriation.

Much is made of ownership and appropriation of space in connection with crime control through defensible space (see Newman, 1971). While many of the cues having to do with maintenance and the like communicate this, there is a question about how appropriation is indicated. Regarding maintenance, for example, we have seen how particular forms of landscaping can be misinterpreted as neglect (Sherif and Sherif, 1963). As another example, it is often suggested that appropriation is indicated by personalization, the presence of personal objects and the like. Yet these cues can be ambiguous: The presence of a set of objects such as "junk" and stripped cars, motorcycles, refrigerators, or washing machines on porches, and the like can indicate either appropriation or the existence of a "slum"; one person's lived-in area is another person's slum. Given our discussion in this chapter, the latter interpretation is more likely since ambiguous cues are matched against a shared schema of "appropriation" or "slum," and the cues just described generally indicate "slum." Thus the meaning of cues is related to culture and context—they are subjectively defined and interpreted. Thus meaning depends on some knowledge of the context and the culture, its rules and schemata. The cues will elicit appropriate responses if understood.

In this connection we can return to graffiti. We have seen that frequently they are seen as signs of highly negative environmental quality, of crime, vandalism, and so on. They can also be seen as an art form, an attempt to overcome anomie, or as signs of appropriation, that is, "territorial markers" (see Ley and Cybriwsky, 1974). In this latter case they can be read: their quality and location display regularities and indicate the distribution of social attitudes as well as predicting subsequent behavior in space. For example, they communicate the ownership of territories and turfs to teenagers and gangs—that is, they are markers of group boundaries, of defended neighborhoods, and hence lead to social behaviors. To most others, however, they do not communicate *those* meanings but others, such as high crime rates, and lead to behavior such as general avoidance of such areas.

In studying crime and defensible space on the neighborhood level (Taylor et al., 1979), it is clear that signs of disintegration of the social order, including physical deterioration, signs of vandalism, and litter, are extremely important in fear of crime. In other words, deterioration in the physical environment and signs of lack of caring about it are interpreted as signs of erosion of the social order and hence perceived as crime, with resultant fear. Perceived crime and its fear has low correspondence to actual crime. Thus all the signs we have been discussing that stand for slum also imply crime: the two meanings are linked. This, then, has clear behavioral consequences, such as avoidance.

The meaning and role of all such cues helps to explain the increasing stress on the importance of management in housing (see Francescato et al., 1979; Sauer, 1977; Brower, 1977; Ahlbrandt and Brophy, 1976; Hole, 1977; Beck and Teasdale, 1977) and, by extension, of urban management. This has to do with the role of management in ensuring good maintenance, low child density, vandalism, litter, and so on. It thus influences the cues present and hence the meaning of areas: Good management leads to good maintenance and is communicated through it. It is interesting that in judging an area as a "mess" in one such study (Sauer, 1977: 26) the now familiar cues are used: garbage and trash strewn around, vandalism, an abandoned car in the middle of the site, bad upkeep, bare earth. As in all other cases, it is clear that these cues communicate environmental quality not only directly but also by indicating the presence of absence of "good" or "bad" people, that is, by inferences regarding the definition of the social situation. This is the significance of the argument above about the differing interpretations of the libertarian suburb (Barnett, 1977), where the particular cues indicate a particular group of people who are, in turn, evaluated as "good" and "bad." In other words, in Anglo-American culture, and increasingly elsewhere, rural image, low perceived density, privacy, good maintenance and appearance, variety and complexity in design, social homogeneity, and high social status indicate good people and hence high environmental quality: They are positive meanings.

The physical elements of suburbia—winding roads, lawns, detached, varied houses, types of front doors and mailboxes, romantic rooflines, garden ornaments, coach lanterns, and many others—all communicate social status, social aspirations, personal identity, individual freedom, nostalgia, and so on. The elements come from history, rural life, patriotism, and the estates of the rich (Venturi and Rauch, 1976). This is, of course, the point stressed throughout: environmental quality variables are such because they have social meaning. Thus, disregarding major disagreement one may have about the validity of meanings of suburbia discussed by Perin (1977; see a review by Rapoport, 1979d), there is considerable agreement about the elements (detached dwellings, social homogeneity, purely residential uses, and the like) and the fact that it is the *meaning* of these that is most important. It is meaning that is the *raison d'être* for the particular definition of environmental quality. The suburban environment is intended to maintain the distinctions among groups, which are judged in terms of the environments in which they live, and these groups, once marked, are included or excluded. All the cues indicate status and lifestyle so that lawns, landscaping, variety of house styles, special recreational facilities, absence of mixed land uses, corner shops, even religious buildings, are all ways of establishing and maintaining a particular image, that is, of communicating social meanings and identity, the maintenance of which is seen as the role of planning (see Werthman, 1968).

As people move through cities (as well as landscapes), they tend to travel along well-defined routes. As a result, therefore, they frequently make judgments on the basis of what is perceived along that route. Thus one frequently judges areas through shopping streets and arterials as "bad" or "good," deteriorating or upgrading based on sets of cues such as types of shops, boarded up or empty shops, protective metal grilles, litter, and so forth. One also infers the ethnic character of areas behind these arterial streets. For example, in Omaha, Nebraska, at the turn of the century, it was found that although the proportion of an ethnic group living in particular areas was significant in judging its ethnic character, even more important was the location of that group's businesses and social and religious institutions—the churches, clubs, bakeries, groceries, butcher shops, restaurants. Their presence along particular stretches of roads led to the identification of the surrounding neighborhood as belonging to Bohemians, Italians, or Jews—even if they constituted a minority of that area: The *visibility* of the cues along the arterial routes was significant (Chudacoff, 1972, 1973).

In the case of an area in Matappan, Massachusetts, changing from being a Jewish area to becoming a black area, it was found that the people remaining became aware of the change when certain stores and institutions disappeared from the shopping areas. These settings did more than fulfill the needs of people; they stood for the nature of the area—they communicated its meaning, as did the nature of the new shops, how late they stayed open, which days they closed, and so on (Ginsberg, 1975). Similarly, business strips often define areas as "skid rows" and as deteriorating, or as high class—or even as back areas, which may exist at the neighborhood scale (for example, lanes), at the urban scale, regional scale, and so on. They have major functions in communicating meanings and they can also define the ethnic, income or racial character of areas. Thus business thoroughfares not only contrast with residential areas, but with each other, and can be interpreted as expressions of culture since their material features have cultural meanings. In the case of a black business street in Chicago (Pred, 1963), it proved possible to identify those cues that characterize low-income shopping streets generally as opposed to those that characterize black shopping streets as opposed to those of other groups.

This could be done impressionistically, that is, through observation, in the way I have been describing. Cues observed included:

sounds generally, noise levels, musical sounds
types of people (e.g., color), their clothing (style, colors, etc.),
    vocal and other nonverbal behaviors
the variety of varied uses (which could be counted)
types of shops
facades of shops, such as shopfronts
types of cars
smells
the visible presence of many activities (as opposed to the absence of
    visible activities in comparable white areas)

As in other cases that we have already discussed (e.g. Anderson and Moore, 1972), it was then possible to move easily to a more systematic, quantitative comparison of the distribution of different uses, service establishment, and shops; to compare specific combinations of uses; and to identify what was sold in groceries or served in restaurants. One could compare maintenance levels of shops, number of vacant shops, empty lots, storefront churches, how bar facades are treated (open versus closed), and many other specific variables. One could clearly discriminate between various types of shopping streets and make judgments and inferences about them and the people in them.

Note, once again, the redundancy of cues in a range of sensory modalities. I would suggest that we customarily use them in very similar ways to judge all kinds of environments in our daily lives. As one example, we use such cues to judge the takeover of areas by ethnic groups. Thus in Southall, an area of London, signs advertising particular kinds of foods the types of people encountered, their behavior, and how they are dressed all quickly suggest an Asian takeover. A typical English pub, with a heavy wooden bar, pitted plastic tile floor, jukebox, and rigid divisions among "public," "saloon," and "private bars" becomes a different place because all the people are Asians, there are no women, the music on the jukebox is Indian. At a larger scale, in a walk through Southall (or other comparable areas), we pass the Kenya Butchery, the oriental store, the Punjabi grocers, Indian driving schools and insurance offices, the Bank of Baroda branch office, posters advertising Indian entertainment. One sees hardly any white faces; newspapers on the back seats of parked cars are in Punjabi, Hindi, or Urdu; newspaper shops are full of Asian papers and magazines; cinemas show Indian films. Smells are of curry, spices, and Indian food; clothing in shops is different; there are temples; supermarkets carry a wide variety of Asian foods. Those doors that are open reveal, behind the facades of typical English suburban architecture, a totally different culture (Sydney Morning Herald 1972; personal observation in Southall, Bethnal Green, and so on).

This is clearly merely a more extreme version of what we have been discussing. Moreover, most of the cues are in the semifixed- and nonfixed-feature realm: The streets and the buildings have not changed. Also, a stroll through that area by any observer—designer, journalist, or layperson—allows the cues and their meanings to be read easily.

Many of these noticeable differences in various sensory modalities are cues that can be seen as examples of erosion or accretion traces used in unobtrusive measures (see Webb et al., 1966). These communicate a variety of meanings. Exterior physical signs in the fixed- and semifixed-feature domains, where people live and their location in public space, that is, where they are found and their temporal distribution (who does what, where, when, and including or excluding whom), their expressive movements, language, activities, clothing and possessions, and many others, communicate urban meanings and are accessible through observation. In Miami, Florida, two years following Castro's takeover of Cuba, cues such as bilingual street signs, the use of Spanish by half the people in streets, signs in shops saying "Se Habla Espanol," stores with Spanish names, Latin American foods on restaurant menus, Cuban foods sold in supermarkets, the manufacture of Cuban types of cigarettes, Spanish radio broadcasts, Spanish newspapers and Spanish-language editorials in English-language newspapers, Spanish services held in forty Miami churches, and so on (Webb et al., 1966: 119) all clearly communicated social change.

Within that city, certain areas with particularly high concentrations of Cubans, such as that called *Habana Chica* (the name itself is a cue!) could be identified by a greater density of the above cues and also the type and volume of music heard, the presence of men conversing around coffee stands and the type of coffee served, the use only of Spanish, aromas of spices, and the general atmosphere and ambience (Rapoport, 1977: 152-153). The strength of such cues would make them difficult to miss and would influence human behavior and communication, encouraging some and discouraging others from entering or penetrating such areas.

What is striking in all these analyses and descriptions is how easy it seems to be, by using one's senses and thinking about what one notices, to read the environment, derive meanings, and make social inferences. The similarity of this to the processes of nonverbal communication as commonly understood does, indeed, seem striking.

7

ENVIRONMENT, MEANING, AND COMMUNICATION

Since traditional nonverbal communication studies in the nonfixed-feature realm have largely been concerned with the role nonverbal behavior plays in human interaction and communication (see Abrahamson, 1966; Scheflen, 1974; Siegman and Feldstein, 1978), it seems useful to ask whether environmental meaning, as a form of nonverbal communication, can also be considered in such terms— that is, whether there is a relationship between environmental meaning and those behaviors related to interaction and communication among people. This question is also most relevant given our stress on context and pragmatics.

Toward the end of Chapter 6, and scattered elsewhere in this volume, there have been some hints that this is, indeed, the case. It is also generally the anthropological view that in all cultures, material objects and artifacts are used to organize social relations through forms and nonverbal communication; that the information encoded in artifacts is used for social marking and for the consequent organization of communication among people. I thus now turn to a consideration of this topic. As usual, however, I begin with an apparently different topic—the nature of "environment."

The nature of "environment"

I have been discussing meaning in the environment, but one needs to ask what is meant by "environment"? In dealing with this question in a particular way, I will also address the issue of the distinction between meaning and communication and, finally, try to relate these three terms.

There are different ways of conceptualizing "the environment," which is too broad a term to be used successfully (as are "culture" and many others; see Rapoport, 1979a, 1979b, 1976b, 1980b, 1980c). Different conceptualizations of the term "environment" have been proposed (Ittelson, 1960; Lawton, 1970; Moos, 1974; Rapoport, 1977), all of which discuss possible components of this term.

Before discussing these, it can be suggested that the environment can be seen as a series of relationships between things and things, things and people, and people and people. These relationships are orderly, that is, they have a pattern and a structure—the environment is *not* a random assemblage of things and people any more than a culture is a random assemblage of behaviors or beliefs. Both are guided by schemata that act as templates, as it were, organizing both people's lives and the settings for their lives. In the case of the environment, the relationships are primarily, although not exclusively, spatial—objects and people are related through various degrees of separation in and by space. But when environments are being designed, *four* elements are being organized (Rapoport, 1977):

    space
    time
    communication
    meaning

There is some degree of ambiguity in the use of the terms "communication" and "meaning." "Communication" refers to verbal or nonverbal communication *among people*, while "meaning" refers to nonverbal communication *from the environment to people*. However, these terms still seem the best available to describe what is being discussed.

While all environments constitute complex interrelationships among these four elements, it is useful conceptually to separate them and discuss them as though they were separate, since this leads to a better understanding of the nature of environments and the relationships between meaning and communication. Since, for our purposes here, the relationship between these two is the most important, I will first briefly discuss space and time (for a more complete discussion, see Rapoport, 1977, 1980c).

Organization of space

Planning and design on all scales—from regions to furniture group-ings—can be seen as the *organization of space* for different purposes and according to different rules, which reflect the activities, values, and purposes of the individuals or groups doing the organizing. At the same time, space organization also reflects ideal images, representing the congruence (or, in cases where the system ceases to work, the lack of congruence) between physical space and social space. It is of interest to note that one can describe a great variety of "types" of space (Rapoport 1970a). This variety and the fact that different groups, whether cultures or subcultures such as designers and the lay public, "see" and evaluate space differently make any definition of space dif-ficult. Intuitively, however, space is the three-dimensional extension of the world around us, the intervals, distances, and relationships between people and people, people and things, things and things. Space organization is, then, the way in which these separations (and linkages) occur and is central in understanding, analyzing, and com-paring built environments.

Organization of time

People, however, live in time as well as space—the environment is also temporal, and can, therefore, also be seen as the *organization of time* reflecting and influencing behavior in time. This may be under-stood in at least two major ways. The first refers to large-scale, cogni-tive structuring of time such as linear flow (typical of our own culture) versus cyclic time (much more typical of many traditional cultures); future orientation versus past orientation; the future as an improve-ment over the past versus the future as likely to be worse. This influ-ences behavior and decisions and, through those, environment. Thus in India, the cyclic view of time (as opposed to our linear conception) has helped preserve elements (plants and animals, for example) that otherwise would have disappeared, and has also helped shape the character of cities (Sopher, 1964). In the case of the United States and Britain, the respective future and past orientations have also led to very different cultural landscapes (Lowenthal, 1968; Lowenthal and Prince, 1964, 1965).

Such time structuring also influences how time is valued and, hence, how finely it is subdivided into limits. Thus we advertise watches as being accurate within one second a year, whereas in traditional Pueblo culture, a week was the smallest relevant time unit (Ortiz, 1972). Such cultural differences clearly influence the second major way in which cultural differences in the organization of time can be considered—the tempos and rhythms of human activities, that is, the number of events per unit time and the distribution of activities in time (day and night, weekday and rest day, seasonal, sacred and profane times, and so on), respectively. Tempos and rhythms distinguish among groups and individuals who have different temporal "signatures" and they may also be congruent or incongruent with each other. Thus people may be separated in time as well as, or instead of, space and groups with different rhythms occupying the same space may never meet. Groups with different tempos may never communicate. Groups with different rhythms may also be in conflict, as when one group, in this case the Swiss, regards a particular time as quiet and for sleep, and another group (in this case Southern Italians) regard it as a time for noise and boisterous activity (Rapoport, 1977). Cultural conflicts and problems may often be more severe at the temporal level than at the spatial, although clearly spatial and temporal aspects interact and influence one another: People live in space-time.

Note also that many behaviors (nonfixed-feature elements) that are used to establish boundaries, assert or define identity, and so on, are, in effect, temporal, although while they are happening they need and use settings and other physical elements. This applies to pilgrimages and other ritual movements, carnivals, festivals, and other rites (see Rapoport, 1981). One example of this is provided by Scotland, where periodic, recurrent ceremonial assemblies based on pilgrimages are used to organize the links between urban centers and hinterlands. At the same time, however, these also need settings. The highland clan gatherings use ancestral castles, highland games an "arena"; lowland Scots of the southwest use the church, while in the Borders area of lowland Scotland the town is the significant setting (Neville, 1979). Thus the meaning of these elements depends on the temporal use they receive—the periodic gatherings.

Organization of communication

The organization of space and time are both aspects of the general question one can ask about human activities—who does what, including or excluding whom, when, and where—they are the *when* and *where*. The who does what with whom is the *organization of com-*

munication among people. Who communicates with whom, under what conditions, how, when, where, and in what context and situation is an important way in which communication and the built environment are related. Environments both reflect communication and modulate it, channel it, control it, facilitate it, inhibit it. Both environments and communication are culturally variable; the nature, intensity, rate, and direction of interaction vary as do the settings appropriate to it. Privacy, as a system of interaction and withdrawal, is also related to it—one can study the various individuals and groups who are linked or separated, the sensory modalities involved, and the mechanisms used: separation in space; physical devices such as walls, doors, and the like; organization of time; rules; manners; and avoidance and psychological withdrawal (Rapoport, 1976b, 1977).

We have been discussing meaning for some time, but it may be useful to restate the principal features of its organization, after reiterating that meaning is communication *from* the environment *to* people, whereas communication, as used here, refers to communication *among* people, whether face to face or in other ways.

Organization of meaning

Space organization, as I have used it above, is a more fundamental property of the environment than is shape, the materials that give it physical expression and other characteristics, which can more usefully be seen as an aspect of the *organization of meaning*. The organization of meaning can then be separated from the organization of space, both conceptually and in fact, as already noted.

While space organization itself expresses meaning and has communicative properties, meaning is often expressed through signs, materials, colors, forms, sizes, furnishings, landscaping, maintenance, and the like—as we have already seen—and by people themselves. Thus spatial meanings can be indicated by walls or other sharp breaks, or by gradients or transitions. They can be indicated by sanctity (the presence of religious symbols), by planting, by various objects or furnishings—of buildings or urban spaces, by treatment of floor or ground surfaces or level changes, by the presence of particular people, and so on—that is, by fixed-, semifixed-, and nonfixed-feature elements (see Figure 28).

Thus both spatial and other systems of cues may identify settings, which then become indicators of social position, ways of establishing group or social identity, ways of defining situations and hence indicat-

VENCE
PUBLIC SPACE (INDICATORS : SHOPS, BENCHES,
OUTDOOR CAFES)

VENCE   SEMI-PRIVATE SPACE
(INDICATORS : HOUSE PLANTS, LAUNDRY, VINE)

LE BROC
SEMI-PUBLIC SPACE (INDICATORS : PEOPLE ON CHAIRS, LAUNDRY,
WATERSOURCE)

PUBLIC, SEMI-PUBLIC & SEMI-PRIVATE SPACES
SOUTHERN FRANCE.
(BASED ON AUTHOR'S SLIDES)

RAPOPORT

Figure 28

ing expected behavior—but only if the cues are comprehensible and can be decoded, although, as I have tried to show, this decoding is not usually too difficult.

The purpose of structuring space and time is to organize and structure communication (interaction, avoidance, dominance, and so on), and this is done partly through organizing meaning. The organization of communication also influences the organization of the other three variables—in fact, all four interact in many, interesting, and complex ways.

The relationship between
meaning and communication

The relationship of the last two, meaning and communication, as aspects of the environment is our principal theme. The argument has been that meaning often communicates the context (who should interact with whom, when, under what conditions), that is, it communicates how. Meaning, as we have seen, also provides information about status, lifestyle, ethnicity, and other variables. These are an important part of both the context and the situation that influences communication. It does this in a way we have not yet discussed—the meaning inherent in settings populated by particular groups and of communicating lifestyle, status, and the like has the purpose of locating people one does not know in social space and, through *that* mechanism, influencing communication.

In this latter connection, an interesting and important question arises: Under what conditions would the environment be *more* or *less* important regarding the meanings it provides? Let us pose this question in terms of when it is *less* important. A number of conditions immediately comes to mind. For example:

(a) Environmental meanings are less important in small places where everyone is known, such as in a village, a small community, an aboriginal camp, or the like. Even in such cases, however, such environmental meaning may be useful. For example, in the mill villages in North Carolina, the distance from the mill and topographic elevation communicated perceived distance in status between overseers' houses and workers' houses, which was further reinforced by the former being larger, having porches, and so on (Glass, 1978: 147); yet, the community was small enough for these differences to be *known* to all. Similarly, we have seen that in the even smaller M'Buti camp, physical cues, such as changed entrance directions, houses turned around, and the building of spite fences (Turnbull, 1961), are used to indicate shifting communication and interaction patterns. People *know* which relationships have changed, but these mnemonics help everyone and certainly help new arrivals or people returning to the camp after an absence to understand the current situation. However, they are certainly *less* important than in larger-scale, more complex environments. This seems clear on intuitive grounds and has already been discussed above (see also Rapoport, 1979a, 1979b). The significance of scale in this connection is beginning to receive recognition in social science (see Berreman, 1978), although it has not been much studied regarding environments. It does seem clear that cultural homogeneity *is* greater in small-scale societies and it therefore follows that the role of physical elements to locate people in social space cannot be as important as it is in larger-scale situations.

(b) Environmental cues are less important where there are rigid, known, and widely accepted social hierarchies. Under those conditions communication is highly predictable and cues from settings are less important. Some ways of communicating status and hierarchy are still needed, however. It thus follows that:

(c) Environmental cues are less important when other cues and indicators are present and work well—accent, clothing, "old school ties," and the like. Anecdotally, I was once told by a graduate student who had been a taxi driver in New York City that the nature of briefcases and attache cases provided a set of cues that helped taxi drivers locate people in social space and thus decide whether to pick them up or not.

Given these conditions, one might then conclude that such cues would be more important in the United States and similar places: Accents tend to be *mainly* (although not entirely) regional and do not locate people in social space; clothing is mass produced and its use is rather complex and nonsystematic; the society is large and complex; cars are available on credit or can be leased—many people have expense accounts. Under those conditions, one would expect that environmental indicators would become more important than elsewhere. It is difficult to obtain a house of a certain type without a set of particular educational, occupational, economic, and social characteristics, and even more difficult to "fake" location—the neighborhood or area of the city in which one lives. This may be an environmental equivalent of the differential difficulty of hiding emotions through nonverbal expression in the nonfixed-feature realm.

These hypotheses, or guesses, are partly supported by anecdotal and personal evidence that in the United States one is often asked upon meeting people, "What do you do?" (which defines education, occupational status, lifestyle, and possible income) and "Where do you live?" which helps define the rest. This receives passing support in some of the literature dealing with social areas in cities (see Timms, 1971; Johnston, 1971a, 1971b; Peach, 1975). In other words, location in physical space becomes an indicator of location in social space. At smaller scales, the presence of people in particular shopping, recreational, dining, and other settings also locates them in social space. Recall, also, that these settings in turn communicate *their* character via environmental cues.

Once the cue becomes known, and the particular regularities in given cultures understood, this becomes easier. There are also some cross-cultural regularities regarding environmental quality of residential areas—altitude, views (if not of industry), water-edge location (if nonindustrial), location in center or periphery, the *known* status of a named area (which may be *associational* rather than perceptual; see Rapoport, 1977: 31-32). At the perceptual level, we have seen repeatedly the role of lawns, maintenance, litter, kinds of houses, and many other variables. The argument implicit in all this is that if people can be located in social space, and hence in a likely context and situation, that is, if they can be categorized, this makes things more predictable (or less unpredictable) and one is more likely to interact with such people than if they cannot be located in social space and remain "strangers."

This argument, based on a priori grounds derived from the evidence reviewed, receives strong support from a study by Lofland (1973). Whereas my argument has dealt mainly, although not exclusively, with residential locations, Lofland's deals mainly with *public places*. The question is how one can locate people encountered in public places in social space, given that one does not interact with strangers, that is, people whom one cannot so locate. Lofland argues that in traditional societies there was a wide range of cues, both traditional and prescribed by law (recall our discussion of sumptuary laws earlier), having to do with clothing, hairstyles, shoes, body scars, tatoos and decorations, and so on that have disappeared. Under those conditions, there is only one mechanism available—public settings become *less* public and more *group specific*. These settings provide the contexts; by seeing people frequent these settings, we can locate them in social space. Hence the proliferation of group-specific settings that traditionally were public.

Lofland's hypothesis was tested, although briefly, by a student of mine (Piwoni, 1976). He compared illustrations and descriptions mainly of medieval public spaces and identified the rather wide range of people who were present, accepted, and involved. He then examined a set of contemporary U.S. public places. It does seem as though these places are becoming more and more specialized and group specific: Each one provides a set of cues that communicates meanings telling people to stay out or enter and, to some extent, predicts the kind of behaviors to be expected and appropriate.

Yet the distinction may be drawn too acutely and made too contrasting. Although the cues may be more subtle, or not present physically, most traditional environments do provide settings that are group specific and the character of which is given by physical cues that remind people of the expected behavior, so that they act almost automatically. One example is the men's sacred building in the Sepik River area of New Guinea known as the Haus Tambaran, where height, shape, decoration, and other strikingly noticeable differences clearly distinguish it from the surrounding dwellings (Rapoport, 1969c: 44; 1979b). In fact, men's houses are found all over New Guinea (Rapoport, 1981), in Afghanistan, India (Singh and Chandhoke, 1966, 1967), Africa (Fernandez, 1977), and elsewhere, and are usually clearly distinguished from other buildings. Among Turkish nomads, also, men's and women's tents can be found (see Cuisenier, 1970), thus helping structure communication even though sex identity is easy to distinguish without the tent or house.

Note that in all these cases, while the difference is noticeable even to the outsider, the complex of relevant behaviors and the social interactions and communications encouraged, discouraged, or prevented are culture specific and can only occur if the cultural code is known. Location, height, size, and decoration do not indicate, for example, social status but sexual and ritual differences, each with their appropriate behaviors learned through enculturation generally and taught through initiation specifically.

In Africa generally, we find settings with sets of cues that identify appropriate behaviors in terms of the distinction between men and women (see Levin, 1971; Fernandez, 1977). That these are not confined only to preliterate culture can be seen from a number of examples from Anglo-American culture. In many of these cases, the cues that indicate the "belongingness" of either men or women may be very subtle—or even nonexistent. In this respect, they are very similar to the traditional examples given above. At the same time, they tend to be primarily—although not exclusively—in the semifixed- (or nonfixed) feature realms.

Thus we find in certain areas of Chicago and East London that the dwelling is very much the woman's domain, where men feel ill at ease (Suttles, 1968; Young and Wilmott, 1962). This was mainly *known*, but was also indicated by the presence of cues such as lace curtains and doilies, furniture covers, and many delicate "what-nots," which were seen as being at odds with the "crude" nature of men. For men there were other settings—such as taverns and pubs, as well as street settings, which were much more important parts of their house-settlement system (see Rapoport, 1977, 1980a, and 1982). In Australia, traditionally, in hotels the public bar was for men only, and women, alone or accompanied by men, drank in "lounges." This was known, but was also indicated by the general decor. Bars fronted the street, were large, cavernous, tiled, with no seating, noisy, undecorated except by beer and liquor advertisements, stressing sports. They have been generally described as looking like large public urinals. Lounges tended to be in the interior, carpeted, having chairs and tables, decorations—all producing a softer, more "feminine," or at least genteel, image. Thus what was *known* was reinforced by physical cues—by *mnemonics*, which were further reinforced by the nonfixed elements: the purely masculine crowd, their behavior, noise levels, and clothing in the one case, the mixed crowd with very different dress codes and very different behavior and noise levels in the other. One easily and quickly adjusted one's behavior accordingly. Knowing these things is important. If one is hungry, one wants to be able easily to identify a place to eat, know the price range, type of food, how one needs to be dressed, and how much it will cost before one wants to know where to enter. As already suggested, the success of chain operations is frequently a function of their great predictability; the tradition in certain places of displaying menus outside and allowing views into the establishment are devices used to communicate these desired meanings. The former method, however, is more interesting theoretically.

The effectiveness of these—as of many other systems of cues—depends not only on adequate redundancy (so that cues are noticed). Their understanding depends on predictability, which, in turn, depends not only on enculturation, but *consistency of use*. This is possibly the most important characteristic that makes chain operations successful. Each time a particular sign, roof shape, building shape, and so on (McDonald's, Kentucky Fried Chicken, Pizza Hut, Hilton, Heritage Bank, or whatever) is used to predict fully and successfully the services, products, behaviors, prices, and so on, the cues reinforce their predictability and hence their effectiveness. They become more successful in producing behavioral invariance—that is, in terms of the argument earlier on, in restricting the range of acceptable and appropriate behaviors (see also Kottak, 1979). In a sense, when the lay public complains that churches, post offices, banks, and so on no longer look like churches, post offices, or whatever, one of the things they are saying is that the expected behaviors are not clear, and also that the designers have neglected meaning—particularly users' meaning.

The above discussion relates to the interaction of meaning and communication. In many traditional societies, the effectiveness of subtle cues depends on their consistency. Some examples have already been given. Consider another—among the Bedouin, the typical tent always has the same divisions in the same order so that one knows where men, women, and animals are located. Tents are also arranged in standardized ways and, in Israel, face east (= front). It is of interest to note that when more permanent dwellings are first constructed, they repeat this order—the same space organization persists.

The men's section (which is also the guest room) is further indicated by other external cues. One that I have observed is a change in the "floor" surface, with sand or other materials altering the "natural" state of the ground. Note that, parenthetically, frequently one finds the equations men = culture and women = nature in various societies. An example already discussed is provided in the case of urban housing in Uganda. Here the distinctions between semipublic, private, and hidden rooms are based on this basic distinction (see Kamau, n.d.) and the nature of these three domains is communicated through physical cues. Thus semipublic spaces, used for entertaining and men, are indicated by decorations, furnishings, and so on—which also indicate social status. In fact, inventories of objects and their arrangements can be made, and the elements and arrangements also indicate sitting versus eating areas. Private spaces are mainly bedrooms and, again, are indicated by furnishings. Different bedrooms (such as the master bedroom) are indicated by the quality of furniture, its amount, and its cleanliness. Hidden spaces—kitchens, showers, and lavatories—are clearly shown by the equipment they contain. In the case of a Maya house—a very small space, 20 feet by 15 feet—the clear division into men's and women's domains is indicated both by consistent location within the space and by cues such as hearth and metate for women and altar for men (see Rapoport, 1979a). Note that in all these cases, communication and interaction are greatly influenced by sex differences.

The second additional cue for the men's/guest part of the tent used among Bedouin is a heap of ashes (from the fire used to make the inevitable tea and coffee or, in some cases, the food accompanying hospitality). In villages or tent clusters, where only one men's section serves as a guest room, this ash heap becomes important. Other cues used are the relative openness of the sections, the furnishings, the people seen, and so on. The ash heap, which indicates "guest room," "intercepts" visitors, that is, strangers, and in this way controls communication (see Figure 29).

In this case, as in that of an Aboriginal or Navaho camp, there is also an invisible, but known, boundary at which one needs to wait in order to be admitted to the camp or settlement in the first place; communication is controlled at various places. All of these depend on consistency of use and of location within the tent and encampment, as well as a knowledge of the rules regarding behavior defined by the situation and a willingness to follow these rules. Without all these conditions, the system would not work in organizing communication.

In the case of an Anglo-American house, there is a whole set of cues—fence, porch, front door, living room door, and so on—that indicates how far one penetrates depending on who one is; communication is controlled (see, for example, my interpretation of Harrington, 1965; in Rapoport, 1977: 200). Other examples can be given, including comparison of fence locations (Rapoport, 1969c; Anderson and Moore, 1972) and many other cues. For example, the traditional Russian house is commonly divided into a "clean" half, where guests are received, and a "dirty" half, where cooking and other similar work takes place. The division is indicated by location—the former being off the street, the latter off the yard—reinforced by separate entrances, with the front entrance being further stressed by a small porch; the "clean" half is also indicated by displays of the family's "best goods" (Dunn and Dunn, 1963). Such systems of cues clearly guide and influence communication patterns. These kinds of cues generally may be very subtle yet control privacy gradients and hence communication very effectively, particularly in cases where there are clear and unambiguous rules, homogeneous populations, clear hierarchies, and consistent use of these devices (Rapoport, 1979a).

At a larger scale, meanings can be communicated through materials in very culture-specific ways, which, once known, enable an under-

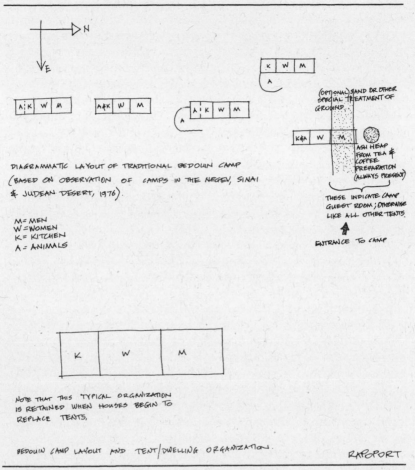

DIAGRAMMATIC LAYOUT OF TRADITIONAL BEDOUIN CAMP
(BASED ON OBSERVATION OF CAMPS IN THE NEGEV, SINAI
& JUDEAN DESERT, 1976).

M = MEN
W = WOMEN
K = KITCHEN
A = ANIMALS

(OPTIONAL) SAND OR OTHER
SPECIAL TREATMENT OF
GROUND.

ASH HEAP
FROM TEA &
COFFEE
PREPARATION
(ALWAYS PRESENT)

THESE INDICATE CAMP
GUEST ROOM; OTHERWISE
LIKE ALL OTHER TENTS.

ENTRANCE TO CAMP

NOTE THAT THIS TYPICAL ORGANIZATION
IS RETAINED WHEN HOUSES BEGIN TO
REPLACE TENTS.

BEDOUIN CAMP LAYOUT AND TENT/DWELLING ORGANIZATION.   RAPOPORT

Figure 29

standing of larger-scale communication patterns. For example, among
the Bedouin, stone or other permanent materials are only used in the
dwellings replacing tents when these are built on land belonging to the
tribe or subgroup of which the individual in question is a member. In
other cases, less durable materials are used. This then indicates the
relation of individuals to the group. Among Bedouin also, tombs of
sheikhs or saints are often used to establish ownership of land (as is
found, for example, in Wadi Firan in the Sinai). This role of tombs is,

once again, culturally specific and neither intuitively clear nor "legible" unless one knows the code. Their importance is, however, stressed through location, form, and color (whitewash) as well as the presence of offerings, occupational debris, and so on. Also, once the code is known, the meanings can be understood easily. One then quickly discovers that such tombs, among the Bedouin groups in the southern Sinai, act as meeting places (shown by having cooking and dining facilities adjacent, cooking utensils, and so on) that reinforce tribal identity and foster interaction and communication among dispersed and nomadic groups. These meetings reaffirm these groups' membership in the tribe and their right to use its resources; they are also occasions for meeting friends, relatives, and visitors from other tribes: "The holy tomb is a very precise image of territorial claims on the land and of the Bedouin's conception of territory as embodied in the group" (Marx, 1976: 25). As such it clearly structures communication. These two functions of tombs or shrines of saints—of marking ownership and structuring interaction and communication—were also found among the Nubians along the Nile before their relocation in New Nubia (Fernea et al., 1973).

Note that many of these cues communicate meanings in culture-specific ways in order to structure and control interaction and communication. Note also that the rules are social, but the cues are frequently physical. What they do, in effect, is to locate people in particular settings that are equivalent to portions of social space and thus define a context and a situation as we saw earlier in the case of offices. In so doing, they categorize people. By categorizing peope in this way, interaction and communication are clearly limited in some way—some forms of interaction and communication become inappropriate. Some groups may even be excluded—that is, if the particular form of categorization is stigmatization, there is no interaction. But the argument is that if there is no categorization, interaction is likely to become even less since one does not interact with strangers (Lofland, 1973).

I have previously discussed conditions under which physical cues from the environment may become more or less important. There is one other such condition not yet discussed. I have argued elsewhere that under conditions of high criticality, physical environments generally become important (Rapoport, 1977, 1979c, 1980c, forthcoming). This also applies to the role of meaning in controlling interaction and communication. A particular form of heightened criticality is environmental stress, and a particular response is what has been called *defensive structuring* (Siegel, 1970). One of the characteristics of this particular response is the greater reliance on particular environmental cues that indicate identity and thus help channel communication processes.

Consider two examples among the many available (for others, and more details, see Rapoport, 1981). Among the Maori in New Zealand, many traditional cultural elements have become condensed or concentrated in a space, the *Marae,* the importance of which has been little noticed by whites precisely because it *is* a space rather than a building or object. It is a spatial-symbolic realm, a spatial expression of an important set of cognitive domains, categories, and elements of the culture, a "remnant microcosm of traditional culture" (Austin, 1976). It also provides the appropriate setting for a range of critically important behaviors, among them rituals, ritual meals, and meetings among various groups. The *Marae* are seen as "symbols of Maoritanga (Maoriness)," "of being a Maori," so that "to be a Maori means to have a home *Marae"* (Austin, 1976: 238-239). Increasingly, Maori are calling for the provision of *Marae,* with their accompanying gateways, meeting houses, and dining halls, in urban areas where they can become indicators of Maori identity and focal points. One could even predict that in time, if no impediments are placed in their way by government policy, Maori would tend increasingly to concentrate in specific urban neighborhoods, leading to the development of specific institutions and other forms. While these and many other semifixed- and nonfixed-feature elements will all help to express and maintain ethnic identity, the *Marae* seems to be the single most important, core element. It should be stressed that it plays a role in structuring interaction and communication in two domains—among Maori and between Maori and non-Maori.

Among the Mayo Indians of Sonora, Mexico, a number of elements are also used to define the ethnic identity of the group: the settlement pattern, churches, cemeteries, and others. The key elements, however, are the house crosses that identify Mayo dwellings (as well as other crosses that mark boundaries and important sites or settings). These crosses and the sacred paths linking them, which are used for periodic ritual movement, are the strongest indicators and definers of ethnic identity among that group (Crumrine, 1964, 1977). In effect, they locate people in social space and, in this way, clearly influence the extent and forms of communication at the highest level of generality of group members versus non-group members, that is, us versus them. It has been argued, in fact, that this is a primary function of culture generally: Through this distinction, culture both prevents (or limits) and encourages communication—the former *among* groups, the second *within* groups.

It will be noted that after discussing the role of public spaces (which are stressed by Lofland, 1973), I returned to examples of residential settings (although as part of the house-settlement system). This is because it seems that in cities, the most important way of locating people in social space is through where they live: their neighborhood, address, associational and perceptual characteristics of the area, street, house, garden, and other elements all communicate and locate people in social space.

I will thus conclude this argument with an example from Canada discussed in some detail. In this study, interaction (that is, communication) was compared in detached houses and apartment buildings (Reed, 1974). The finding was that, counterintuitively, interaction was *higher* in houses. At this point, I do not wish to discuss the validity of this finding or the support it might receive from other studies. What I wish to do is to accept the finding, and compare the reasons given to the argument of this monograph.

Five sets of reasons are given for the higher levels of interaction and communication in detached dwellings, which can be described (in somewhat modified form) as follows:

(1) the physical structure or layout of the residential type
(2) the symbolic (better, *communicative*) aspects of the residential units
(3) the relative homogeneity or heterogeneity of the respective populations
(4) the nature of the information control provided by the respective units
(5) the mobility of the respective populations and their length of residence

I will now interpret these findings in terms of some of our discussion.

One can argue that, with the exception of point 1, all of them relate to my argument. One can further argue that (a) even the first point leads to higher probabilities of chance encounters, that is, we are dealing with a *direct* effect of the space organization on organization of communication, and (b) several of the others depend on the particular form of housing and its spatial organization. The other points all represent more *indirect* effects and can be understood in terms of the distinction between wanted and unwanted interaction, that is, in terms of privacy defined as the *control of unwanted interaction* (see Rapoport,

1976b, 1977). Let us examine the remaining four reasons in somewhat more detail.

(2) If, in order to interact with people, one needs to locate them in social space, then it follows that one needs information about people. Location and the nature of the residential structure, the quality of streets, and other associational and perceptual cues already discussed allow some *general* inferences to be made. In addition, however, houses also allow personalization, that is, the manipulation of a large number of cues in the semifixed realm that communicate *specific* information about people—their preferences, status, lifestyles, and so on. In apartments, which are identical and have little or no possibility of personalization, this information is lacking. This could be overcome partially if the population were highly homogeneous, but this is where the next point comes in.

(3) It is found that apartments tend to house more heterogeneous populations than do groups of houses. This makes people in them not only less identifiable by physical cues, but also less predictable socially. These two also interact—one way of judging the homogeneity of a population is precisely through semifixed-feature elements—maintainance, lawns, personalization, planting, colors, and so on—particularly if they add up to a recognizable character, that is, are not random.

(4) In apartments, due to the form of the space organization (point 1) and particularly the lack of common open space, it is more difficult to observe the comings and goings of people to specific dwellings—of visitors, deliveries, time spent on maintenance and gardening, time spent on recreation—and the forms of recreation. There is thus difficulty in judging *lifestyles*, and hence the location of people in social space again becomes more difficult—a problem compounded by the greater heterogeneity, or *diversity of lifestyles*. This lack of visual information about how to place people in social space is compounded by the reverse phenomenon in other sensory modalities: In apartments it is more difficult to control unwanted information through olfactory and aural channels. As a result, unwanted information may be communicated that might be embarrassing. This further inhibits interaction. Thus it is the *control* over the cues that seems significant: One might almost say that while houses allow "front" meanings, apartments reveal "back" meanings.

Since the communication of meaning through environmental and other cues is an aspect of the management of the flow of information, we are generally discussing *front* rather than *back* behavior. Many of the examples of the negative identity (stigma) attributed to people via environmental cues (for example, the definition of slums) is frequently related to front/back reversals, so that meanings culturally defined as inappropriate by the receiving group are present.

(5) The high rate of mobility in apartments means not only greater uncertainty about who people are, and thus greater unpredictability; it also means that there is less opportunity both to establish informal normative structure and to maintain it by the socialization of newcomers through sanctions.

Generally, then, four of these five points (and many are related to the first) are due to meanings being communicated, mainly by semifixed and nonfixed elements, which then influence interaction, that is, communication—which is, of course, where we came in.

CONCLUSION

What seems significant about this last example, the many others given, and still others that could have been used, but were not, is that suddenly a considerable number of things fit into place. A large framework begins to emerge, linking many apparently diverse and unrelated concepts, theories, disciplines, and findings, which was, in fact, one of the objectives described in the preface. In fact, this framework begins to *predict* things that existing empirical studies confirm. Clearly, studies specifically set up to test predictions, and to study this whole approach, would prove even more useful.

One different way of conceptualizing some of the arguments in this monograph is as follows:

Perceptual ←——————————→ *Associational*
noticeable differences (reinforced by redundancy) that in themselves have some significance and meaning by drawing attention to themselves through *contrast* and through the selection of which cues are made noticeable ·

the *decoding* of the meaning of elements, their associations with use and behavior, derived partly from consistent use, partly from the cultural rules associated with settings, that is, the context and the situation

definition of the setting, the mnemonic functions of which activate subroutines for culturally appropriate, more or less routinized behavior, including the location of people in social space and hence communication; hence the importance of the built environment and its early appearance in the development of the human species

Clearly, the goal has been to set out this approach and framework as clearly and succinctly as possible. As a result, I have left out much, and simplified considerably. Yet I hope the utility of the approach has been demonstrated. Its utility, in my view, is twofold. First, it is *specific.* This has to do with the relative simplicity of using the nonverbal communication model. In fact, the very criticism occasionally leveled against nonverbal communication research—that it lacks theory, is overly simple, and so on—is, in some ways, an advantage. It approaches such behavior in the first instance through observation, recording, and then analysis. It is thus relatively simple and straightforward to use. It is also relatively easy to transfer the approach from purely nonfixed-feature elements to semifixed- and fixed-feature elements. At the same time, there is sufficient theory, both in nonverbal communication and man-environment studies, to enable conceptual structures to develop. It is also an approach that lends itself to comparative and cross-cultural approaches and that makes it easier to broaden the sample by using historical, archaeological, and ethnographic material.

For example, once a group and its profile in terms of lifestyle and environmental quality preferences have been established, one can frequently define the group's activity systems and the systems of settings, domains, and so on that accommodate them. Through observation and analysis of these settings and the behaviors occurring in them (who does what, where, when, and including or excluding whom), the relevant cues can quickly be discovered and understood. They can then be provided or it can be made easy for the group to provide these for themselves. One could study the percentage of settings with great predictability in either satisfactorily or unsatisfactorily communicating both the expected behavior and its permitted range or latitude.

Second, the utility of this approach is *general.* This has to do with the fact that it fits into the way of thinking described in the preface. This approach, which is basically humanistic, has to do with all products of human culture. Its method is interpretive, being based on the work of many others. One thus uses many small pieces of information from diverse sources to show how they interrelate, or how different fields and disciplines interrelate, revealing unsuspected connections. Thus one can build frameworks and conceptual models that seem valid cross-culturally and historically and thus help relate primitive, vernacular, and high-style environments, traditional and modern examples.

REFERENCES

Aaronson, B. S. (1970) "Some affective stereotypes of color." International Journal of Symbology 2 (August): 15-28.

Abrahamson, M. (1966) Interpersonal Accommodation. New York: Van Nostrand Reinhold.

Ahlbrandt, R. S. and P. C. Brophy (1976) "Management: an important element of the housing environment." Environment and Behavior 8 (December): 505-526.

Anderson, E. N. (1972) "On the folk art of landscaping." Western Folklore 31 (July): 179-188.

Anderson, J. R. and C. K. Moore (1972) "A study of object language in residential areas." (mimeo)

Appleyard, D. and R. Y. Okamoto (1968) Environmental Criteria for Ideal Transportation Systems. Berkeley: Institute of Urban and Regional Development, University of California.

Architects Journal (1979) "Martlesham Heath: selling the village image." Vol. 170 (September): 485-503.

Architectural Record (1979) Vol. 166 (September): 126-129.

Architectural Review (1976) Vol. 159 (February).

Argyle, M. (1967) The Psychology of Interpersonal Behavior. New York: Penguin.

———and R. Ingham (1972) "Gaze, mutual gaze and proximity." Semiotica 6, 1: 19-32.

Austin, M. R. (1976) "A description of the Maori Marae," pp. 229-241 in A. Rapoport (ed.) The Mutual Interaction of People and Their Built Environment. The Hague: Mouton.

Bachelard, G. (1969) The Poetics of Space. Boston: Beacon.

Backler, A. L. (1974) A Behavioral Study of Locational Changes in Upper Class Residential Areas: The Detroit Example. Bloomington: Department of Geography, Indiana University.

Barker, R. G. (1968) Ecological Psychology. Palo Alto, CA: Stanford University Press.

Barkow, J. H. (1975) "Prestige and culture—a biosocial interpretation." Current Anthropology 16 (December): 553-572.

Barnett, P. M. (1975) "The Worcester three-decker: a study in the perception of form." Design and Environment 6 (Winter).

Barnett, R. (1977) "The libertarian suburb: deliberate disorder." Landscape 22 (Summer): 44-48.

Barth, F. (1969) Ethnic Groups and Boundaries. Boston: Little, Brown.

Barthes, R. (1970) Elements of Semiology. Boston: Beacon.

———(1970-1971) "Semiologie et urbanisme." Architecture d'Aujourd 'hui 42 (December/January): 11-13.

Basso, K. H. and H. A. Selby [eds.] (1976) Meaning in Anthropology. Albuquerque: University of New Mexico Press.

Bates, E. (1976) Language and Context: The Acquisition of Pragmatics. New York: Academic.

Baudrillard, J. (1968) Le Systéme des Objects. Paris: Denöel/Gonthier.

Beck, R. J. and P. Teasdale (1977) User Generated Program for Lowrise Multiple Dwelling Housing: Summary of a Research Project. Montreal: Centre de Recherches et d'Innovation Urbaines, Université de Montréal.

Becker, F. D. (1977) User Participation, Personalization and Environmental Meaning: Three Field Studies. Ithaca, NY: Program in Urban and Regional Studies, Cornell University.

Beckley, R. M. (1977) A Comparison of Milwaukee's Central City Residential Areas and Contemporary Development Standards: An Exploration of Issues Related to Bringing the Area Up to "Standard." Milwaukee: Urban Research Center, University of Wisconsin.

Berlin, B. and P. Kay (1969) Basic Color Terms: Their Universality and Evolution. Berkeley: University of California Press.

Bermant, C. and M. Weitzman (1979) Ebla: A Revelation in Archaeology. New York: Times Books.

Bernstein, B. (1971) Class, Codes and Control, Vol. 1: Theoretical Studies Towards a Sociology of Language. London: Routledge & Kegan Paul.

Berreman, G. D. (1978) "Scale and social relations." Current Anthropology 19 (June): 225-245.

Birdwhistell, R. L. (1970) "Kinesics," pp. 379-385 in D. Sills (ed.) International Encyclopedia of the Social Sciences, Vol. 8. New York: Macmillan.

———(1972) Kinesics and Context. Philadelphia: University of Pennsylvania Press.

Birenbaum, A. and E. Sagarin [eds.] (1973) People in Places: The Sociology of the Familiar. New York: Praeger.

Blanch, R. J. (1972) "The origins and use of medieval color symbolism." International Journal of Symbology 3 (December): 1-5.

Blanton, R. E. (1978) Monte Albán: Settlement Patterns at the Ancient Zapotec Capital. New York: Academic.

Blomeyer, G. (1979) "Architecture as a political sign system." International Architect 1, 1: 54-60.

Blumer, H. (1969a) Symbolic Interactionism: Perspective and Method. Englewood Cliffs, NJ: Prentice-Hall.

———(1969b) "Fashion: from class differentiation to collective selection." Sociological Quarterly (Summer): 275-291.

Bonta, J. P. (1973) "Notes for a theory of meaning in design." Vs. Quaderni de Studi Semiotici 6: 26-58.

———(1975) An Anatomy of Architectural Interpretation: A Semiotic Review of the Criticism of Mies Van Der Rohe's Barcelona Pavilion. Barcelona: Gustavo Gili.

———(1979) Architecture and Its Interpretation: A Study of Expressive Systems in Architecture. London: Lund Humphries.

Boudon, P. (1969) Pessac de le Corbusier. Paris: Dunod.

Bourdieu, P. (1973) "The Berber house," pp. 98-110 in M. Douglas (ed.) Rules and Meanings. New York: Penguin.

Boyden, S. V. (1974) "Conceptual basis of proposed international ecological studies in large metropolitan areas." (mimeo)

Britten, A. (1973) Meanings and Situations. London: Routledge & Keagan Paul.

Broadbent, G. (1977) "A plain man's guide to the theory of signs in architecture." Architectural Design 48:

———R. Bunt, and C. Jencks [eds.] (1980) Signs, Symbols and Architecture. Chichester: John Wiley.

Brower, S. N. (1977) The Design of Neighborhood Parks. Baltimore: Baltimore City Planning Commission, Department of Planning.

———and P. W. Williamson (1974) "Outdoor recreation as a function of the urban housing environment." Environment and Behavior 6 (September): 295-345.

Bruner, J. S. (1973) Beyond the Information Given. New York: W. W. Norton.

Burby, R. J., S. H. Weiss, et al. (1976) New Communities U.S.A. Lexington, MA: D. C. Heath.

Burgess, J A. (1978) Image and Identity: A Study of Urban and Regional Perception with Particular Reference to Kingston-upon-Hull. Hull, England: University of Hull.

Campbell, D. T. (1961) "The mutual methodological relevance of anthropology and psychology," in L. K. Hsu (ed.) Psychological Anthropology. Homewood, IL: Dorsey.

Canetti, E. (1962) Crowds and Power (C. Stewart, trans.). London: Gollancz.

Carr, S. (1973) City Signs and Lights: A Policy Study. Cambridge: MIT Press.

Carson, D. H. (1972) "Residential descriptors and urban threats," pp. 154-168 in J. F. Wohlwill and D. H. Carson (eds.) Environment and the Social Sciences: Perspectives and Applications. Washington, DC: American Psychological Association.

Chapin, F. S. (1938) "Effects of slum clearance and rehousing on family and community relationships in Minneapolis." American Journal of Sociology 42 (March): 744-763.

Chenu, L., M. J. Dozio, P. Feddersen, and K. Noschis (1979) Identité et Comportement en Milieu Urbain. Paris: UNESCO.

Childs, T. (1979) Cold Turkey. New York: Harper & Row.

Choay, F. (1970-1971) "Remarques a-propos de semiologie urbaine." Architecture d'Aujourd 'hui 42 (December/January): 9-10.

Chudacoff, H. P. (1972) Mobile Americans. New York: Oxford University Press.

———(1973) "A new look: residential despersion and the concept of visibility in a medium-sized city." Journal of American History 60 (June): 77-91.

Clarke, D. L. (1968) Analytical Archaeology. London: Methuen.

Collier, J. (1967) Visual Anthropology. New York: Holt, Rinehart & Winston.

Cook, M. (1971) Interpersonal Perception. New York: Penguin.

Cooper, C. (1971) The House as Symbol of Self. Working Paper 120. Berkeley: Institute of Urban and Regional Development, University of California.

———(1978) "The emotional content of house/self relationships," part 2, p. 419 in R. L. Brauer (ed.) Priorities for Environmental Design Research: EDRA 8. Washington, DC: EDRA.

Cowburn, W. (1966) "Popular housing." Arena: Journal of the Architectural Association of London (September/October).

Craik, K. H. and E. H. Zube [eds.] (1976) Perceiving Environmental Quality. New York: Plenum.

Crowe, J. (1979) Close to Death. New York: Dodd, Mead.

Crumrine, N. R. (1964) The House Cross of the Mayo Indians of Sonora, Mexico: A Symbol of Ethnic Identity. Anthropology Paper 8. Tucson: University of Arizona.

———(1977) The Mayo Indians of Sonora. Tucson: University of Arizona Press.

Cuisenier, J. (1970) "Une tente turque d'Anatolie centrale." L'Homme 10 (April/June): 59-72.

Cunningham, C. E. (1973) "Order in the Atoni house," pp. 204-238 in R. Needham (ed.) Right and Left. Chicago: University of Chicago Press.

Daniel, T. C. et al. (n.d.) "Quantitative evaluation of landscapes: an application of signal detection analysis to forest management alternatives." (mimeo)

da Rocha Filho, J. (1979) "Architectural meaning: the built environment as an expression of social values and relations." Master's thesis, University of Wisconsin—Milwaukee.

Darwin, C. (1872) The Expression of the Emotions in Man and Animals. London: John Murray.

Davis, G. and R. Roizen (1970) "Architectural determinants of student satisfaction in college residence halls," pp. 28-44 in J. Archea and C. Eastman (eds.) EDRA 2. Pittsburgh: Carnegie-Mellon University.

Davis, M. [ed.] (1972) Understanding Body Movement: An Annotated Bibliography. New York: Arno.

Deetz, J. (1968) "Cultural patterning of behavior as reflected by archaeological materials," pp. 31-42 in K. C. Chang (ed.) Settlement Archaeology. Palo Alto, CA: National Press.

De Long, A. J. (1970) "Dominance in territorial relations in a small group." Environment and Behavior 2 (September): 170-191.

———(1974) "Kinesic signals at utterance boundaries in preschool children." Semiotica 11, 1.

———(1978) "Context, structures and relationships," pp. 187-214 in A. H. Esser and B. Greenbie (eds.) Designing for Communality and Privacy. New York: Plenum.

Desor, J. A. (1972) "Towards a psychological theory of crowding." Journal of Personality and Social Psychology 21, 1: 79-83.

Di Matteo, M. R. (1979) "A social-psychological analysis of physician-patient rapport: toward a science of the art of medicine." Journal of Social Issues 35, 1: 12-33.

Douglas, M. (1972) "Symbolic orders in the use of domestic space," pp. 513-522 in P. J. Ucko et al. (eds.) Man, Settlement and Urbanism. London: Duckworth.

———(1973a) Natural Symbols. New York: Vintage.

———[ed.] (1973b) Rules and Meanings. New York: Penguin.

———(1974) "Deciphering a meal," pp. 61-81 in C. Geertz (ed.) Myth, Symbol and Culture. New York: W. W. Norton.

———(1975) Implicit Meanings: Essays in Anthropology. London: Routledge & Kegan Paul.

———and Baron Isherwood (1979) The World of Goods. New York: Basic Books.

Duffy, F. (1969) "Role and status in the office." Architectural Association Quarterly 1, 4: 4-14.

————and J. Freedman (1970) "Patterns and semiology," pp. 60-72 in H. Sanoff and S. Cohn (eds.) EDRA 1. Chapel Hill, NC: EDRA.

Duncan, H. D. (1968) Symbols in Society. London: Oxford University Press.

Duncan, J. S. (1973) "Landscape taste as a symbol of group identity." Geographical Review 63 (July): 334-355.

————(1976) "Landscape and the communication of social identity," pp. 391-401 in A. Rapoport (ed.) The Mutual Interaction of People and Their Built Environment. The Hague: Mouton.

————and N. G. Duncan (1976) "Social worlds, status passage and environmental perspectives," pp. 206-213 in G. T. Moore and R. G. Golledge (eds.) Environmental Knowing. Stroudsburg, PA: Dowden, Hutchinson & Ross.

Duncan, S. (1969) "Nonverbal communication." Psychological Bulletin 72 (August): 118-137.

Dunn, S. P. and E. Dunn (1963) "The great Russian peasant: culture change or cultural development." Ethnology 2.

Dunster, D. (1976) "Sign language." Architectural Design 46 (November): 667-669.

Eco, U. (1972) "A componential analysis of the architectural sign." Semiotica 24: 97-117.

————(1973) "Function and sign: semiotics of architecture," pp. 130-153, 200-203 in J. Bryan and R. Sauer (eds.) Structures Implicit and Explicit, Vol. 2. Philadelphia: Falcon.

————(1976) A Theory of Semiotics. Bloomington: Indiana University Press.

Efron, D. (1941) Gesture and Environment. New York: King's Crown. (New edition, 1971. Gesture, Race and Culture. The Hague: Mouton.)

Eibl-Eibesfeld, I. (1970) Ethology: The Biology of Behavior. New York: Holt, Rinehart & Winston.

————(1972) "Similarities and differences between cultures in expressive movements," in R. A. Hinde (ed.) Nonverbal Communication. Cambridge: Cambridge University Press.

————(1979) "Similarities and differences between cultures in expressive movements," pp. 37-48 in S. Weitz (ed.) Nonverbal Communication. New York: Oxford University Press.

Eichler, E. P. and M. Kaplan (1967) The Community Builders. Berkeley: University of California Press.

Eidt, R. C. (1971) Pioneer Settlement in Northeast Argentina. Madison: University of Wisconsin Press.

Ekman, P. (1957) "A methodological discussion of nonverbal behavior." Journal of Psychology 43: 141-149.

————(1965) "Differential communication of affect by head and body cues." Journal of Personality and Social Psychology 2, 2: 726-735.

————(1970) "Universal facial expressions of emotion." California Mental Health Research Digest 8 (Autumn): 151-158.

————(1972) "Universals and cultural differences in facial expressions of emotion," in J. Cole (ed.) Nebraska Symposium on Motivation. Lincoln: University of Nebraska Press.

————(1976) "Movements with precise meanings." Journal of Communication 26 (Summer): 14-26.

————(1977) "Biological and cultural contributions to body and facial movement," pp. 39-84 in J. Blacking (ed.) The Anthropology of the Body. London: Academic.

————(1978) "Facial signs: facts, fantasies and possibilities," pp. 124-156 in T. Sebeok (ed.) Sight, Sound and Sense. Bloomington: Indiana University Press.

————and W. V. Friesen (1967) "Head and body cues in the judgement of emotion: a reformulation." Perceptual and Motor Skills 24: 711-724.

————(1968) "Nonverbal behavior in psychotherapy research." Research in Psychotherapy 3: 179-216.

————(1969a) "Nonverbal leakage and clues to deception." Psychiatry 32 (February): 88-105.

————(1969b) "The repertoire of non-verbal behavior: categories, origins, usage and coding." Semiotica 1, 1: 49-98.

————(1971) "Constants across cultures in the face and emotion." Journal of Personality and Social Psychology 17, 2: 124-129.

————(1972) "Hand movements." Journal of Communication 22 (December): 353-374.

————(1974a) "Nonverbal behavior and psychopathology," pp. 203-232 in R. J. Friedman and M. M. Katz (ed.) The Psychology of Depression: Contemporary Theory and Research. Washington, DC: Winston & Sons.

————(1974b) "Detecting deception from the body or face." Journal of Personality and Social Psychology 29, 3: 288-298.

————(1975) Unmasking the Face. Englewood Cliffs, NJ: Prentice-Hall.

————(1976) "Measuring facial movement." Environmental Psychology and Nonverbal Behavior 1 (Fall): 56-75.

————and P. Ellsworth (1972) Emotion in the Human Face. New York: Pergamon.

Ekman P., W. V. Friesen, and K. R. Scherer (1976) "Body movement and voice pitch in deceptive interaction." Semiotica 16, 1: 23-37.

Ekman, P., W. V. Friesen, and S. S. Tomkins (1971) "Facial affect scoring technique: a first validity study." Semiotica 3, 1: 37-58.

Ekman, P., E. R. Sorenson, and W. V. Friesen (1969) "Pan-cultural elements in facial displays of emotion." Science 164 (April): 86-88.

El Guindi, F. and H. A. Selby (1976) "Dialectics in Zapotec thinking," pp. 181-196 in K. H. Basso and H. A. Selby (eds.) Meaning in Anthropology. Albuquerque: University of New Mexico Press.

Ellis, W. R., Jr. (1972) "Planning, design and black community style: the problem of occasion-adequate space," in W. Mitchell (ed.) Environmental Design: Research and Practice (EDRA 3). Los Angeles: University of California, Los Angeles.

————(1974) "The environment of human relations: perspectives and problems." Journal of Architectural Education 27 (June): 11ff.

Ermuth, F. (1974) Satisfaction and Urban Environmental Preferences. Downsview, Ontario: Atkinson College, York University.

Esber, G. S. (1972) "Indian housing for Indians." The Kiva 37 (Spring): 141-147.

Fathy, H. (1973) Architecture for the Poor. Chicago: University of Chicago Press.

Fauque, R. (1973) "Pour une nouvelle approche semiologique de la ville." Espaces et Societés 9 (July): 15-27.

Fernandez, J. W. (1971) "Persuasions and performances: of the beast in everybody . . . and the metaphors of every man," pp. 39-60 in C. Geertz (ed.) Myth, Symbol and Culture. New York: W. W. Norton.

————(1974) "The mission of metaphor in expressive culture." Current Anthropology 15 (June): 119-145.

————(1977) Fang Architectonics. Working Paper 1. Philadelphia: Institute for the Study of Human Issues.

Fernea, R. A. et al. (1973) Nubians in Egypt. Austin: University of Texas Press.

Firey, W. (1961) "Sentiment and symbolism as ecological variables," pp. 253-261 in G. A. Theodorson (ed.) Studies in Human Ecology. Evanston, IL: Row, Peterson.

Firth, R. W. (1973) Symbols: Public and Private. Ithaca, NY: Cornell University Press.

Flannery, K. V. (1976) "Contextual analysis of ritual paraphernalia from formative Oaxaca," pp. 333-344 in K. V. Flannery (ed.) The Early Mesoamerican Village. New York: Academic.

Fleming, A. (1972) "Vision and design: approaches to ceremonial monument typology." Man 7, 1: 57-73.

Foddy, W. H. (1977) "The use of common residential area open space in Australia." Ekistics 43 (February): 81-83.

Fox, R. (1970) "The cultural animal." Encounter 35 (July): 34-42.

Francescato, G. et al. (1979) Residents' Satisfaction in HUD-Assisted Housing: Design and Management Factors. Washington, DC: U.S. Department of Housing and Urban Development.

Frederiksen, N. (1974) "Toward a taxonomy of situations," pp. 29-44 in R. H. Moos and P. M. Insel (eds.) Issues in Social Ecology: Human Milieus. Palo Alto, CA: National Press.

Friedman, H. S. (1979) "Nonverbal communication between patients and medical practitioners." Journal of Social Issues 35, 1: 82-99.

Geertz, C. (1966a) Person, Time and Conduct in Bali. New Haven, CT: Yale University Press.

————(1966b) "Religion as a cultural system," pp. 1-46 in M. Banton (ed.) Anthropological Approaches to the Study of Religion. New York: Praeger.

————[ed.] (1971) Myth, Symbol and Culture. New York: W. W. Norton.

Ghosh, B. and K. C. Mago (1974) "Srirangam: urban form and pattern in an ancient Indian town." Ekistics 38: 377-384.

Gibson, J. J. (1950) The Perception of the Visual World. Boston: Houghton Mifflin.

————(1968) The Senses Considered as Perceptual Systems. London: Allen & Unwin.

————(1977) "The theory of affordance," in R. Shaw and J. Bransford (eds.) Perceiving, Acting and Knowing. New York: Halsted.

Giglioli, P. P. [ed.] (1972) Language and Social Context. New York: Penguin.

Ginsberg, Y. (1975) Jews in a Changing Neighborhood. New York: Macmillan.

Giteau, M. (1976) The Civilization of Angkor. New York: Rizzoli.

Glass, B. (1978) "Southern Mill hills: design in a 'public' place," pp. 138-149 in D. Swaim (ed.) Carolina Dwelling: Towards Preservation of Place: Celebration of the North Carolina Vernacular Landscape. Student Publication 26. Raleigh: School of Design, North Carolina State University.

Goffman, E. (1959) The Presentation of Self in Everyday Life. Garden City, NY: Doubleday.

————(1963) Behavior in Public Places: Notes on the Social Organization of Gatherings. New York: Macmillan.

Goldberg, F. J. and J. R. Stabler (1973) "Black and white symbolism in Japan." International Journal of Symbology 4 (November): 37-46.

Goldman, I. (1975) The Mouth of Heaven: An Introduction to Kwakiutl Religious Thought. New York: John Wiley.

Goodenough, W. G. (1957) "Cultural anthropology and linguistics," pp. 167-173 in P. L. Garvin (ed.) Report of the 7th Annual Round Table Meeting on Linguistics and Language Study. Washington, DC: Georgetown University.

Goodman, P. (1959) "The meaning of functionalism." Journal of Architectural Education 14 (Autumn). (Reprinted in RIBA Journal [1973] 80 [February]: 32-38.)

Greenfield, P., L. Reich, and R. Olver (1972) "On culture and equivalence," pp. 217-235 in P. Adams (ed.) Language and Thinking. New York: Penguin.

Greimas, A. J. et al. (1970) Sign-Language-Culture. The Hague: Mouton.

Griaule, M. and G. Dieterlen (1954) "The Dogon," pp. 83-110 in D.Forde (ed.) African Worlds: Studies in the Cosmological Ideas and Social Values of African Peoples. Oxford: Oxford University Press.

Groat, L. N. (1979) 'A study of meaning in contemporary architecture: do post-contemporary buildings really exist for anyone besides architectural critics?" Master's thesis, University of Surrey.

———and D. Canter (1979) "Does post-modernism communicate?" Progressive Architecture (December): 84-87.

Gumperz, J. J. and D. Hymes [eds.] (1972) Directions in Sociolinguistics: The Ethnography of Communication. New York: Holt, Rinehart & Winston.

Hall, E. T. (1961) The Silent Language. Greenwich, CT: Fawcett.

———(1966) The Hidden Dimension. Garden City, NY: Doubleday.

———(1976) Beyond Culture. Garden City, NY: Doubleday.

Hamburg, D. A. (1975) "Ancient man in the twentieth century," in V. Goodall (ed.) The Quest for Man. New York: Praeger.

Hammond, N. (1972) "The planning of a Maya ceremonial center." Scientific American 226 (May): 82-91.

Harper, R. G., A. N. Wiens, and J. D. Matarazzo (1978) Nonverbal Communication: The State of the Art. New York: John Wiley.

Hayward, D. G. (1978) "An overview of psychological concepts of home," pp. 418-419 in R. L. Brauer (ed.) Priorities for Environmental Design Research, Part 2: Workshop Summaries. EDRA 8. Washington, DC: EDRA.

Hazard, J. (1972) "Furniture arrangement as a symbol of judicial roles," pp. 291-298 in R. Gutman (ed.) People and Buildings. New York: Basic Books.

Healan, D. M. (1977) "Architectural implications of daily life in ancient Tollán, Hidalgo, Mexico." World Archaeology 9 (October): 140-156.

Herbert, G. (1975) Martienssen and the International Style. Capetown and Rotterdam: A. A. Balkema.

Hill, A. D. (1964) The Changing Landscape of a Mexican Municipio: Villa Las Rosas, Chiapas. Research Paper 91. Chicago: Department of Geography, University of Chicago.

Hillman, J. (1976) "The £450m. cut in standards." The Guardian (February 16).

Hinde, R. A. [ed.] (1972) Non-Verbal Communication. Cambridge: Cambridge University Press.

Hiz, H. (1977) "Logical basis of semiotics," pp. 40-53 in T. A. Sebeok (ed.) A Perfusion of Signs. Bloomington: Indiana University Press.

Hodges, H.W.M. (1972) "Domestic building materials and ancient settlements," pp. 523-530 in P. Ucko et al. (eds.) Man, Settlement and Urbanism. London: Duckworth.

Hoffman, G. and J. A. Fishman (1971) "Life in the neighborhood: a factor-analytic study of Puerto Rican males in the New York Area." International Journal of Comparative Sociology 12 (June): 85-100.

Holdsworth, D. W. (1975) "House and home in Vancouver." Presented at the British-Canadian Symposium on Historical Geography, Kingston, Ontario, September. (mimeo)

Hole, V. (1977) "Local housing strategies." BRE News 40 (Summer): 2-5.

Howard, W. A. et al. (1974) Residential Environmental Quality in Denver Utilizing Remote Sensing Techniques. Denver: Department of Geography, University of Denver.

Hull, R. W. (1976) Africian Cities and Towns Before the European Conquest. New York: W. W. Norton.

Hymes, D. [ed.] (1964) Language in Culture and Society. New York: Harper & Row.

Ilan, Z. (1978) "Bosnian settlers in the Plain of Sharon." Israel Land and Nature 3 (Spring): 102.

Ingham, J. M. (1971) "Time and space in ancient Mexico: the symbolic dimension of clanship." Man 6, 4: 615-629.

International Bibliography on Semiotics (1974) in Vs. Quaderni di Studi Semiotici, Vols. 8-9.

Isbell, W. H. (1978) "The prehistoric ground drawings of Peru." Scientific American 238 (October): 140-153.

Ittelson, W. H. (1960) "Some factors influencing the design and function of psychiatric facilities." Brooklyn College, Department of Psychology.

Jaanus, H. and B. Nieuwenhuijse (1978) "Determinants of housing preference in a small town," pp. 252-274 in A. H. Esser and B. B. Greenbie (eds.) Design for Communality and Privacy. New York: Plenum.

Jackovics, T. W. and T. F. Saarinen (n.d.) "The sense of place: impressions of Tucson and Phoenix, Arizona." (mimeo)

Jackson, J. B. (1951) "Ghosts at the door." Landscape 1 (Autumn): 3-9.

James, J. (1973) "Sacred geometry on the island of Bali." Journal of the Royal Asiatic Society: 141-154.

———(1978) "Significance in sacred sites: the churches around Positano." Annals of Science 35: 103-130.

James, L. D. et al. (1974) Community Well-Being as a Factor in Urban Land Use Planning. Atlanta: Environmental Resources Center, Georgia Institute of Technology.

Janz, W. (1978) "The extension of self into house fronts." Term paper, University of Wisconsin—Milwaukee.

Jencks, C. (1977) The Language of Post-Modernist Architecture. New York: Rizzoli.

———(1980) "The architectural sign," pp. 71-118 in G. Broadbent et al. (eds.) Signs, Symbols and Architecture. Chichester: John Wiley.

———and G. Baird [eds.] (1969) Meaning in Architecture. London: Barrie & Rockliffe.

Jett, S. C. (1978) "The origins of Navajo settlement patterns." Annals, Association of American Geographers 68 (September): 351-362.

Johnson, H. G., P. Ekman, and W. V. Friesen (1975) "Communicative body movements: American emblems." Semiotica 15, 4: 335-353.

Johnston, R. J. (1971a) Urban Residential Patterns. London: George Bell.

———(1971b) "Mental maps of the city: surburban preference patterns." Environment and Planning 3: 63-69.

Joiner, D. (1971a) "Office territory." New Society (October 7): 660-663.
———(1971b) "Social ritual and architectural space." RIBA Journal of Research and Teaching 1 (April): 11-22.
Jopling, C. F. (1974) "Aesthetic behavior as an adaptive strategy." Presented at the XLI Congreso Internacional de Americanistas, Mexico, D. F., September 2-7. (mimeo)
Kamau, L. J. (1976) "Conceptual patterns in Yoruba culture," pp. 333-364 in A. Rapoport (ed.) The Mutual Interaction of People and Their Built Environment. The Hague: Mouton.
———(1978/79) "Semi-public, private and hidden rooms: symbolic aspects of domestic space in urban Kenya." African Urban Studies 3, 105-115.
Kaplan, P. P. (1975) "The symbolism of color." Intenational Journal of Symbology 6 (March): 1-9.
Kaufman, L. (1971) "Tacesics, the study of touch: a model for proxemic analysis." Semiotica 4, 2: 149-161.
Kearney, M. (1972) The Winds of Ixtepeji: World View and Society in a Zapotec Town. New York: Holt, Rinehart & Winston.
Keesing, R. M. (1979) "Linguistic knowledge and cultural knowledge: some doubts and speculations." American Anthropologist 81: 14-36.
Kelly, G. (1955) The Psychology of Personal Constructs. New York: W. W. Norton.
Kendon, A., R. M. Harris, and M. R. Key [eds.] (1975) Organization of Behavior in Face to Face Interaction. The Hague: Mouton.
Kimber, C. (1966) "Dooryard gardens of Martinique." Yearbook, Association of Pacific Coast Gardeners 28: 97-118.
———(1971) "Interpreting the use of space in dooryard gardens: a Puerto Rican example." (mimeo)
——1973) "Spatial patterning in the dooryard gardens of Puerto Rico." Geographical Review 63 (January): 6-26.
King, A. D. (1977) "The westernization of domestic architecture in India." Art and Archaeology Research Papers (June): 32-41.
Knobel, L. (1979) "The tragedy of Bentley Wood." Architectural Review 166,993: 275, 310-311.
Koestler, A. (1964) The Act of Creation. New York: Macmillan.
Kottack, C. P. (1979) "Rituals at McDonald's." Natural History 87 (January): 75ff.
Krampen, M. (1979) Meaning in the Urban Environment. London: Pion.
Krauss, R. M. and S. Glucksberg (1977) "Social and non-social speech." Scientific American 236 (February): 100-105.
Kuper, H. (1972) "The language of sites in the politics of space." American Anthropologist 74 (June): 411-425.
Ladd, F. (1972) "Black youths view their environment: some views on housing." AIP Journal 38 (March): 108-116.
———(1976) Residential History: A Personal Element in Planning and Environmental Design. Urban Planning, Policy Analysis, and Administration Policy Note P76-2. Cambridge, MA: Harvard University, Department of City and Regional Planning.
Lamb, M. E., S. J. Suomi, and G. R. Stephenson [eds.] (1979) Social Interaction Analysis: Methodological Issues. Madison: University of Wisconsin Press.
Lamphere, L. (1969) "Symbolic elements in Navajo ritual." Southwestern Journal of Anthropology 25 (Autumn): 279-305.

Landsberg, M. E. (1980) "The icon in semiotic theory." Current Anthropology 21 (February): 93-95.

Lannoy, R. (1971) The Speaking Tree: A Study of Indian Culture and Society. London: Oxford University Press.

Largey, G. P. and D. R. Watson (1972) "The sociology of odors." American Journal of Sociology 77 (May): 1021-1034.

Lawton, M. P. (1970) "Planning environments for older people." AIP Journal 36: 124-129.

Leach, E. (1972) "The influence of cultural context on non-verbal communication in man," in R. A. Hinde (ed.) Nonverbal Communication. Cambridge: Cambridge University Press.

———(1976) Culture and Communication: The Logic by Which Symbols Are Connected. Cambridge: University Press.

Lee, D. (1969a) "The Nubian house: persistence of a cultural tradition." Landscape 18 (Winter): 36-39.

———(1969b) "Village morphology and growth in Northern Sudan." Proceedings, Association of American Geographers 1: 80-84.

———(1969c) "Factors influencing choice of house type: a geographic analysis from the Sudan." Professional Geographer 21 (November): 393-397.

———(1974) "Geographical Record: Africa." Geographical Review 64, 4: 577-579.

Leeming, F. (1977) Street Studies in Hong Kong: Localities in a Chinese City. Hong Kong: Oxford University Press.

Leone, M. P. (1973) "Archaeology as the science of technology: Mormon town plans and fences," pp. 125-150 in C. L. Redman (ed.) Research and Theory in Current Archaeology. New York: John Wiley.

Lévi-Strauss, C. (1957) Tristes Tropiques. Paris: Plon.

Levin, M. D. (1971) "House form and social structure in Bakosi," pp. 143-152 in P. Oliver (ed.) Shelter in Africa. London: Barrie & Jenkins.

Ley, D. and R. Cybriwski (1974) "Urban graffiti as territorial markers." Annals, Association of American Geographers 64 (December): 491-505.

Littlejohn, J. (1967) "The Temne house," pp. 331-347 in J. Middleton (ed.) Myth and Cosmos. Garden City, NY: Natural History Press.

Lloyd, B. B. (1972) Perception and Cognition: A Cross-Cultural Perspective. New York: Penguin.

Lofland, L. H. (1973) A World of Strangers: Order and Action in Urban Public Space. New York: Basic Books.

Lowenthal, D. (1968) "The American scene." Geographical Review 58, 1: 61-88.

———and H. C. Prince (1964) "The English landscape." Geographical Review 54, 3: 309-346.

———(1965) "English landscape tastes." Geographical Review 55, 2: 186-222.

McCully, R. S. (1971) Rorschach Theory and Symbolism. Baltimore: Williams & Wilkins.

MacDonald, W. L. (1976) The Pantheon. Cambridge, MA: Harvard University Press.

McLaughlin, H. (1976) "Density: the architect's urban choices and attitudes." Architectural Record (February): 95-100.

McQuillan, D. A. (1978) "Territory and enthnic identity: some new measures of an old theme in the cultural geography of the United States," pp. 136-169 in J. R. Gibson (ed.) European Settlement and Development in North America. Toronto: University of Toronto Press.

Madge, J. (1968) "The social sources of anxiety." Angst 6 (March): 1-4.
Manis, M. (1971) An Introduction to Cognitive Psychology. Belmont, CA: Brooks/ Cole.
Mann, L. (1969) Social Psychology. Sydney: John Wiley.
Manning, J. and L. Aschoff (1980) "Seamy side: a polluted potential." Milwaukee Sentinel (January 2).
Marcus, J. (1973) "Territorial organization of the lowland Maya." Science 180 (June): 911-916.
Marshall, L. (1960) "!Kung Bushman bands." Africa 30 (October): 325-355.
Marx, E. (1976) "Holy tombs as political rallying points among Bedouin of South Sinai." Presented at the ASA Conference on Regional Cults and Oracles, Manchester, England, March-April. (mimeo)
Maslow, A. H. and N. L. Mintz (1956) "Effects of aesthetic surroundings I: initial effects of three aesthetic surroundings upon perceiving 'energy' and 'wellbeing' in faces." Journal of Psychology 41: 247-254.
Mehrabian, A. (1972) Nonverbal Communication. Chicago: Aldine.
Mellaart, J. (1964) "A neolithic city in Turkey." Scientific American 210 (April): 94-104.
———(1967) Çatal Hüyük: A Neolithic Town in Anatolia. London: Thames & Hudson.
Memmott, P. C. (1979) "Lardil properties of place: an ethnological study in man-environment relations." Ph.D. dissertation, University of Queensland.
Metcalf, J. (1977) "Standards for older housing and its surroundings." BRE News 40 (Summer): 6-10.
Michelin, R. L. et al. (1976) "Effects of seating arrangement on group participation." Journal of Social Psychology 99: 174-186.
Michelson, W. and P. Reed (1970) The Theoretical Status and Operational Usage of Lifestyle in Environmental Research. Research Paper 36. Toronto: Center for Urban and Community Studies, University of Toronto.
Milgram, S. (1970) "The experience of living in cities." Science 167 (March): 1461-1468.
Miller, G. A. (1956) "The magical number seven plus or minus two: some limits on our capacity for processing information." Psychological Review 63: 81-97.
———and P. N. Johnson-Laird (1976) Language and Perception. Cambridge, MA: Belknap.
Milwaukee Journal (1973) "Homeowner wants a different view." September 26.
———(1976) "Is the living room on the way out?" November 21.
———(1979) "Court says blocking street would be 'badge of slavery." November 6.
Milwaukee Sentinel (1978) "Residents disagree on bicycle path." March. 1.
Miner, H. (1956) "Body ritual among the Nacirema." American Anthropologist 58: 503-507.
Mintz, N. L. (1956) "Effects of aesthetic surroundings II: prolonged and repeated experiences in a 'beautiful' and an 'ugly' room." Journal of Psychology 41: 459-466.
Molloy, J. T. (1976) "Which twin gets the best job?" Milwaukee Journal (November 21).
Moos, R. H. (1974) "Systems for the assessment and classification of human environments: an overview," pp. 5-28 in R. H. Moos and P. M. Insel (eds.) Issues in Social Ecology: Human Milieus. Palo Alto, CA: National Press Books.

Morris, D., P. Collett, P. Marsh, and M. O'Shaughnessy (1979) Gestures: Their Origins and Distribution. New York: Stein & Day.

Moss, L. (1965) "Space and direction in the Chinese garden." Landscape 14 (Spring): 29-33.

Müller, R. (1961) Die Heilige Stadt: Roma Quadrata, Himmlisches Jerusalem und di Mythe des Weltnabel. Stuttgart: Kohlhanner.

Murch, G. M. (1973) Visual and Auditory Perception. Indianapolis: Bobbs-Merrill.

Needham, R. [ed.] (1973) Right and Left: Essays on Symbolic Classification. Chicago: University of Chicago Press.

Neisser, U. (1967) Cognitive Psychology. Englewood Cliffs, NJ: Prentice-Hall.

Nesbitt, P. D. and G. Steven (1974) "Personal space and stimulus intensity at a Southern California amusement park." Sociometry 37, 1: 105-115.

Neville, G. K. (1979) "Community form and ceremonial life in three regions of Scotland." American Ethnologist 6 (February): 93-109.

New Jersey County and Municipal Government Planning Commission (1974) Housing and Suburbs. Trenton: Author.

Newman, O. (1971) Crime Prevention Through Architectural Design. Washington, DC: U.S. Department of Justice, Law Enforcement Assistance Administration.

New York Times (1975) "Verdicts linked to speech style: anthropologists say patterns influence juries." December 14.

Nicolson, M. H. (1959) Mountain Gloom and Mountain Glory. Ithaca, NY: Cornell University Press.

Norcross, C. (1973) Townhouses and Condominiums: Residents' Likes and Dislikes. Washington, DC: Urban Land Institute.

Ohnuki-Tierney, E. (1972) "Spatial concepts of the Ainu of the northwest coast of Southern Sakhalin." American Anthropologist 74 (June): 426-457.

Olver, R. and J. Hornsby (1972) "On equivalence," pp. 306-320 in P. Adams (ed.) Language in Thinking. New York: Penguin.

Ortiz, A. (1972) "Ritual drama and the Pueblo world view," in A. Ortiz (ed.) New Perspectives on the Pueblos. Albuquerque: University of New Mexico Press.

Osgood, C., G. Suci, and P. Tannenbaum (1957) The Measurement of Meaning. Urbana: University of Illinois Press.

Peach, C. [ed.] (1975) Urban Social Segregation. London: Longman.

Peckham, M. (1976) Man's Rage for Chaos: Biology, Behavior and the Arts. New York: Schocken.

Perin, C. (1977) Everything in Its Place: Social Order and Landuse in America. Princeton, NJ: Princeton University Press.

Perinbanayagam, R. S. (1974) "The definition of the situation: an analysis of the ethnomethodological and dramaturgical view." Sociological Quarterly 15 (Autumn): 521-541.

Peterson, G. L. (1967a) "A model of preference: quantitative analysis of the perception of residential neighborhoods." Journal of Regional Science 7, 1: 19-31.

———(1967b) "Measuring visual preferences of residential neighborhoods." Ekistics 27 (March): 169-173.

———and R. D. Worrall (1969) "On a theory of accessibility preference for selected neighborhood services." Presented at the Joint National Meeting, Operations Research Society (35th Annual Meeting)/American Astronautical Society (15th National Meeting), June. (mimeo)

Pétonnet, C. (1972a) "Reflexions au sujet de la ville vue par en dessous." l'Annee Sociologique 21: 151-185.

———(1972b) "Espace, distance et dimension dans une societé musulmane." l'Homme 12 (June): 47-84.

Piwoni, J. (1976) "Forms of urban plazas in the U.S." Term paper, University of Wisconsin—Milwaukee.

Plant, J. (1930) "Some psychiatric aspects of crowded living conditions." Journal of Psychiatry 9, 5: 849-868.

Poyatos, F. (1976) "Analysis of a culture through its culturemes: theory and method," pp. 265-274 in A. Rapoport (ed.) The Mutual Interaction of People and Their Built Environment. The Hague: Mouton.

Pred, A. (1963) "Business thoroughfares as expressions of urban Negro culture." Economic Geography 39 (July): 217-233.

Preziosi, D. (1979) The Semiotics of the Built Environment: An Introduction to Architectonic Analysis. Bloomington: Indiana University Press.

Prussin, L. (1972) "West African mud granaries." Paideuma 18: 144-169.

Rainwater, L. (1966) "Fear and house-as-haven in the lower class." AIP Journal 32 (January): 23-31.

Rapoport, A. (1964-1965) "The architecture of Isphahan." Landscape 14 (Winter): 4-11.

———(1967a) "Some consumer comments on a designed environment." Arena: Journal of the Architectural Association of London 82 (January): 176-178.

———(1967b) "Whose meaning in architecture?" Interbuild/Arena (Architectural Association, London), Interbuild 14, 10; Arena 83 (October): 44-46.

———(1968a) "The personal element in housing—an argument for open-ended design." Journal of the Royal Institute of British Architects (July): 300-307.

———(1968b) "Sacred space in primitive and vernacular architecture." Liturgical Arts 36 (February): 36-40.

———(1969a) "The notion of urban relationships." Area: Journal of the Institute of British Geographers 1, 3: 17-26.

———(1969b) "An approach to the study of environmental quality," pp. 1-3 in H. Sanoff and S. Cohn (eds.) EDRA 1. Chapel Hill, NC: EDRA.

———(1969c) House Form and Culture. Englewood Cliffs, NJ: Prentice-Hall.

———(1969d) "Facts and models," pp. 136-146 in G. Broadbent and A. Ward (eds.) Design Methods in Architecture. London: Lund Humphries.

———(1969e) "Some aspects of the organization of urban space," pp. 121-139 in G. J. Coates and K. M. Moffett (eds.) Responses to Environment. Raleigh: School of Design, North Carolina State University.

———(1970a) "The study of spatial quality." Journal of Aesthetic Education 4 (October): 81-96.

———(1970b) "Symbolism and environmental design." International Journal of Symbology 1, 3: 1-9. (Reprinted, Journal of Architectural Education 27, 4 [1975]; partly summarized, Ekistics 39, 232 [1975].)

———(1972) "Environment and people," pp. 3-21 in A. Rapoport (ed.) Australia as Human Setting. Sydney: Angus & Robertson.

———(1973) "Images, symbols and popular design." International Journal of Symbology 4, 3: 1-12. (Summarized, Ekistics 39, 232 [1975].)

———(1975a) "Australian Aborigines and the definition of place, pp. 7-37 in P. Oliver (ed.) Shelter, Sign and Symbol. London: Barrie & Jenkins.

———(1975b) "An 'anthropological' approach to environmental design research," pp. 145-151 in B. Honikman (ed.) Responding to Social Change: EDRA 6. Stroudsburg, PA: Dowden, Hutchinson & Ross.

———(1975c) "Towards a redefinition of density." Environment and Behavior 7 (June): 133-158.

———(1976a) "Environmental cognition in cross-cultural perspective," pp. 220-234 in G. T. Moore and R. G. Gollege (eds.) Environmental Knowing. Stroudsburg, PA: Dowden, Hutchinson & Ross.

———(1976b) "Socio-cultural aspects of man-environment studies," pp. 7-35 in A. Rapoport (ed.) The Mutual Interaction of People and Their Built Environment. The Hague: Mouton.

———(1977) Human Aspects of Urban Form. Oxford: Pergamon.

———(1978a) "The environment as an enculturating medium," Part 1, pp. 54-58 in S. Weidemann and J. R. Anderson (eds.) Priorities for Environmental Design Research: EDRA 8. Washington, DC: EDRA.

———(1978b) "Culture and the subjective effects of stress." Urban Ecology 3: 241-261.

———(1978c) "Nomadism as a man-environment system." Environment and Behavior 10 (June): 215-247.

———(1979a) "On the cultural origins of architecture," pp. 2-20 in J. C. Snyder and A. J. Catanese (eds.) Introduction to Architecture. New York: McGraw-Hill.

———(1979b) "On the cultural origins of settlements," pp. 31-61 in A. J. Catanese and J. C. Synder (eds.) Introduction to Urban Planning. New York: McGraw-Hill.

———(1979c) "An approach to designing Third World environments." Third World Planning Review 1, 1: 23-40.

———(1979d) "Review of Perin's Everything in Its Place." Journal of Architectural Research 7 (March).

———(1979e) "On the environment and the definition of the situation." International Architect 1, 1: 26-28.

———(1980a) "Toward a cross-culturally valid definition of housing," pp. 310-316 in R. R. Stough and A. Wandersman (eds.) Optimizing Environments: Research, Practice and Policy: EDRA 11. Washington, DC: EDRA.

———(1980b) "Vernacular architecture and the cultural determinants of form," in A. D. King (ed.) Buildings and Society: Essays on the Social Development of the Built Environment. London: Routledge & Kegan Paul.

———(1980c) "Cross-cultural aspects of environmental design," in I. Altman et al. (eds.) Environment and Culture. New York: Plenum.

———(1980-1981) "Neighborhood heterogeneity or homogeneity." Architecture and Behavior 1, 1: 65-77.

———(1981) "Identity and environment: a cross-cultural perspective," in J. S. Duncan (ed.) Housing and Identity: Cross-Cultural Perspectives. London: Croom-Helms.

———(1982) "Urban design and human systems—on ways of relating buildings to urban fabric," pp. 161-184 in P. Laconte et al. (eds.) Human and Energy Factors in Urban Planning: A Systems Approach. The Hague: Nijhoff.

—––(1983) "The effect of environment on behavior," pp. 200-201 in J. B. Calhoun (ed.) Environment and Population: Problems of Adaptation. New York: Praeger.

—––and N. Watson (1972) "Cultural variability in physical standards," pp. 33-53 in R. Gutman (ed.) People and Buildings. New York: Basic Books.

—––(forthcoming) "Defining vernacular design," in M. Turan (ed.) On Vernacular Architecture: Paradigms of Environmental Response. Aldershott, Eng.: Gower.

Raymond, H. et al. (1966) L'Habitat Pavillonnaire. Paris: Centre de Recherche d'Urbanisme.

Reed, P. (1974) "Situated interaction: normative and non-normative bases of social behavior in two urban residential settings." Urban Life and Culture 2 (January): 460-487.

Rees, D. W., L. Williams, and H. Giles (1974) "Dress style and symbolic meaning." International Journal of Symbology 5 (March): 1-8.

Relph, E. (1976) Place and Placelessness. London: Pion.

Reser, J. (1977) "The dwelling as motif in Aboriginal bark painting," pp. 210-219 in P. J. Ucko (ed.) Form in Indigenous Art. Canberra, Australia: Institute of Aboriginal Studies.

Richardson, M. (1974) "The Spanish American (Colombian) settlement pattern as a societal expression and as a behavioral cause," pp. 35-51 in H. J. Walker and W. G. Haag (Eds.) Man and Cultural Heritage: Papers in Honor of Fred B.Kniffen. Geoscience and Man, Vol. V. Baton Rouge: School of Geoscience, Louisiana State University.

Richardson, J. and A. L. Kroeber (1940) "Three centuries of women's dress fashions." Anthropological Records 5, 2.

Roach, M. E. and J. B. Eicher [eds.] (1965) Dress, Adornment and the Social Order. New York: John Wiley.

—––(1973) The Visible Self: Perspectives on Dress. Englewood Cliffs, NJ: Prentice-Hall.

Rosch, E. and B. B. Lloyd [eds.] (1978) Cognition and Categorization. Hillsdale, NJ: Lawrence Erlbaum.

Rose, D. M. (1968) "Culture and cognition: some problems and a suggestion." Anthropological Quarterly 41 (January): 9-28.

Rosenthal, R. (1966) Experimenter Effects in Behavioral Research. New York: Appleton-Century-Crofts.

Rossi, A. S. (1977) "A biosocial perspective on parenting." Daedalus 106 (Spring): 1-32.

Royce, J. (1965) Psychology and the Symbol. New York: Random House.

Royse, D. C. (1969) "Social inferences via environmental cues." Ph.D. dissertation, Massachusetts Institute of Technology.

Rubin, B. (1979) "Aesthetic ideology and urban design." Annals, Association of American Geographers 69 (September): 339-361.

Ruesch, J. and W. Kees (1956) Nonverbal Communication: Notes on the Visual Perception of Human Relations. Berkeley: University of California Press.

Rykwert, J. (1976) The Idea of a Town. Princeton, NJ: Princeton University Press.

Sabloff, J. A and W. L. Rathje (1976) "The rise of a Maya merchant class," Scientific American 237 (October): 72-83.

Sadalla, E. K. (1978) "Population size, structural differentiation, and human behavior." Environment and Behavior 10 (June): 271-291.

Sarles, H. (1969) "The study of language and communication across species." Current Anthropology 10, 1-2.

Sauer, L. (1972) "The architect and user needs," pp. 147-170 in W. M. Smith (ed.) Behavior, Design and Policy Aspects of Human Habitats. Green Bay: University of Wisconsin.

———(1977) "Differing fates for two nearly identical housing developments." AIA Journal (February): 26.

Scheflen, A. E. (1972) Body Language and the Social Order. Englewood Cliffs, NJ: Prentice-Hall.

———(1973) The Stream and Structure of Communicational Behavior. Bloomington: University of Indiana Press.

———(1974) How Behavior Means. Garden City, NY: Doubleday.

Schnapper, D. (1971) Italie Rouge et Noire: Les Modèles Culturels de la Vie Quotidienne à Bologne. Paris: Gallimard.

Schneider, D. M. (1976) "Notes toward a theory of culture," pp. 197-220 in K. H. Basso and H. A. Selby (eds.) Meaning in Anthropology. Albuquerque: University of New Mexico Press.

Schroder, J. T. (1976) "The impact of tree removal on neighborhoods." Term paper, University of Wisconsin—Milwaukee.

Scully, V. (1963) The Earth, the Temple and the Gods. New Haven, CT: Yale University Press.

Sebeok, T. A. [ed.] (1977a) A Perfusion of Signs. Bloomington: Indiana University Press.

———[ed.] (1977b) How Animals Communicate. Bloomington: Indiana University Press.

Seligmann, C. (1975) "An aedicular system in an early twentieth century American popular house." Architectural Association Quarterly 7 (April/June): 11-17.

———(1976) "A visit to Denmark: some speculations on symbolic aspects of the environment." Arkitekten (Copenhagen) 78 (April 6).

Shands, H. C. and J. D. Meltzer (1977) "Unexpected semiotic implications of medical inquiry," pp. 77-89 in T. A. Sebeok (ed.) A Perfusion of Signs. Bloomington: Indiana University Press.

Shepard, P. (1969) English Reaction to the New Zealand Landscape Before 1850. Pacific Viewpoint Monograph 4. Wellington: Victoria University.

Sherif, M. and C. W. Sherif (1963) "Varieties of social stimulus situations," pp. 82-106 in S. B. Sells (ed.) Stimulus Determinants of Behavior. New York: Ronald Press.

Siegel, B. J. (1970) "Defensive structuring and environmental stress." American Journal of Sociology 76: 11-46.

Siegman, A. W. and S. Feldstein [eds.] (1978) Nonverbal Behavior and Communication. Hillsdale, NJ: Lawrence Erlbaum.

Simoons, F. J. (1965) "Two Ethiopian gardens." Landscape 14 (Spring): 15-20.

Singh, K. B. and S. K. Chandhoke (1966) "Village housing scheme in Lalgarh—an assessment." Newsletter, Rural Housing Wing, School of Planning and Architecture, University of New Delhi 6 (July).

———(1967) "Bhawanpura research-cum-demonstration project—an assessment." Newsletter, Rural Housing Wing, School of Planning and Architecture, University of New Delhi 7 (January).

Snyder, P. Z., E. K. Sadalla, and D. Stea (1976) "Socio-cultural modifications and user needs in Navajo housing." Journal of Architectural Research 5 (December).
———(1977) "House form and culture revisited," in P. Suedfeld and J. A. Russell (eds.) The Behavioral Basis of Design: EDRA 7. Stroudsburg, PA: Dowden, Hutchinson & Ross.
Sommer, R. (1965) "Further studies in small group ecology." Sociometry 28: 337-348.
———and M. Estabrook (1974) "The colored compass." International Journal of Symbology 5 (July): 37-52.
Sopher, D. (1964) "Landscapes and seasons: man and nature in India." Landscape 13 (Spring): 14-19.
Spiro, M. E. [ed.] (1965) Context and Meaning in Cultural Anthropology. New York: Macmillan.
Spradley, J. P. [ed.] (1972) Culture and Cognition: Rules, Maps and Plans. San Francisco: Chandler.
Stabler, J. R. and F. J. Goldberg (1973) "The black and white symbolic matrix." International Journal of Symbology 4 (July): 27-35.
Stabler, J. R. and E. E. Johnson (1972) "The meaning of black and white to children." International Journal of Symbology 3 (December): 11-21.
Steinitz, C. (1968) "Meaning and congruence of urban form and activity." AIP Journal 34 (July): 233-248.
Stenning, D. J. (1959) Savannah Nomads. Oxford: Oxford University Press.
Stewart, N. R. (1965) "The mark of the pioneer." Landscape 15 (Autumn): 26-28.
Strodtbeck, F. L. and L. H. Hook (1961) "The social dimensions of a twelve man jury table." Sociometry 24: 397-415.
Suchman, R. G. (1966) "Cultural differences in children's color and form preferences." Journal of Social Psychology 70: 3-10.
Suttles, G. D. (1968) The Social Order of the Slum. Chicago: University of Chicago Press.
———(1972) The Social Construction of Communities. Chicago: University of Chicago Press.
Sydney Morning Herald (1972) "London's 'Little Asia.' " September 6.
Swithebank, M. (1969) Ashanti Fetish Houses. Accra: Ghana Universities Press.
Tambiah, S. J. (1973) "Classification of animals in Thailand," pp. 127-166 in M. Douglas (ed.) Rules and Meanings. New York: Penguin.
Taylor, R. et al. (1979) "Towards a resident-based model of community crime prevention: urban territoriality, social networks and design." Center for Metropolitan Planning and Research, Johns Hopkins University. (mimeo)
Thourlby, W. (1980) You Are What You Wear. New York: Signet.
Tiger, L. (1969) Men in Groups. New York: Random House.
———and R. Fox 1(1971) The Imperial Animal. New York: Delta.
Tiger, L. and J. Shepher (1975) Women in the Kibbutz. New York: Harcourt Brace Jovanovich.
Time (1967a) Reynolds Aluminum advertisement, May 5.
———(1967b) September 29: 23.
———(1967c) "Space: quarantine for moon travellers," December 29: 34.
Timms, D. (1971) The Urban Mosaic. Cambridge: Cambridge University Press.
Todd, I. A. (1976) Çatal Hüyük in Perspective. Menlo Park, CA: Cummings.
Trudgill, P. (1974) Sociolinguistics—An Introduction. New York: Penguin.

Tuan, Y. F. (1974) Topophilia. Englewood Cliffs, NJ: Prentice-Hall.
———(1977) Space and Place: The Perspective of Experience. Minneapolis: University of Minnesota Press.
———(1978) "Sign and metaphor." Annals, Association of American Geographers 68 (September): 363-372.
Turnbull, C. M. (1961) The Forest People. London: Reprint Society.
Turner, J. (1967) "Barriers and channels for housing development in modernizing countries." AIP Journal 33 (May).
Turner, V. (1968) Drums of Affliction: A Study of Religious Process Among the Ndembu of Zambia. London: Oxford University Press.
Tyler, S. A. [ed.] (1969) Cognitive Anthropology? New York: Holt, Rinehart & Winston.
Uphill, E. (1972) "The concept of the Egyptian palace as a 'ruling machine,' " pp. 721-734 in P. Ucko et al. (eds.) Man, Settlement and Urbanism. London: Duckworth.
Venturi, R. and D. Rauch (1976) Signs of Life: Symbols in the American City. Publication accompanying exhibition of the same name at the Renwick Gallery of the National Collection of Fine Arts, Smithsonian Institution, Washington, D.C., February-September.
Venturi, R. et al. (1972) Learning from Las Vegas. Cambridge: MIT Press.
———(1976) "A house is more than a home." Progressive Architecture (August): 62-67.
Vogt, E. Z. (1970) "Levi-Strauss among the Maya." Man 5 (September): 379-392.
———(1976) Tortillas for the Gods: A Symbolic Analysis of Zinacanteco Rituals. Cambridge, MA: Harvard University Press.
von Raffler-Engel, W. (1978) "On the structure of non-verbal behavior." Man-Environment Systems 8 (March): 60-66.
von Simson, O. (1953) The Gothic Cathedral. New York: Pantheon.
Wagner, J. (1975) "The sex of time-keeping." International Journal of Symbology 6 (November): 23-30.
———[ed.] (1979) Images of Information: Still Photography in the Social Sciences. Beverly Hills, CA: Sage.
Wallis, M. (1973) "Semantic and symbolic elements in architecture: iconology as a first step towards an architectural semiotic." Semiotica 8, 3: 220-238.
Warr, P. B. and C. Knapper (1968) The Perception of People and Events. London: John Wiley.
Warren, R. M. and R. P. Warren (1970) "Auditory illusions and confusions." Scientific American 223 (December): 30-36.
Webb, E. J. et al. (1966) Unobtrusive Measures: Nonreactive Research in the Social Sciences. Chicago: Rand McNally.
Weick, K. E. (1968) "Systematic observational methods," pp. 357-451 in G. Lindzey (ed.) Handbook of Social Psychology. Reading, MA: Addison-Wesley.
Weisner, T. (1974) "Periodic migration and child behavior." Presented at the Conference on Psychosocial Consequences of Sedentarization of Nomads, UCLA, December 12-14.
Weitz, S. [ed.] (1979) Nonverbal Communication: Readings with Commentary. New York: Oxford University Press.
Wellman, S. (1978) "The boundaries of race: process of ethnicity in England." Man 13 (June): 200-217.

Werthman, C. (1968) "The social meaning of the physical environment." Ph.D. dissertation, University of California, Berkeley.

Wheatley, P. (1971) The Pivot of the Four Quarters. Chicago: Aldine.

Whiting, J.W.M. (1964) "Effects of climate on certain cultural practices," pp. 511-544 in W. H. Goodenough (ed.) Explorations in Cultural Anthropology. New York: McGraw-Hill.

Wilhelm, G. (1975) "Dooryard gardens and gardening in the Black community of Brushy, Texas." Geographical Review 65 (January): 73-92.

Williams, J. E., J. K. Morland, and W. L. Underwood (1970) "Connotations of color names in the U.S., Europe and Asia." Journal of Social Psychology 82 (October): 3-14.

Wittkower, R. (1962) Architectural Principles in the Age of Humanism. London: Tiranti.

Wohlwill, J. F. and I. Kohn (1973) "The environment as experienced by the migrant: an adaptation-level view." Reprints of Research in Social Psychology 4 (January): 135-164.

Wollheim, R. [ed.] (1972) The Image in Form: Selected Writings of Adrian Stokes. New York: Penguin.

Woodburn, J. (1972) "Ecology, nomadic movement and the composition of the local group among hunters and gatherers: an East African example and its implications," pp. 193-206 in P. Ucko et al. (eds.) Man, Settlement and Urbanism. London: Duckworth.

Young, M. and P. Wilmott (1962) Family and Kinship in East London. New York: Penguin.

Zeisel, J. (1973) "Symbolic meaning of space and the physical dimension of social relations," pp. 252-263 in J. Walton and D. E. Carns (eds.) Cities in Change—Studies on the Urban Condition. Boston: Allyn & Bacon.

EPILOGUE

This book was originally published at the end of 1982, though it was completed in 1980. In connection with its reissue it seemed sensible briefly to review the developments in the literature, in other relevant fields, and in my thinking since that time. It also seemed sensible to do so by means of an epilogue so that the book could be brought up to date without rewriting it. This offered not only practical but also conceptual advantages: If it proved possible to add an epilogue without rewriting the book, that would suggest that the basic argument has stood up, and it has in fact proved possible to do so.

Space limitations meant that I had to be selective. This epilogue is therefore limited to three principal themes. First, I summarize and further develop an argument, published in a chapter in 1988, which qualifies and partly modifies some of the argument in Chapter 2. Second, I refer to some more recent work on meaning that seems generally to support, complement, expand, and even strengthen the overall argument of the book. This also serves to update the bibliography with a list of new references, found at the end of the Epilogue. Third, I elaborate, albeit in a very preliminary and brief form, two suggestions that I made almost offhandedly in the original book and that I did not pursue at the time. These concern possible general mechanisms, proposed in other fields, which make more plausible the suggested processes whereby cues in settings guide behavior and whereby global affective responses to environments are primary.

A change in the argument in Chapter 2

The change in Chapter 2 is best seen in the wider context of the possible approaches discussed in that chapter. In it I refer only briefly to method-driven studies of meaning (e.g., the use of semantic differentials, personal constructs, and the like), which have no strong conceptual or theoretical bases (pp. 35–36). Because they are eclectic and fairly straightforward in approach, these can be "claimed" by the nonverbal communication (NVC) approach, even though they never use or even refer to it (e.g., Lee, 1982; Hucek, 1983; Nasar, 1988, 1989). Using the distinction (p. 38) between syntactics, semantics, and pragmatics, one can argue that the "eclectic" approach and NVC essentially address pragmatics (and possibly some semantics), that symbolic approaches essentially deal with semantics, and that semiotics largely deals only with syntactics. Of course, both NVC and symbolic approaches address structure. Context is critical, and as I argue throughout this book, the meaning of elements depends on contexts (both cultural and of other elements) and contrasts and noticeable differences *among* elements. Moreover, the Hymes (1964) model of communication (p. 52 above) can be reduced to a minimal set that *all* sound approaches to meaning, however identified, share: sender, receiver, channel, and context.

Following the brief mention of method-driven approaches, I identify and discuss the three approaches mentioned above: semiotic/linguistic, symbolic, and nonverbal communication. Further consideration of the latter two, stimulated by some questions raised by a student, led me to a rather significant revision (Rapoport, 1988). Two things are involved. The first proposes that the term "meaning" is too global; one needs to distinguish among types or levels of meaning. It follows that built environments, and material culture generally, may communicate *several distinct types of meaning*. Given that, the second change reconsiders the evaluation of symbolic approaches presented on pages 43–48 of this book.

The description and criticism of semiotics, and the linguistic approach from which it derives,[1] still seem valid as written. First, semiotics is even more dominant, and it has become almost synonymous with the study of meaning in the built environment. Almost everyone uses it—or claims to—pays lip service to it, and puts even nonsemiotic work in a semiotic framework or "decorates" the work with references to semiotics. In the text I refer to examples (e.g., Bonta, 1975, 1979; Krampen, 1979) and suggest that in them references to semiotics can be eliminated, and that this not only does not weaken the argument or findings but in fact strengthens them. This also applies, for example, to one study among others that I discuss below (Duncan, Lindsey, and Buchan, 1985), which was originally presented at a semiotics conference and which contains quite unnecessary references to semiotics (see also Lang, 1982). In my copy I have, in fact, crossed out every mention of semiotics and refer to and use the paper frequently.

Second, I still do not know of any good empirical or other study that really uses semiotics to study built environments (but see Gottdiener and Lagopoulos, 1986). This is because, third, as argued in the book, it seems essentially unusable and is almost impossible to understand. I argued (on p. 37) that there had been no advance between 1969 and 1980, and this still seems to be the case (although work is certainly being done and published). At best this approach is stagnating; in fact, it seems to be an exemplar of what Lakatos (1971: 100) calls a "degenerating research program."[2]

In retrospect, however, the criticism of the symbolic approach (pp. 43–48) may need to be qualified in one sense, although it is indeed not useful for understanding users' meanings in everyday environments, the domain of this book. Such meanings are most usefully studied using NVC approaches (particularly because the more general problems with the study of symbols also seem valid). Symbolism, however, may represent a *different type of meaning* that some built environments may communicate, and it may be most relevant regarding those other types of meaning in certain environments. The term "symbolic" refers, then, not so much to an *approach* as to a *distinct type or level of meaning*.

In fact, it seems that one is typically dealing with several distinct levels of meaning, so that "meaning" is too global a term regarding built environments and material culture generally. These seem to communicate meaning at three distinct levels, which need to be clearly distinguished, although they are ideal types structuring a continuum (for analogous cases, see Rapoport, 1977: 37, Fig. 1.13; and Rapoport, in press b: Figs. 2, 3). They are:

(1) "High-level" meanings related to, for example, cosmologies, cultural schemata, worldviews, philosophical systems, and the sacred.
(2) "Middle-level" meanings, those communicating identity, status, wealth, power, and so on—that is, the latent rather than the instrumental aspects of activities, behavior, and settings.
(3) "Low-level" everyday and instrumental meanings: mnemonic cues for identifying uses for which settings are intended and hence the social situations, expected behavior, and the like; privacy, accessibility; penetration gradients; seating arrangements; movement and way-finding; and other information which enables users to behave and act appropriately and predictably, making co-action possible.[3]

This book is concerned primarily with (2) and (3), although unfortunately it does not *explicitly* distinguish between them. Nonverbal models are most useful for the study of these meanings. What I call symbolic approaches may, however, refer to high-level meanings, what they are and how they are communicated; they may need other approaches, although as I will argue later, these still need to be relatively straightforward, and the general approach advocated in this book may still be quite relevant.

There seem to be suggestive links between these levels of meaning and Gibson's (1968) hierarchy ranging from the concrete object through the use object, value object, and symbolic object (p. 15 above and Rapoport, 1977, esp. pp. 19–20). There is also a suggestive and interesting link to Binford's discussion in a number of publications, the first in 1962, of three levels of function: *technomic* (instrumental or technical use), *socio-technic* (use in a social rather than a technical sense), and *ideo-technic* (ideology, symbolism, etc.). However, he restricts "meaning" to the ideo-technic, whereas I propose three levels of meaning.[4]

This point can be elaborated, and many and varied examples can be given of how the same buildings or other settings may communicate all, two, or even just one of these meanings, and how useful this distinction among levels is likely to be; readers are referred to the chapter in question, which also provides relevant references (Rapoport, 1988). Two conclusions should, however, be discussed.

The first is that typically in any given case only a few people know the high-level meanings even in traditional contexts. All, however, need to understand low-level meanings in order to behave appropriately and to co-act. (To make the point, I use a number of examples of religious buildings, in which high-level meanings can be expected to be at their maximum.) It follows that no matter what high-level, symbolic meanings may be present, and how important they may be, and no matter how important (or unimportant) middle-level meaning may be, low-level meanings *must be present* if the environment is to work for users, visitors, and the majority "not in the know"; all need to know how to behave or act. The reverse is not the case: high-level meanings do not need to be known for settings to work. It follows that low-level meanings are always present—they are the one constant, while the other two levels tend to be much more variable.

The second point concerns the relationships among levels of meanings. In some cases—many small-scale, preliterate groups, for example—middle-level meanings may be relatively unimportant, as this book suggests; only low-level and high-level meanings may be present. In others, only low-level meanings may be present. Also, one might hypothesize more generally that as other symbolic systems become more widely available—writing, for example (Goody, 1977), or what has been called World Three (Popper, 1972)—high-level meanings *in the built environment* may become less important.

This question of the possibly greatly reduced importance of high-level symbolic meanings in present-day environments is briefly discussed below. More generally, the significant point is that it becomes relatively easy to begin to think of which meanings are likely to be important in which cases, as are the likely courses of change (i.e., prediction).

For example, middle-level meanings often tend to increase in importance in present-day environments due to the scale, complexity, and heterogeneity of the system. Since people are not known, and social hierarchies are more fluid, communicating status, identity, and the like through environmental cues may become more important. Low-level meanings may also gain in importance because behavior is less routinized and because cues in complex systems with more heterogeneous populations require higher redundancy in order to remind people how to behave (see pp. 149–152 above; cf. Rapoport, 1977). Low- and middle-level meanings also gain *relative* prominence if high-level meanings become less important.

In studying any built environment (in the broad sense used in this book, i.e., including semifixed and nonfixed elements) one needs to assume that all three levels *may* be present. In any given case it may even be possible, as already suggested, to "predict" their relative importance; which are present and how important these are become empirical questions. Also to reiterate, *low-level, everyday instrumental meanings are always present in any built environment*, although the cues may be very subtle (see, e.g., pp. 183–193 above).

In order clearly to understand the relation between built environments and human behavior over the full range of environments, cross-culturally and historically, all three levels of meaning need to be considered, studied, and understood; they are complementary rather than conflicting or competing. In starting out to study an example of that component of material culture that is the built environment, one must not prejudge which of the three levels of meaning will be present, even if hypotheses are made. In most traditional environments—those studied by historians, archaeologists, and anthropologists—high-level meanings can be expected to be important or significant. In most present-day environments, I would suggest, high-level meanings are likely to be absent, or at least relatively unimportant. Thus the three levels of meaning can vary independently of one another (or partly so). Their presence or absence and their relative importance could be profiled. For example, I hypothesize that in the contemporary United States, high-level meanings are generally absent, middle-level meanings tend to be extremely important and prominent, and low-level meanings are "normal," although expressed with very high levels of redundancy.

A contrary view has been put forward, arguing that cosmological structures are still present in contemporary environments (Doxtater 1981). In my view, however, the examples he gives are in fact exemplars of middle-level meanings, such as identity, status, and the nature of social units and their values (Doxtater, 1981: 38). Three students in a session of the doctoral proseminar at which I talked about this topic recently proposed an alternative hypothesis—that rather than high-level meanings disappearing or becoming unimportant in contemporary situations—in the United States, for example—as I suggest, it is their *content* that changes. For example, the types of high-level meanings I described earlier—cosmologies, cultural schemata, worldviews, philosophical systems, the sacred, and so on, are replaced by the importance of the individual, equality, health, comfort, mastery over nature (or partnership with it), and the like. In fact, under that hypothesis one could argue that status, individual or group identity (see Rapoport, in press d), wealth, power, and the like are some of the new high-level meanings rather than what I call middle-level meanings.

This is an intriguing suggestion that, in time, one might pursue, although there is an immediate problem with such a "flexible" definition and use of a concept. If a concept can acquire ever new and different content, it becomes difficult, if not impossible, to use it. It may thus be preferable to keep my original definition of high-level meanings, although its constituent elements certainly need to be broadened. Also, in any case, one will not be dealing with a monothetic set but rather with a polythetic set—only some of the multiple attributes need be represented in any given case (Clarke, 1978: 36; Rapoport, in press b). One would also expect cross-cultural variability.

Moreover, at the moment I still believe that the decline of high-level meanings in the United States (and more generally with "modernization") is real. This is how I interpret two recent studies. Jackson (1984) compares two U.S. ideal landscapes—those of the 19th and 20th centuries. It seems clear from his analysis that the change is essentially one of progressive loss of symbolic content, whether sacred (for parks, roads, crossings, and so forth) or political (for public space or country courthouses). This symbolic content is replaced by what I would call low-level meanings, of which the "highest" is an "agreeable environmental experience" (Jackson, 1984: 20). The whole analysis, involving many other types of settings in the U.S. cultural landscape, can also be interpreted as a reduction in high-level meanings and concomitant greater emphasis on, as well as an actual increase in, low-level meanings and, as in suburbia and in office environments, middle-level meanings (see Rapoport, 1985a, 1985b).

A similar interpretation also seems to apply to a more detailed study of political meaning involving an analysis of 75 U.S. city council chambers. Over time there has been a clear loss of symbolic, high-level meanings in favor of low-level meanings (Goodsell, 1988). This can admittedly be interpreted in terms of the alternative hypothesis, as a new set of high-level meanings—democracy and egalitarianism, for example.

I also interpret as the loss of high-level meanings a recent study of housing in Singapore in relation to the religious practices of three groups: Chinese, Malays, and Hindu Indians (Chua, 1988). Though the study clearly shows that meaning is, indeed, a most important function of housing, these seem to be low-level meanings, such as cues about how to behave, rather than high-level philosophical or cosmological meanings, which are clearly absent.[5]

It would clearly be worthwhile to test these two alternative hypotheses. Whichever is correct, generally or in any given case, however, *the idea of levels of meanings remains*. It is, I believe, important and useful, not least in generating hypotheses to be tested. It is also the major change in this book.

I have not yet discussed the third approach, nonverbal communication, with which this book is concerned. Since, however, this approach is not modified in any way but rather supported and confirmed by more recent work, it will be discussed in the next section.

Review of some more recent work

The first and most important point is that further work seems not simply to support but to strengthen the centrality of meaning in environment-behavior relations as a most important mechanism linking people and environments. It seems clearer than ever that, as I suggested, meaning is not something additional to "function" but is possibly the most important function. All the material reviewed in this section needs to be seen in this light. Another of my main points that receives support is the centrality of culture, the fact that meaning must be studied within its appropriate cultural context and that, within general patterns, it is culture specific.

One point that is only implicit in the text needs to be made explicit. Although meaning, like all environment-behavior relations, includes subjective experience, it is only usefully studied or considered if it can be adequately generalized to groups. Purely individual or idiosyncratic associations or meanings are of interest only to the individuals concerned and are not part of the domain of EBS and research on it.

The new work, and earlier work which I only discovered since the completion of this book, from which this limited review draws follows semiotic, symbolic, and nonverbal approaches to the study of meaning and also includes method-driven, eclectic studies. The review is neither exhaustive nor systematic; for one thing, it generally does not deal with work in semiotics. I briefly consider some studies of symbolism, some of which use NVC approaches and some, while they do not explicitly fit the latter, study meaning in terms of pragmatics and in straightforward ways. They can therefore be incorporated into my approach even when they formally claim allegiance to other approaches, even semiotics; this has been discussed above. Recall also that in the text I use a variety of findings from some studies claiming allegiance to semiotics and from quite a few coming from the symbolic tradition. This is also the case in this section (e.g., Lang, 1982; Duncan, Lindsey, and Buchan, 1985; Broda, Carrasco, and Matos, 1987; Cherulnik and Wilderman, 1986; Despres, 1987a; Nasar, 1988). In that sense my approach in this book, as in my work generally, is eclectic; I use whatever works and makes sense. I only draw the line at work I find wrong, incomprehensible, or unusable. In both the positive and negative senses, the label means less than the content.

This certainly applies to work on symbolism, which continues—and continues to be useful in the sense that it can be used in conjunction with both eclectic work and work based on NVC. This is not surprising, given the discussion in the first section of this epilogue. Nor is it surprising that most of it does not seem to be applied to contemporary everyday settings[6] but to traditional societies, either in the past (e.g., studies in archaeology; see Rapoport, in press a) or those still in existence. Such studies (e.g., Pieper, 1980; Vinnicombe, 1976; Lewis-Williams, 1981, 1983; Hockings, 1984, 1987; Marcus, 1976; Broda, Carrasco, and Matos, 1987; Isbell, 1978) can all be incorporated into the corpus of work on meaning with which this book is concerned. This even applies to studies based on approaches even more "remote"—e.g., textual analysis, in this case of the urban landscape of Kandy (Sri Lanka; see Duncan, 1984), or a structuralist analysis of Maori art (Hanson, 1983).

In most cases the approach is very straightforward and direct, whatever the theoretical rationale, and it is even possible, post facto, to distinguish among the levels of meaning discussed earlier. Moreover, also as already mentioned both in the book and the epilogue, the term "symbol" can often easily be replaced by other terms, such as "cues," "indicators," "expressions of" and the like—and then understood in an NVC framework. This is the case, for example, with "symbolic aesthetics" (Lang, 1982) and also with discussions of the social meaning of dwellings (and what I would argue is the need to consider the larger system of settings) in Longana, Vanuatu, in the South Pacific (Rodman, 1985a, 1985b). These studies also reemphasize the importance of the cultural context in understanding the various cues that are used. This becomes clear from a special issue on home interiors in Europe in *Environment and Behavior* (1987), in which one finds differences between the United States and Western Europe generally and between France and Italy. One also finds differences in the perceived residential quality of neighborhoods between the United States and Saudi Arabia (Zube et al., 1985); that study also again illustrates the difference between insiders and outsiders (e.g., Rapoport, 1977), which has now been studied empirically (e.g., Brower, 1989).

In a study of the Great Temple of Tenochtitlán (Broda, Carrasco, and Matos, 1987) the temple is considered as ritual space embodying a cosmic vision (a typical high-level symbolic meaning). That cosmic vision is then analyzed and shown to be central to the Aztec world generally. Such continuity also emerges from a similar analysis of the Maya (Marcus, 1976) which shows how a single schema seems to underlie, and can be used to understand, environments on many scales, from the state or realm to the building. Similarly, Nemeth 1987 analyzes a cultural landscape that reflects neo-Confucian ideology and celestial prototypes not only on Cheju Island, Korea (the locale of the study), but also in the past throughout medieval China and Korea. The same neo-Confucian model, prototype, or schema was applied to the region, city, town, village, farmstead, and tomb, again reinforcing points made in this book (see also Wood, 1969; and Ingham, 1971). Nemeth's study also confirms that the settings incorporating this schema acted as a mnemonic—a central point of this book. The metaphysical, philosophical, and religious meanings involved are examples of high-level meanings and reinforce the question I raised about how many users knew this esoteric material (Rapoport, 1988); I suspect very few did. None of these studies discuss low-level meanings. Neither does a study of prehistoric ceremonial centers in the Andes (Isbell, 1978), where the concern is with cosmology (a typical high-level meaning), and the point is also made that symbols (meanings) are context specific. Isbell's study emphasizes the great continuity of these cosmological schemata, not in space (as in the previous studies) but over time. It begins with more recent cases (e.g., 16th-century Cuzco, with its pattern of the Puma on the urban scale and a 20th-century ethnographic example). Having identified the schema, Isbell finds it in two prehistoric ceremonial centers 2500 and 3000 years before Cuzco and the ethnographic example, respectively. Although the approach is structuralist, Isbell identifies the symbols in straightforward and direct ways (cf. Flannery and Marcus, 1983; Rapoport, in press a).

In the case of nonverbal communication, two doctoral students have done literature reviews as part of independent studies (Despres, 1987b; Devlin, 1988). Despres (1987b) concludes that NVC was a prolific area of research in the decade 1977 to 1986. She further concludes that none of the studies deals specifically with environments and objects (semifixed elements), which are generally neglected or ignored. While she is able to identify 19 books and 36 doctoral dissertations which have some potential relevance for the study of environmental meaning, she also finds that among the 36 dissertations, explicit references to environments and physical settings comprise only 7 percent, and object displays only 4 percent, of the subject matter. While the work includes literature reviews, syntheses, empirical and methodological work, and even textbooks (e.g., Poyatos, 1983; Wiemann and Harrison, 1983; Kendon, 1981; Wolfgang, 1984; Katz and Katz, 1983), it ignores the mutual relationship between people and settings as a form of NVC. In my terms this work is still largely restricted to non-fixed elements—communication among people. This body of research is very active indeed and is growing. For example, Ekman and his group (whom I discuss on pp. 97ff. and 101ff.) have published a great deal since 1981, mainly on facial expressions (see Bull and Rumsey, 1988). It is also significant that this work has now reached daily newspapers (e.g., Goleman, 1989b).

Devlin (1988) identifies 13 new books and papers (e.g., Ridgeway et al., 1985; Blanck et al., 1986), including a textbook aimed at high school teachers (Vargus, 1986)—a most significant development. She also reanalyzes some of Despres' entries (e.g., Scherer and Ekman, 1982). Again, with very few exceptions (e.g., Ames, 1980; cf. Ames, 1978), material culture is either ignored or explicitly rejected. She also identifies 12 doctoral dissertations on NVC during 1986 and 1987.

Given that these two reviews are highly selective, it seems clear that there is much research in many areas of NVC but little or nothing on the built environment (see Poyatos, 1988, in which my chapter is the only one dealing with material culture). The built environment is still being neglected, as it was when this book was written (e.g., pp. 48ff., esp. p. 50).

Some studies have been influenced, directly or indirectly, by my work (e.g., Farbstein and Kantrowitz, 1986; Goodsell, 1988). Most studies, however, do not explicitly use NVC but confirm many of the points made in this book: that settings communicate, that cultural contexts are critical, and that semifixed elements and their arrangements are dominant (i.e., that the relationships are at least as important as the elements). To give just one example, this is clear from a special issue of *Environment and Behavior* in 1987 on home interiors in Europe which implicitly also makes another important point: Although the preface and the six papers take different approaches to the topic, they can be read together—and their findings can fit into an NVC framework.

There is also work on semifixed elements of all kinds (e.g., Ames, 1978, 1980). Some of this work uses the term "symbols" but, like some described in the text, fits perfectly into my model and can be reworded in the way suggested (e.g., Csikszentmihalyi and Rochberg-Halton, 1981; Hucek, 1983). A study of clothing (Wobst, 1977, which is discussed on pp. 63–64 of the text) not only puts it into a broad anthropological context and relates it to a large new body of work but also confirms its importance and that of other semifixed elements. Moreover, it supports my more general theoretical argument for the importance of redundancy (see Robinson et al., 1984).

One study of dwellings in Vancouver, which explicitly takes a semiotic approach (Duncan, Lindsey, and Buchan, 1985), makes a number of useful points, and serves to support two of my major points. The first is that semifixed elements do indeed seem to be the most important in communicating meaning both inside the dwelling (e.g., furnishings and decorations) and outside (landscaping and outdoor objects). The second is that people are indeed able very easily to understand meanings communicated by dwellings, landscaping, furnishings, and the like. The levels of agreement found (between 59 and 86 percent, depending on cues and location) are extremely high—much higher than I would have expected, and at the levels of satisfaction with physical comfort aimed for in the design of heating, ventilation, and air conditioning.

Very high levels of agreement (between 48 and 56 percent) were also found in a study of how dwellings communicate identity (Sadalla et al., 1987; cf. Rapoport, 1981; Duncan, 1981). Given the very high levels of agreement, these two studies implicitly seem to contradict the argument (see Bonta, 1975) that environments do not communicate meanings but rather that people project meanings onto them. On the other hand, they seem to support the argument in this book that environments and settings do communicate meanings and, moreover, that if they do so successfully, they greatly constrain possible meanings (see Wollheim, 1972: 123, and Perinbanayagam, 1974, in my discussion on pp. 59–63).

The two studies (Duncan, Lindsey, and Buchan, 1985; Sadalla et al., 1987) disagree about whether exteriors or interiors show greater agreement, that is, communicate more effectively. The former finds that exteriors elicit more agreement because it is more important to communicate meanings to outsiders than to those invited inside, who already know one. The latter finds that interiors elicit more agreement because one has more control there. The reasons for this difference are unclear but may include the type of area studied or the culture (one study is from Canada, the other from the United States). They may also be artifacts of the methods used. Further research to clarify this disagreement would be useful.'

Both studies agree that attributes of dwellings, furnishings, and landscaping communicate identity and other meanings. They also agree about the greater importance of semifixed elements vis-à-vis fixed features. This is also the case with a study of Lincoln Park in Chicago (Suchar and Rotenberg, 1988). Because this is a gentrifying neighborhood, three distinct groups were identified for whom dwellings had different overall meanings, and hence distinctiveness was achieved through objects, that is, semifixed elements. These distinguish among dwellings as stages for social performance, as settings for expressing unique individuality, and as providing an atmosphere of private family life and domesticity. These become styles and seem to correspond to what Jopling (1974; cited in the text), in the case of Puerto Ricans in Boston, calls an aesthetic complex.

In spite of the emphasis on semifixed elements, these studies and others begin to consider fixed-feature elements (see Ostrowetsky and Bordreuil, 1980, which discusses the meaning of particular regional house styles in France [cf. Rapoport, in press e]). This is also the case with a study that confirms my argument on page 76 on the meaning of the neo-Quebecois style in Quebec (Despres, 1987a). Parentheti-cally, while this is discussed in terms of "symbolic representation," it illustrates my argument, which is couched in terms of NVC and cues; moreover, the study cites this book. The emphasis on fixed-feature elements is also found in other studies (see Groat, 1982; Cherulnik and Wilderman, 1986; Nasar, 1988, 1989).

In all these studies one finds an extension from semifixed elements to fixed-feature elements in terms of the meanings of various dwelling styles. In other words, the likely temporal sequence that I discuss in the book seems to be starting, and the sequence of the application of NVC approaches seems to be the one predicted: from nonfixed to semifixed and eventually to fixed-feature elements. There is also another extension of the domain to be discussed later: from domestic settings to other building types.

The study by Cherulnik and Wilderman (1986) emphasizes what I would now identify as middle-level meanings and finds that the origi-nal fixed-feature elements still elicit judgments consistent with the orig-inal owners' socioeconomic status; that is, the original meaning of the various cues persists, among them size, ornateness, and materials (see Barnett, 1975). This study and those by Nasar (1988, 1989) all refer to "symbols" where I refer to cues, because they discuss what I would regard as middle-level meanings, not only the wealth and status but also, in the Nasar studies, the desirability, perceived friendliness, and leadership qualities of the presumed residents, which are interpreted differently according to the different styles of dwellings. The different styles are also ranked differently in terms of preference, and while there seems to be no difference between Los Angeles and Columbus, Ohio, judgments vary among groups, and as I argued, architects' judg-ments are very different from nonarchitects'.

All studies of this type (see Nasar, 1983) not only seem to be very consistent about the positive and negative qualities of cues, at least in the United States and in Anglo-American culture more generally, they also strongly suggest that what is often called the "aesthetic quality" of environments is in fact much more an aspect of *meaning*. Its com-ponents (Rapoport, 1985a, 1989) indicate either liked or disliked en-vironments on the basis of status, well-being, perceived safety, and so on. The attributes of the environment are, then, the cues that communicate such meanings to users. This is, of course, an aspect of my distinction between perceptual and associational aspects: this distinction has been used by others, and similar points made, although using the concept of "symbols" ("symbolic aesthetics") and a semiotic approach (Lang, 1982). Here again the central substantive point and the content can be expressed easily in an NVC framework without difficulty or loss; it can also, of course, be extended from "architecture" to semifixed elements and material culture generally and hence to the cultural landscape.

This is clearly the case in a study of the residential aspects of the normalization of mentally retarded people (Robinson et al., 1984). The various architectural elements and whether they are liked or work are to be understood in terms of their meanings. Attributes with negative meanings are associated with the negative image of institutionality; attributes with positive meanings are associated with positive images of domesticity ("homelike"). This is much as suggested in this book (on the basis of Davis and Roizen's 1970 study). Robinson et al., 1984, also emphasize the importance of redundancy for settings to communicate appropriate meanings.

The centrality of the meaning of architectural and other environmental elements usually considered in aesthetic rather than associational terms, and the consequent differences between designers and users, become very clear in a study of Maiden Lane, a problem housing estate in London (Hunt Thompson Associates, 1988). In this case one finds a complete reversal in the interpretation of the look of the project. The features praised by architects and the architectural press are described by 71 percent of the residents in extremely negative terms—and these are associational, that is, they have to do with meaning. Among them are "prison," "concentration camp," "battery farm," and "mental institution." The feel of the project also elicits negative emotional terms from 53 percent of the residents: "depressing," "closed in," "claustrophobic." Many of the more specific comments are clearly congruent with my discussion and illustrations in the book (e.g., pp. 14–18). Among the changes recommended, many seem clearly meant to change those qualities of the project that communicate negative meanings (including the institutional character discussed above; see Robinson et al., 1984).

More generally, it is significant that recommended changes in housing projects often seem to involve changing those elements that have negative meanings to elements that have positive meanings. This is much the case with Lucien Kroll's work at Perseigne d'Alençon in

France (*Revue de l'habitat social*, 1981) as it is with a project in Boston (Deitz, 1984), to mention just two.

All the studies cited, and others, identify the various attributes or elements that communicate meaning. In effect they are engaged in the development of what in this book I call lexicons, repertoires, or palettes of elements. These include, for example, style, landscaping and plant materials, ornateness, furnishings, size, materials, and color. The latter, which I discuss on pages 111–114, is clearly a major attribute that communicates meaning very effectively, being a major noticeable difference (Rapoport, 1977).

Color has recently received attention. Thus one study of color (Foote, 1983) implicitly discusses redundancy and emphasizes *communication*. Although it does not adopt an NVC approach, it can easily fit into the framework of this book. It is also significant in that it concentrates on nondomestic settings (banks; savings and loan associations; hotels and motels; churches; restaurants; educational, public, and government institutions; funeral homes; and a range of shops). Other studies have investigated the meanings communicated by the style of suburban office buildings (Nasar and Kang, 1989). Thus the study of meaning is being extended to new types of environments. While this book does discuss offices, restaurants, and religious buildings, the emphasis is on dwellings and urban areas.

In connection with religious buildings, the book discusses a number of elements of the repertoire or palette that can be, or have been, used; one of these is height (see pp. 107–111). A striking recent example of this is the new church at Yamoussoukro, Ivory Coast (Brooke, 1988), in which size, scale, and above all, height are emphasized; the important point seems to be that the church is the world's largest and tallest—significantly larger and taller than St. Peter's in Rome.

Color has also been shown to communicate ethnic identity (in this case, that of Mexican Americans) and through longitudinal studies, even to communicate levels of acculturation to the United States (Arreola, 1984). Also, as discussed in the text, fences are part of this particular repertoire. Thus fences and fence varieties can also be used as indicators of the Mexican-American identity of residents (Arreola, 1981). In fact, eventually it becomes apparent that a whole set, or system, of elements is involved in communicating Mexican-American identity—what is called a housescape (Arreola, 1988). This includes property enclosure, exterior house color, and yard shrines, among other elements; it is the most recent evolution of a historic landscape that has links to pre-Columbian Mexico and to Spain. In my terms, this once again emphasizes the importance of redundancy. In addition, as I suggest more generally, the meaning of fences, like other attributes or cues, is contextual (see p. 130 and Fig. 19 in text). This also applies to color, so that a given color can be conforming or nonconforming, depending on context. This recently led to legal action in Britain, where bright colors on listed buildings (such as the Royal Crescent in Bath) have been held by the courts to be "development"; if "inappropriate," consent may be refused (*Practice*, 1983: 3).

One of the first longitudinal studies of vernacular design (in Greece; Pavlides, 1985) found that meaning was a most important aspect of the built environment and that status was the most important meaning, especially in more recent environments. This, of course, supports my argument in the first section of this epilogue. Moreover, the elements communicating status *change over time*—from type of dwelling, size of house and of spaces, decoration, kind of wall cavities and protrusions, degree of elaborateness, and the like to degree of modernization, that is, the use of modern materials such as cement and paint, the removal of "old-fashioned" features, and the introduction of furniture and appliances (i.e., semifixed elements) that are absent and hence not very important in traditional dwellings (see Rapoport, in press d), piped water, and electricity. The role played by modern elements in a situation like this and in developing countries generally is a point made in this book (e.g., pp. 142–144) and has been greatly developed since then in Rapoport, 1983. That paper also further develops, in a major way, the notion of the *culture core*, discussed briefly on page 83 of this book. This has proved to be of great importance in studying and understanding meaning in the situations of rapid culture change characteristic of developing countries. All these elements, however, are shown (by Pavlides, 1985) to be important indicators of status, and it is clearly both possible and essential to begin to develop lexicons or repertoires of such indicators. Two other points in that study further strengthen my argument. First, it becomes clear that, with a single exception, sets of elements are consistent, and hence that redundancy is most important and both reinforces and makes more precise the meanings communicated. Second, subgroups knew the house features in their own category best. *General* status or rank could be determined broadly by everyone; subtle distinctions became more important *within* each group, where minute details were noticed. This tends to support my argument about the importance of cultural context and great cultural and group specificity. It also supports a point made implicitly in this book and explicitly elsewhere (e.g., Rapoport, 1977) and already mentioned earlier in this epilogue: that there are differences between insiders and outsiders (e.g., Brower, 1989). Since designers are the quintessential outsiders, it follows that there are differences between designers and the lay public (e.g., Groat, 1982; Lee, 1982; Hunt Thompson Associates, 1988).

I myself have considerably expanded two other points made in this book. The first is conceptual; the second concerns a body of evidence and examples. As part of my argument for broadening the definition of the built environment as a subset of material culture, including semifixed feature elements and also people, I also briefly suggested (pp. 88–89) that it be extended to include the cultural landscape as an expression of the system of settings in which systems of activities take place. This I have since greatly elaborated, showing its importance generally and demonstrating how its various components act together to communicate various meanings (e.g., Rapoport, 1983, 1985a, 1986a, in press c, in press e). This is also my reading of a number of the studies reviewed in this epilogue.

As part of my redefinition of the domain of EBS, I not only extended it to cover the system of settings/cultural landscapes but also to include all types of environments, all cultures, and most recently, the full time span. As part of the latter I had begun to use archaeological evidence and material in this book. I further developed this in the chapter dealing with levels of meaning (Rapoport, 1988), and it plays a major role in a forthcoming book on the relation between EBS and historical data (Rapoport, in press a, especially Chapter 5).

There are two reasons for using this evidence. The first is that it greatly expands the time depth of the evidence one can use, and this helps to make the evidence broader and more diverse, and hence any generalizations more valid. The second reason concerns the relation between the study of meaning and archaeology. If meanings can be identified in archaeological material, when so little is left, then one can have greater confidence in the approach. Conversely, if environment-behavior studies and archaeology can be used together, they can help to interpret archaeological data in terms of meaning (their *ideotechnic function* [Binford, 1962]). Ethnoarchaeology is one such attempt, which unfortunately has had little interaction with EBS (Kent, 1984, 1987; Rapoport, 1988, in press a, in press c).

Some preliminary ideas on mechanisms

In dealing with the scientific understanding and explanation of any phenomenon, one's analysis and proposals become much more convincing if plausible general mechanisms can be identified or proposed.

This is because they can help to explain how any suggested processes work. Thus any findings bearing on mechanisms have major implications, and the identification of possible mechanisms becomes a most important task.

The major process proposed in this book is that if cues in settings are noticed and understood, the social situation appropriate to that setting is identified, and appropriate (i.e., expected or congruent) behavior is brought to attention and elicited. In effect a repertoire of appropriate behaviors is retrieved from storage; the setting is seen as acting as a mnemonic activating all this culturally acquired knowledge. While settings do not determine appropriate behavior, there are major pressures to conform, and appropriate action is amazingly often the result, making co-action possible. This is not surprising; after all, a major function of culture is to routinize behavior, reserving cognitive channel capacity for more important matters (see Rapoport, 1986b). This process is elaborated in the text, and much evidence is adduced to suggest that it is very likely and, indeed, probable: it seems to be the best explanation of a great variety of findings, otherwise puzzling occurrences, and so on. However, no mechanism was identified that might make this process work.

Some suggestions about a possible mechanism come from work in artificial intelligence and cognitive science—a large, interdisciplinary, increasingly sophisticated, and rapidly growing field. In it, some mechanisms have been proposed in different connections which work in ways analogous to what is proposed in this book. The coincidence and overlap is, at the very least, intriguing and promising. Should these suggested mechanisms be confirmed, it would make my proposed process that much more likely and convincing. It also means that a whole new large body of work—conceptual, theoretical, and empirical—becomes potentially relevant; this in itself is most important and promising.

Clearly this will be a very brief and preliminary discussion, without the topic being developed to any significant extent, as it deserves to be. The purpose of this discussion is merely to point out the existence of this congruence with work in cognitive science and hence of a possible mechanism. It is also encouraging that after developing this material my attention was drawn to some work from Germany (Kaminsky, 1987; Kruse, 1988).[7] While rather different in detail and not drawing the interpretation I do, it is broadly similar in emphasizing the link with Barker's concept of behavior settings, as I do on page 85 of this book.

The mechanism that I propose is based on the concepts of "frames" (Minsky, 1975) and "scripts" (Schank and Abelson, 1977, 1979; Abelson, 1976, 1981) and how they are related (e.g., Mandler, 1984). Through these it is also related to the concept of schemata more generally, of which they are a specific type (Brewer and Nakamura, 1984). There is a very large literature on schemata in psychology, which go back at least to Sir Frederick Bartlett in 1932 (Bartlett, 1967) and on which Lewin, Tolman, Piaget, Kelly, Boulding, and others based their work. Moreover, I have long argued that the concept of schemata, not necessarily as defined in psychology but also in their anthropological meaning, is central in EBS (see Rapoport, 1977, and references in it). Schemata are very important in cognitive anthropology and in anthropology more generally if one sees culture, the major concern of anthropology, as a framework within which particulars take on meaning as a way of life, as a blueprint or design for life, and hence as leading to routinized behavior (see Rapoport, 1986b).

The papers by Minsky, Abelson, and Schank are still referred to in all discussions in the literature and have been used extensively for all kinds of purposes. For example, Thagard (1988: 198) points out that schema theory, while not universally accepted, is supported by a great deal of evidence that people process information by using something like schemata, which help to encode and retrieve information. Furthermore, schemata seem to be framelike structures (Minsky, 1975) and have been postulated to play an important role in perception, discourse understanding, learning, remembering (see Bartlett, 1967), and problem solving, among other things.

The concept of scripts (Schank and Abelson, 1977, 1979; Abelson, 1976, 1981), which are related to frames, introduces behavior and involves a typical and organized sequence of events. An individual expects these to occur on the basis of prior learning and experience, and enculturation, and they typify what in this book I call a situation. The point is made that well-learned scripts lead to a "mindless" state— people respond automatically with behaviors expected in the situation. Schank and Abelson (1977: 5) use a restaurant visit as their example: the visit elicits a restaurant script, which has other scripts embedded in it and is itself embedded in the general frame or schema for a restaurant.

The congruence with my postulated process is almost complete. In my case the frame is the situation identified by users on the basis of cues in the setting, which acts as a mnemonic. This then reminds users how to act, the script is then the appropriate behavioral repertoire drawn upon to match the situation, and the automatic or "mindless" response is culturally routinized behavior.

The ideas of schema or frame theory have also been applied to part of the built environment and material culture—industrial design, that is, various artifacts and machines, equipment, light switches, door handles, and the like (Norman, 1988). In this application three propositions are made (pp. 115–116):

(1) There is a logic or order to individual structures in the human mind; these are "schemas" or "frames."

(2) Human memory is associative—each schema points and refers to many others to which it is related and which help define the components or "network."

(3) Much of the human power of deductive thought comes from using the information in one schema to deduce properties in another.

The many examples in Norman 1988 which deal with small-scale elements of the built environment closely resemble my arguments in this book, and his analysis of industrial design extends and complements mine of landscapes, settlements, buildings, and interiors.

Thus, without further elaboration and pending further research and development, enough has been said at least to make a case that the process by which settings communicate meaning and how this influences behavior, which I developed in this book quite independently, fits perfectly into a powerful mechanism being uncovered by research in cognitive science.

There is another aspect of meaning that I propose in this book. I begin with the argument that a global affective response, sometimes based on subliminal perception, typically precedes any more detailed analysis and even sets the tone or feeling for more conscious perception (see Russell and Snodgrass, 1987). It follows that environmental evaluation and preference are more a matter of overall affective response than of detailed analysis; they are more a matter of latent than of manifest functions, and they are largely affected by images and ideals, in the sense that the "success" of environments depends on their congruence with appropriate images (Rapoport, 1977: 50, 60). In this book (pp. 14–15) I then argue that these global affective responses are based on the *meaning* that environments, and particular aspects of them, have for people. I adduce much evidence for this position, which is also discussed in the previous section of this epilogue.

Once again, more recent work in psychology, brain science, and cognitive science has made available two developments which strengthen the postulated process. The first is that there is now much additional evidence of the importance of affect generally (for one review, see Russell and Snodgrass, 1987; see also n. 8). The second again concerns possible mechanisms at the level of brain structure, neurotransmitters, and the like. The literature on both these topics is voluminous and cannot possibly be reviewed here, although it would be both interesting and useful.[8] All I will do, therefore, is to refer to a recent newspaper account that, in popular form, summarizes some of the research (Goleman, 1989a). This research strongly argues for the primacy of affect and its ability even to override thought and to operate independently of it. It also confirms the role of subliminal perception, understood as affective reactions that occur prior to thoughts being processed, or even before having registered fully what causes the emotional reaction. It also begins to describe, and even diagram, the parts of the brain involved (e.g., the thalamus and amygdala) and the pathways between them, which avoid the neocortex and which provide the mechanism for the global affective response. What seems important is that there is a vast amount of work in brain anatomy, neurobiology, neurophysiology, neurochemistry, cognitive neurobiology, and so on which provides the bases for a mechanism to explain the process that I postulated, and much empirical evidence in its favor. This once again strengthens the likelihood that the particular processes proposed, or something very much like them, are in fact those operating in the way meaning from the built environment influences preference and behavior.

Conclusion

This epilogue is relatively brief, and although it updates the discussion through the middle of 1989, the updating is neither systematic nor complete. This is partly because work and publication continue, and at an accelerating rate, in any field that is alive and progressing, and partly because to be thorough I would need to review quite a few different fields. Also, while many references could be added, it does not seem that they would change anything—they would just provide further support, examples, and elaboration, and this seems unnecessary. There was also a limit set for the size of this epilogue; a complete and systematic review could have doubled the size of the book.

There is also another reason. Over the years I have tended to use my earlier work as "predictions" tested to the extent that my conclusions, proposals, and hypotheses have been supported. It thus seems quite in order to leave this ongoing process at the point it has reached and to hope that this new edition of the book will be used in the same way, not just by me but by others.

The material I have reviewed in this epiloque suggests that although some significant modifications to a part of Chapter 2 proved necessary, these do not seem to invalidate any of the central arguments of the book. The concept of levels of meaning as briefly described above actually helps to clarify the central argument and is also helpful in identifying the likely meanings in given situations.

It seems clearer than ever that people seem to obtain meanings from the environment and to understand it directly and easily. In most cases people notice and interpet cues in settings in straightforward, effortless, and simple ways and to act appropriately. This process is usually self-evident and unproblematic, at least in a given cultural context. This is shown by my use, in earlier work and in this book, of material from television and film, newspapers, magazines, novels, advertising, and the like. I have continued to collect and analyze such material, and it continues to show this self-evident use of meaning (e.g., Rapoport, 1985a, 1985b, in press f). As just one example, a recent newspaper story described the "symbolic" lowering of the special, higher dais for prosecutors in Italian courts, which will now be at the same level as that of the defense counsel (Hoffmann, 1989). This change reflects major changes in Italian law and clearly illustrates and reinforces the discussion of courtrooms in four other societies in this book (on pages 124–126 and in Fig. 18). It is noteworthy that a great many resources are being expended to lower the dais a few inches. It is also of interest that this change is traced to the impact of the "Perry Mason" television series. More than ever it seems that attempts to complicate the issue, to make it esoteric, difficult, and arcane, are part of a general tendency toward obfuscation in both the social sciences and the humanities. But that is a topic for another day.

Given all this, it follows that the study of these processes and meanings should be equally simple, easy, and straightforward. This justifies my emphasis on the methodological simplicity and directness of the NVC approach as one of its major attractions. This is desirable conceptually because it is "natural" in the sense that it is like the way users interpret environmental cues in their everyday use of settings. It is also desirable pragmatically for the reasons given in this book. This does not mean that the full repertoire of methods cannot, and should not, be used, including cognitive mapping, projective tests, studies of environmental memory, observation, experiments, and so on. Methodological sophistication can go with simplicity of approach even in the study of high-level meanings. Thus nonverbal communication is the preferred, although perhaps not the only, approach for the study of the everyday low- and middle-level meanings that built environments have for users, which is the subject of this book. In addition, not only is NVC clearly a progressive research program but, both inherently and seen broadly and eclectically as I suggest, it is able to accommodate much work that seems to use other approaches.

These arguments for a relatively straightforward and direct approach to the study of meanings—as contrasted with, say, the supposedly theory-driven approach of semiotics—does not mean, as one reviewer of this book thought, that I was opposed to theory (Bedford, 1984). That is, of course, the exact opposite of my position. Without engaging in polemics, I will make just two points. The first is that there is explanatory theory, which is based on research and supported by empirical data and which leads to understanding and prediction, and then there is "theory," which is really nothing more than opinion, ideology, and the like. I was criticizing the latter, what passes for theory in too many fields. Second, the construction of explanatory theory cannot begin until there is sufficient empirical data to suggest directions and to constrain such theory construction. This, I argue in the text, is the case with linguistics, in which it is often necessary to have a "natural history" stage (see Rapoport, 1986b). Such data are clearly best obtained using the NVC approach as I have developed it.

The discovery of possible mechanisms for the processes proposed, by research in neuroscience, cognitive science, and related fields, is also important. It at least begins to suggest possible explanations for how the processes that I postulated work and thus should be most helpful in theory development. It will be worthwhile to look for further work along these lines and to do a more thorough and explicit job in relating these different bodies of work. Furthermore, this also suggests that the study of meaning is not only straightforward but can also be explicitly scientific and that it benefits from work in other sciences. There are clearly other views; in fact, they may even be dominant (e.g., Hodder, 1986), but in my view, they do not stand up to analysis (see Rapoport, in press a).

It also continues to be the case that very little NVC work concerns the built environment and material culture. This is clear from the reviews by Despres (1987b) and Devlin (1988), and from the book edited by Poyatos (1988), in which my chapter is the only one to address those domains (Rapoport, 1988). I thus end with a plea that those interested in studying meaning in the built environment, and it is central in any understanding of environment-behavior interaction, try using nonverbal communication approaches.

Notes

1. I realize that there is disagreement with "lumping" semiotics and linguistics together, and there are, in fact, some differences between the two fields. It seems to me, however, that the starting point of semiotics is linguistics and that major linguistic influences permeate the former.

2. My use of this concept in this connection does not mean that I necessarily accept Lakatos' more general views about science, the history of science, and so on.

3. The point has been made to me that the terms "high-level," "middle-level," and "low-level" present a problem by implying some hierarchy of value. While not intended, this may be so, but I have been unable to come up with better terms.

4. There is also a possible link with Tuan's (1978) distinction between signs, affective signs, and symbols, although I have not pursued this. In any case, and in the light of this discussion, my suggestion on page 35 that the first two should be combined now seems inappropriate. This is, however, a relatively minor point and does not invalidate the rest of my argument.

5. Note that even in the examples of traditional *religious* settings that I discuss where high-level meanings have been shown to be present, my argument is that most users utilized very similar low-level cues (Rapoport, 1988). Admittedly, these settings accommodate users' needs rather better than the housing in Singapore—as did traditional culture-specific dwellings. But that is another topic.

6. When "symbols" are mentioned or used in studies of contemporary everyday settings, they seem to be used as a synonym for "meaning" rather than in any technical sense.

7. These were drawn to my attention by a Visiting Fellow in our department, Fridrich Dieckmann.

8. A recent review of the literature by one of my doctoral students, Paul Maas ("Aesthetic emotions," completed in late September 1989), contains 465 references covering both aspects, of which about 400 are directly relevant to the point I am making here.

References

Abelson, R. P. (1976) "Script processing in attitude formation and decision making," in J. S. Carroll and J. W. Payne (eds.) Cognition and Social Behavior. Hillsdale, NJ: Erlbaum.

———(1981) "Psychological status of script concept." American Psychologist 36: 715–729.

Ames, K. L. (1978) "Meaning in artifacts: hall furnishings in Victorian America." Journal of Interdisciplinary History 9 (1): 19–46.

———(1980) "Material culture as nonverbal communication: a historical case study." Journal of American Culture 3 (4): 619–641.

Arreola, D. D. (1981) "Fences as landscape taste: Tucson's Barrios." Journal of Cultural Geography 2 (1): 96–105.

———(1984) "House color in Mexican-American barrios." Presented at a conference on Built Form and Culture Research, University of Kansas, Lawrence, 18–20 October. (mimeo)

———(1988) "Mexican American townscapes." Geographical Review 78 (3): 299–315.

Bartlett, F. (1967) Remembering. Cambridge: Cambridge University Press; originally published 1932.

Bedford, M. (1984) "Analyzing the built form." RIBA Journal 91 (3): 16.

Binford, L. R. (1962) "Archaeology as anthropology." American Antiquity 28 (2): 217–266.

Blanck, P. D., R. Buck, and R. Rosenthal [eds.] (1986) Nonverbal Communication in the Clinical Context. University Park: Pennsylvania State University Press.

Brewer, W., and G. Nakamura (1984) "The nature and function of schemas," pp. 119–160 in R. Wyer and T. Srull (eds.) Handbook of Social Cognition. Hillsdale, NJ: Erlbaum.

Broda, J., D. Carrasco, and E. Matos (1987) The Great Temple of Tenochtitlán: Center and Periphery in the Aztec World. Berkeley: University of California Press.

Brooke, J. (1988) "Ivory Coast church to tower over St. Peter's," New York Times December 19.

Brower, S. (1989) "Residents' and outsiders' perceptions of the environment," pp. 189–203 in S. M. Low and E. Chambers (eds.) Housing, Culture and Design. Philadelphia: University of Pennsylvania Press.

Brower S., K. Dockett, and R. B. Taylor (1983) "Residents' perceptions of territorial features and perceived local threats." Environment and Behavior 15 (4): 419–437.

Bull, R., and N. Rumsey (1988) The Social Psychology of Facial Appearance. New York: Springer Verlag.

Cherulnik, P. D., and S. K. Wilderman (1986) "Symbols of status in urban neighborhoods: contemporary perceptions of nineteenth-century Boston." Environment and Behavior 18 (5): 604–622.

Chua, B. H. (1988) "Adjusting religious practices to different house forms in Singapore." Architecture and Behavior 4 (1): 3–25.

Clarke, D. L. (1978) Analytical Archaeology. 2d ed. London: Methuen.

Csikszentmihalyi, M., and E. Rochberg-Halton (1981) The Meaning of Things: Domestic Symbols and the Self. New York: Cambridge University Press.

Deitz, P. (1984) "A gentle redesign for a 1949 project," New York Times, June 21.

Despres, C. (1987a) "Symbolic representations of the suburban house: the case of the Neo-Quebecois house," pp. 152–159 in J. Harvey and D. Henning (eds.) Public Environments. EDRA 18. Washington, DC: EDRA.

———(1987b) Nonverbal Communication as Applied to Environmental Meaning: An Annotated Bibliography of Recent Publications (1977–1986). Unpublished paper, Department of Architecture, University of Wisconsin-Milwaukee (February).

Devlin, K. (1988) "Nonverbal Communication: An Approach to Environmental Meaning (Annotated Bibliography and Discussion)." Unpublished paper, Department of Architecture, University of Wisconsin-Milwaukee (May).

Doxtater, D. (1981) "A cosmos in the corporation," pp. 36–45 in A. E. Ostenberg, C. P. Tiernan, and R. A. Findlay (eds.) Design Research Interactions. EDRA 12. Washington, DC: EDRA.

Duncan, J. S. (1984) "Texts and contexts in eighteenth century Kandy." Presented at the Conference on Built Form and Culture Research, University of Kansas, Lawrence, October. (mimeo)

———[ed.] (1981) Housing and Identity: Cross-Cultural Perspectives. London: Croom Helm.

Duncan, J. S., S. Lindsey, and R. Buchan (1985) "Decoding a residence: artifacts, social codes and the construction of the self." Espaces et societés No. 47: 29–43.

Environment and Behavior (1987) "Home interiors: a European perspective," special issue, 19 (2): 147–262.

Farbstein, J., and M. Kantrowitz (1986) "The image of post office buildings: first findings—focus group," pp. 259–264 in J. Wineman et al. (eds.) The Costs of Not Knowing. EDRA 17. Washington, DC: EDRA.

Flannery, K. V., and J. Marcus [eds.] (1983) The Cloud People: The Divergent Evolution of the Zapotec and Mixtec Civilizations. New York: Academic Press.

Foote, K. E. (1983) Color in Public Spaces: Toward a Communication-Based Theory of the Urban Built Environment. University of Chicago, Department of Geography Research Paper, no. 205. Chicago.

Goleman, D. (1989a) "Brain's design emerges as a key to emotions." New York Times, August 15.

———(1989b) "Sensing silent cues emerges as a key skill." New York Times, October 10.

Goodsell, C. T. (1988) The Social Meaning of Civic Space: Studying Political Authority Through Architecture. Lawrence: University Press of Kansas.

Goody, J. (1977) The Domestication of the Savage Mind. Cambridge: Cambridge University Press.

Gottdiener, M., and A. Ph. Lagopoulos (1986) The City and the Sign: An Introduction to Urban Semiotics. New York: Columbia University Press.

Groat, L. (1982) "Meanings in post-modern architecture: an examination using the multiple sorting task." Journal of Environmental Psychology 2: 3–22.

Hanson, F. A. (1983) "When the map is the territory: art in Maori culture," pp. 74–89 in D. K. Washburn (ed.) Structure and Cognition in Art. Cambridge: Cambridge University Press.

Hockings, J. (1984) Built Form and Culture: A Case Study of Gilbertese Architecture. Ph.D. diss., Department of Architecture, University of Queensland (Australia).

———(1987) "Built form and culture." Architecture and Behavior 3 (4): 281–300.

Hodder, I. (1986) Reading the Past: Current Approaches to Interpretation in Archaeology. Cambridge: Cambridge University Press.

Hoffman, P. (1989) "In Italy 'Perry Mason' is inspiring," New York Times, October 16.

Hucek, A. (1983) "Domestic Objects and the Presentation of Self: A Study of Designers and Non-Designers." Senior thesis, Minneapolis College of Art and Design (Fall).

Hunt Thompson Associates (1988) Maiden Lane: Feasibility Study for the London Borough of Camden. London: Hunt Thompson Associates.

Isbell, W. H. (1978) "Cosmological order expressed in prehistoric ceremonial centers," pp. 267–297 in Actes du 42 Congres International des Americanistes, vol. 4. Paris.

Jackson, J. B. (1984) Discovering the Vernacular Landscape. New Haven, CT: Yale University Press.

Kaminski, G. (1987) "Cognitive bases of situation processing and behavior setting participation," pp. 218–240 in G. R. Semeni and B. Krahé (eds.) Issues in Contemporary German Social Psychology. Beverly Hills, CA: Sage.

Katz, A. M., and V. T. Katz (1983) Foundations of Nonverbal Communication: Readings, Exercises and Commentary. Carbondale and Edwardsville: Southern Illinois University Press.

Kendon, A. [ed.] (1981) Nonverbal Communication, Interaction and Gestures: Selections of Semiotica. New York: Mouton.

Kent, S. (1984) Analyzing Activity Areas: An Ethnoarchaeological Study of the Use of Space. Albuquerque: University of New Mexico Press.

———(1987) "Understanding the use of space: an ethnoarchaeological perspective," pp. 1–60 in S. Kent (ed.) Method and Theory for Activity Area Research: An Ethnoarchaeological Approach. New York: Columbia University Press.

Kruse, L. (1988) "Behavior settings, cognitive scripts, linguistic frames." Presented at the Symposium on Ecological Psychology, 10th IAPS Conference, Delft, The Netherlands, July. (mimeo)

Lakatos, I. (1971) "History of science and its rational reconstruction," pp. 91–136 in R. D. Buck and R. S. Cohen (eds.) Boston Studies in the Philosophy of Science, vol. 8. Dordrecht: Reidel.

Lang, J. (1982) "Symbolic aesthetics in architecture," pp. 172–182 in P. Bart, A. Chen, and G. Francescato (eds.) Knowledge for Design. EDRA 13. Washington, DC: EDRA.

Lee, L.-S. (1982) "The image of city hall," pp. 310–317 in P. Bart, A. Chen, and G. Francescato (eds.) Knowledge for Design. EDRA 13. Washington, DC: EDRA.

Lewis-Williams, J. D. (1981) Believing and Seeing: Symbolic Meanings in Southern San Rock Paintings. London: Academic Press.

———(1983) The Rock Art of Southern Africa. Cambridge: Cambridge University Press.

Mandler, J. M. (1984) Stories, Scripts and Scenes: Aspects of Schema Theory. Hillsdale, NJ: Erlbaum.

Marcus, J. (1976) Emblem and State in the Classic Maya Lowlands. Washington, DC: Dumbarton Oaks.

Minsky, M. (1975) "A framework for representing knowledge," pp. 211–277 in P. H. Winston (ed.) The Psychology of Computer Vision. New York: McGraw-Hill.

Nasar, J. L. (1983) "Adult viewers' preferences in residential scenes: a study of the relationship of attributes to preference." Environment and Behavior 15 (5): 589–614.

———(1988) "Architectural symbolism: a study of house-style meanings," pp. 163–171 in D. Lawrence et al. (eds.) Paths to Co-existence. EDRA 19. Washington, DC: EDRA.

———(1989) "Symbolic meanings of house styles." Environment and Behavior 21 (3): 235–257.

Nasar, J. L., and J. Kang (1989) "Symbolic meanings of building style in small suburban offices." Presented at the 20th EDRA Conference, Black Mountain, NC, April. (mimeo)

Nemeth, D. J. (1987) The Architecture of Ideology: Neo-Confucian Imprinting on Cheju Island, Korea. University of California, Publications in Geography, no. 26. Berkeley.

Norman, D. A. (1988) The Psychology of Everyday Things. New York: Basic Books.

Ostrowetsky, S., and J. S. Bordreuil (1980) Le Néo-Style Regional: Reproduction d'une Architecture Pavillonnaire. Paris: Dunod.

Pavlides, E. (1985) Vernacular Architecture and Its Social Context: A Case Study from Eressos, Greece. Ph.D. diss., University of Pennsylvania.

Pieper, J. [ed.] (1980) Ritual Space in India. AARP, 17. London.

Popper, K. R. (1972) Objective Knowledge: An Evolutionary Approach. Oxford: Clarendon Press.

Poyatos, F. (1983) New Perspectives in Nonverbal Communication. New York: Pergamon Press.

———[ed.] (1988) Cross-Cultural Perspectives in Nonverbal Communication. Toronto: C. J. Hogrefe.

Practice (1988) "Planning." Journal of the Royal Institute of British Architects, supplement 95 (October): 3.

Rapoport, A. (1983) "Development, culture change and supportive design." Habitat International 7 (5/6): 249–268.

———(1985a) "Thinking about home environments: a conceptual framework," pp. 255–286 in I. Altman and C. M. Werner (eds.) Home Environments, vol. 8 of Human Behavior and Environment. New York: Plenum.

———(1985b) "On diversity" and "Designing for diversity," pp. 5–8, 30–36 in B. Judd, J. Dean, and D. Brown (eds.) Housing Issues I: Design for Diversification. Canberra: Royal Australian Institute of Architects.

———(1986a) "The use and design of open spaces in urban neighborhoods," pp. 159–175 in D. Frick (ed.) The Quality of Urban Life: Social, Psychological and Physical Conditions. Berlin: de Gruyter.

———(1986b) "Culture and built form—a reconsideration," pp. 157–175 in D. G. Saile (ed.) Architecture in Cultural Change: Essays in Built Form and Culture Research. Lawrence: University Press of Kansas.

———(1988) "Levels of meaning in the built environment," pp. 317–336 in F. Poyatos (ed.) Cross-Cultural Perspectives in Nonverbal Communication. Toronto: C. J. Hogrefe.

———(1989) "Environmental quality and environmental quality profiles." Presented at the seminar Quality in the Built Environment, University of Newcastle upon Tyne (Great Britain), July. (to appear in proceedings)

———(in press a) History and Precedent in Environmental Design. New York: Plenum.

———(in press b) "Defining vernacular design," in M. Turan (ed.) On Vernacular Architecture. Aldershot: Gower.

———(in press c) "Systems of activities and systems of settings," in S. Kent (ed..) Domestic Architecture and Use of Space. Cambridge: Cambridge University Press.

———(in press d) "On the attributes of 'tradition,'" in N. Alsayyad and J. P. Bourdier (eds.) Dwellings, Settlements and Tradition. Lanham, MD: University Press of America.

———(in press e) "On regions and regionalism," in N. C. Markovich, W.F.E. Preiser, and F. A. Sturm (eds.) Pueblo Style and Regional Architecture. New York: Van Nostrand Reinhold.

———(in press f) "Indirect approaches to environment-behavior research." National Geographical Journal of India, 1989 special issue on "Literature and Humanistic Geography," 35 (pts. 3–4).

Revue de l'habitat social (1981) "Alençon: l'impossible rehabilitation de Perseigne." No. 63 (May): 32–47.

Ridgeway, C. L., J. Berger, and L. Smith (1985) "Nonverbal cues and status: an expectation states approach." American Journal of Sociology 90 (5): 955–978.

Robinson, J. W., et al. (1984) Towards an Architectural Definition of Normalization: Design Principles for Housing Severely and Profoundly Retarded Adults. Minneapolis: University of Minnesota (September).

Rodman, M. C. (1985a) "Contemporary custom: redefining domestic space in Longana, Vanuatu." Ethnology 24 (4): 269–279.

———(1985b) "Moving houses: residential mobility and the mobility of residences in Longana, Vanuatu." American Anthropologist 87: 56–87.

Russell, J. A., and J. Snodgrass (1987) "Emotion and the environment," pp. 245–280 in D. Stokols and I. Altman (eds.) Handbook of Environmental Psychology, vol. 1. New York: Wiley.

Sadalla, E. J., et al. (1987) "Identity symbolism in housing." Environment and Behavior 19 (5): 569–587.

Schank, R. C., and R. P. Abelson (1977) Scripts, Plans, Goals and Understanding: An Inquiry into Human Knowledge Structures. Hillsdale, NJ: Erlbaum.

———(1979) "Scripts, plans and knowledge," pp. 421–432 in N. Johnson-Laird and P. C. Wason (eds.) Thinking: Readings in Cognitive Science. Cambridge: Cambridge University Press.

Scherer, K. R., and P. Ekman [eds.] (1982) Handbook of Methods in Nonverbal Behavior Research. Cambridge: Cambridge University Press.

Suchar, C. S., and R. Rotenberg (1988) "Judging the adequacy of shelter: a case from Lincoln Park." Presented at the meeting of the Society for Applied Anthropology, Tampa, FL, April. (mimeo)

Thagard, P. (1988) Computational Philosophy of Science. Cambridge, MA: MIT Press/Bradford Books.

Varady, D. P. (1986) "Neighborhood confidence: a critical factor in neighborhood revitalization." Environment and Behavior 18 (4): 480–501.

Vargus, M. F. (1986) Louder than Words: An Introduction to Nonverbal Communication. Ames: Iowa State University Press.

Vinnicombe, P. (1976). People of the Eland: Rock Paintings of the Drakensberg Bushmen as a Reflection of Their Life and Thought. Pietermaritzburg: University of Natal Press.

Wiemann, J. M., and R. P. Harrison [eds.] (1983) Nonverbal Interaction. Beverly Hills, CA: Sage.

Wobst, H. M. (1977) "Stylistic behavior and information exchange," pp. 317–342 in C. E. Cleland (ed.) For the Director: Research Essays in Honor of James B. Griffin. University of Michigan, Museum of Anthropology, Anthropological Papers, no. 61.

Wolfgang, A. [ed.] (1984) Nonverbal Behavior: Perspectives, Applications, Intercultural Insights. Lewiston, NY: Hogrefe.

Wood, D. (1969) "The image of San Cristobal." Monadnock 43: 29–45.

Zube, E. H., J. Vining, C. S. Law, and R. B. Bechtel (1985) "Perceived urban residential quality: a cross-cultural bimodal study." Environment and Behavior 17 (3): 327–350.

INDEX

NOTE: The following index is reproduced from the original edition. It covers subjects only and includes neither names found in the text nor references to the new epilogue.

ABOUT THE AUTHOR

Amos Rapoport is Distinguished Professor in the School of Architecture and Urban Planning at the University of Wisconsin-Milwaukee. He has taught at the Universities of Melbourne and Sydney in Australia, at the University of California, Berkeley, and at University College, London, and has held visiting appointments in Israel, Turkey, Great Britain, Argentina, Brazil, Canada, India, and elsewhere. He has also lectured by invitation and been a Visiting Fellow in many countries.

Professor Rapoport is one of the founders of the new field of Environment-Behavior Studies. His work has focused mainly on the role of cultural variables, cross-cultural studies, and theory development and synthesis. In addition to the present book, he is the author of House Form and Culture (originally published in 1969 and translated into five languages), Human Aspects of Urban Form (1977), and History and Precedent in Environmental Design (1990). In addition, he has published over two hundred papers, chapters, and essays, many of them invited, and is the editor or coeditor of four books.

He has been the editor in chief of Urban Ecology and associate editor of Environment and Behavior, and he has been on the editorial boards of many professional journals. In 1980 the Environmental Design Research Association honored him with its Distinguished Career Award. Professor Rapoport has been the recipient of a Senior Fellowship from the National Endowment for the Arts and a Graham Foundation Fellowship. During the academic year 1982–83 he was a Visiting Fellow of Clare Hall, Cambridge University, of which he is now a Life Member. He has also been a member of the program committee (1987–1988) and the jury (1989) for the International City Design Competition.